THE PASSION OF
MY TIMES

ALSO BY
WILLIAM L. TAYLOR

Hanging Together: Equality in an Urban Nation

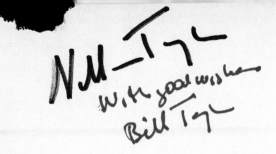

THE PASSION OF MY TIMES

*An Advocate's Fifty-Year Journey
in the Civil Rights Movement*

WILLIAM L. TAYLOR

CARROLL & GRAF PUBLISHERS
NEW YORK

THE PASSION OF MY TIMES
An Advocate's Fifty-Year Journey in the Civil Rights Movement

Carroll & Graf Publishers
An Imprint of Avalon Publishing Group Inc.
245 West 17th Street
11th Floor
New York, NY 10011

AVALON
publishing group incorporated

First Carroll & Graf edition 2004
First Carroll & Graf trade paperback edition 2006

Library of Congress Cataloging-in-Publication Data is available.

ISBN-13: 978-0-78671-685-2
ISBN-10: 0-7867-1685-1

Interior design by Maria E. Torres
Printed in the United States of America
Distributed by Publishers Group West

For Simone and Jesse Hart
In memory of Harriett

Contents

As life is action and passion it is required
that one should share in the passion
and action of one's times at peril
of being judged not to have lived.

—Oliver Wendell Holmes

Prologue

In his book *Giant Killers*, Michael Pertschuk writes of how, in the summer of 1982, a season of liberal despair about the ascendancy of the Reagan administration, he was startled to witness the entry into a restaurant on Capitol Hill of a "whooping throng: Ralph Neas and Bill Taylor and a bunch of their cohorts from the Leadership Conference on Civil Rights . . . They were actually celebrating. They were celebrating the Senate's passage of amendments to the 1965 Voting Rights Act"—amendments that not only extended voting protections but strengthened the law. They had done so, Pertschuk adds, in the teeth of opposition from Republican leaders in the Senate and President Reagan. "So infectious was their delight," Pertschuk says of our group, "that we all ended up smiling like idiots."

Pertschuk had it right. This was one of those rare moments when all of us involved in civil rights work could say we had accomplished something of great benefit to our clients and to the nation. Seventeen years earlier I had been engaged in taking the testimony of black people in the South—people who had been physically assaulted or humiliated for daring to try to register to vote. The 1965 Voting Rights Act changed all that and enfranchised hundreds of thousands of black citizens. But the key provisions of the act were regarded as emergency legislation. The assertion of federal authority was viewed as temporary, with power over voting to be restored to the states after the crisis was over. In 1982, starting as underdogs, we were able to persuade Congress that these measures had to be continued for another twenty-five years and that a restrictive Supreme Court decision on voting should be overturned.

The battle did not end in 1982. In the presidential election of 2000, people of color in Florida and elsewhere were effectively disenfranchised by archaic voting practices and antiquated machinery. And, to my astonishment, the twenty-five-year extension will soon expire and

Congress will again be faced with the question of continuing the key provisions of the Voting Rights Act.

My fifty-year journey in civil rights has been marked more by struggle than by such moments of triumph as the one I have described. But I do not feel like Sisyphus pushing the boulder up the hill only to have it roll back down again. The 1982 Voting Rights extension embedded in our law the fundamental concept of fairness and nondiscriminatory treatment in our political processes. That commitment to electoral participation for all helps distinguish the United States from so many other nations where democratic processes have not been established. Fifty years ago, the United States could not in good conscience have claimed such a distinction.

I am convinced that we are not going back to the era when discrimination and repression were dominant. There are many battles still to be fought, but experience suggests that they are worth fighting and that they can be won.

Introduction

A White Guy Like Me

I have had the good fortune to be a participant, not just a spectator, in the enormous social transformations of American life that occurred during the last half of the twentieth century. I see the changes in my everyday life and in the status of people of color, women, and people with disabilities. When I take a walk in my middle-class neighborhood in Washington, D.C., or when I go shopping, I encounter as many people of color as I do whites. When I go to sessions of the D.C. Bar, many of them are led by African Americans (and women). When I travel around the country to make speeches to educators or community groups, people of color play prominent roles in those. When I go to my medical center, I am likely to be cared for by a woman physician. Some years ago, Gallaudet College, an institution for the deaf, established a branch in my neighborhood, and students on the street engaged in animated conversations in sign language, where once they would have been hidden away.

The dry statistics show that the African-American middle class quadrupled over that half century, that other people of color, including Hispanics and Asian Americans, have advanced economically and politically, and that women now play prominent roles in all walks of life. It is not, however, just a matter of statistics; the quality of American life has changed dramatically for a great many people.

At the same time, there are millions of poor people of color who have been left largely untouched by the civil rights revolution. I do not see them on a daily basis as I tend to see more affluent people. But I know from my experience in central cities in years past that they are there and that they continue to live in poverty, facing discrimination on a daily basis. I also learned a great deal from the accounts of my late wife, Harriett, who was a trial judge in the District of Columbia for seventeen years and who handled landlord-tenant cases, child abuse and neglect cases, and drug and murder prosecutions, as well as other matters. She described vividly the frustrations of living in a resource-starved, dysfunctional society, and the potential talent among young people that was buried in this environment.

While much of this seems familiar, I believe that a very large segment of middle-class Americans blocks out these images, both positive and negative. Many people of a conservative bent have convinced themselves that the battle for civil rights has been won and that no further measures are needed to secure equal opportunity. In the minds of conservatives, ghetto residents have literally become Ralph Ellison's invisible man or are stereotyped as so shiftless as to be beyond help.

What may be more surprising is the propensity of some liberals to believe that the last half century has brought no real progress for African Americans. In some cases this view may stem from a gloomy habit of mind that tends to see everything through dark lenses. In other cases, this kind of rhetorical excess may be thought of as a strategic means of creating a sense of urgency to engage in new battles. If so, I think it will be counterproductive. If the extraordinary legal, political, and community efforts of the civil rights movement over the past half century have ended in abject failure, if American society is irredeemably racist, what chance is there that new efforts will succeed?

More than anything, I think that both the conservative and liberal extremes stem from a self-imposed isolation that prevents people from seeing clearly the society in which they live. We all create cocoons for ourselves—families and communities that enable us to escape the hard knocks of competing in the workaday world and to establish relationships with people who share our values. But to the extent that these communities are homogenous, that they are stratified along lines of class and color, they exclude from our vision large parts of society. Certainly, television as well as books and newspapers can expand our knowledge, but in some ways I have come to think of television and much of the other popular media as fun-house mirrors—reflecting but distorting at the same time.

So there will be an element of advocacy in this memoir—something that will not surprise people who know me. I want to convince people whose minds are open that the work of providing opportunity to those who are worst off in this society is not done. And I want to convince the pessimists that change is possible—that if the Kings and Marshalls could overcome the enormous barriers of the last century, modern advocates should not despair.

I also want through this memoir to examine how the process of institutional change has worked in civil rights. I have been involved in big court cases, in major legislative efforts, in planning civil rights strategy, and in persuading people with power or influence to do the right thing. Without becoming overly enmeshed in minutiae, I hope to offer some useful insights into these processes.

Working for social change teaches lessons of humility. The huge transformations that have occurred during my lifetime have not primarily been a product of rational planning and calculation. Change has been triggered by the enormous leadership qualities of Martin Luther King Jr. in the United States, Nelson Mandela in South Africa, and Mahatma Gandhi in India, and even more so by the loyalty they inspired, the repression their work evoked, and the ways in which all of this touched the national conscience. The contribution that the rest of us have made has been to know how to take advantage of the tidal waves of change, to craft and implement the laws and policies that enable people to improve their own lives.

Within the limits of my capacity for personal introspection, I will also seek to address a question that Roger Wilkins, a friend of fifty years, suggested I write about: "What leads a white guy like you to spend his whole professional life working on behalf of black people?" In the next chapter I will discuss some of the early influences that shaped my future: growing up Jewish in New York City in an era of anti-Semitism at home while the Holocaust raged in Europe; being part of a family and a nation that watched admiringly as FDR used the powers of government to help people crushed by the Depression; learning about civil rights by following the career and courage of Jackie Robinson as he broke the color line in baseball.

I also know that I had my sights trained on a career of public service at a fairly early age. When in college I met the woman who would become my wife, she told me of her hopes to become a lawyer. In the 1950s this was still regarded as a pioneering move for women, and members of Harriett's family discouraged her. When I urged her to pursue her dream, some friends thought I was an early feminist. In fact, as I told Harriett then, since I expected to have a very limited income as a public-interest lawyer, it would be good to have two wage earners in the family.

In part it was fortuitous timing—graduating from law school in the year of the historic Supreme Court decision in *Brown*—that got me into civil rights work. Why have I stayed in it? There were times, particularly early in my career, when some of the people whom I admired most were suggesting other possibilities for me. When I was getting ready to leave the NAACP Legal Defense Fund in 1958, Thurgood Marshall said he would contact a couple of large law firms that he thought I might find congenial. Years later, when I was preparing to leave the U.S. Commission on Civil Rights, Father Ted Hesburgh of Notre Dame and John Hannah of Michigan State said they thought I might make a good college president and offered to help. Nobody made me an offer I could not refuse and nothing came of those suggestions. I have no idea what path I might have followed if something outside of civil rights work had been presented to me in an irresistible fashion.

Still I think the reasons I have persevered are far more positive than negative or merely from the lack of something else to do. At the end of the 1960s when the black power movement gained ascendancy, many African Americans, including some of my closest friends, decided that white participation in the movement was too often patronizing or hypocritical and that in any event they preferred to act without whites, and they pushed us away. At that point I was impelled to examine my own reasons for being a civil rights lawyer. I decided that I was doing the work I did not for anyone else, but for myself—to help shape the kind of world that I wanted to live in and would want my children and grandchildren to live in. Fortunately, the black-white tensions of the late '60s and early '70s have subsided, and many people are working together harmoniously and with a sense of common purpose. But if a new era of tension were to arise I think my resolve would not weaken and my feelings would be the same.

The fact is that I love the professional life I have led. Trying to puzzle out the dilemma of race has provided me with a lifelong education, not simply in the law, but in the way institutions function and have an impact on peoples' lives. I love going to new places and learning how people live. In recent years I have loved teaching and working with young people who are seeking purposes in life that are greater than themselves. And, of course, there are those rare wonderful moments when I can see the tangible results of our efforts on the lives of people who have sought only to be given a chance.

Like everyone else, I have had ups and downs. But I have rarely experienced a day when I got up thinking I didn't have any work to pursue that was not useful and interesting and that I would rather stay in bed.

This is not meant to be a preachy book. It is a memoir about my experience and the perspectives it has given me. Over the course of a half century in civil rights work, I have witnessed acts of courage and heroism as well as acts of hypocrisy and cowardice. Some people have learned to live and work together in coalitions despite differing backgrounds and agendas, while others split over differences that may seem trivial in retrospect. Often, people have behaved in unexpected and funny ways. I have always liked to tell stories, and this seems like a good time and place to tell them. If an occasional moral pops up, so be it.

In Your Case
I'll Make an Exception

I hate to ruin anyone's career, but in your case I'm prepared to make an exception.
—Harry D. Gideonse, president of Brooklyn College, to the author, October 1950

I have tried to answer Roger Wilkins's question on at least one level, by describing the rewards and satisfactions that have kept me at the civil rights trade all these years. But obviously the question can be posed at other levels. What was the environment that shaped me and helped define my choices, and what were the forces beneath the surface (such as a need for the spotlight or character traits that could be described either as perseverance or stubbornness) that may have guided me on this path? The simple answer to the latter part of that question is that I don't know and I have no great interest in finding out. If, as Socrates said, "the unexamined life is not worth living," I think the overly examined one has some problems as well.

But I can identify some key events of my childhood and youth that I'm sure affected the course of my life. Perhaps the pivotal event took place a few days after my nineteenth birthday in October 1950, during my junior year at Brooklyn College. In 1950, the Brooklyn College campus was a place of ferment. Many of the students were veterans returning from World War II service. It was the beginning of the McCarthy era and, in June 1950, the United States entered the Korean War.

The president of the college was Harry D. Gideonse, an economist who had been an associate of Robert Hutchins at the University of Chicago. Gideonse viewed his mission as ridding the college of any taint of communism or radicalism, and he appeared to see that taint everywhere on campus. In the spring of l950, he forced the history department to replace its chairman, Jesse Clarkson, a well-respected teacher who had criticized Gideonse's treatment of professors whose views he scorned. When the college newspaper, the *Vanguard*, published the story against the recommendation of its faculty advisor, the newspaper's publication was suspended, as were its top editors.

After an outcry, the paper was allowed to resume publishing but with the proviso that it had to run editorials on both sides of any controversial issue and that its last editorial board could not continue to serve. I was then the sports editor and my colleagues elected me to be the editor in chief. The issues confronting the college were multiple: Could communist or leftist groups continue to function on campus when the nation was at war? Should people indicted under the Smith (anticommunist) Act be allowed to make speeches on campus? Should there be a Reserve Officers Training Corps on campus and should participation by male students be mandatory?

On these and other issues, the *Vanguard* took a civil libertarian position—that compulsion should be avoided and that speech should not be restrained. We lasted only two issues on my watch. After the second issue, two students who had taken positions opposing ours complained that they were not given enough space. The administration swooped down on our offices, locked us out, and banned the newspaper from campus.

When a reporter from the *New York Times* asked me for a reaction I said, "The dissolution of *Vanguard* can only be construed as an attempt by the college administration to gain control of any student opinion which does not agree with that of the administration." The very next day, when the article appeared, Gideonse summoned me to his office. He said that my statement was "a deliberate lie" and that, while he hated to ruin anyone's career, in my case he was prepared to make an exception.

While Gideonse's words were meant to intimidate me, for reasons I still cannot explain I did not feel intimidated. The *Vanguard* editors prepared and filed their appeals before the designated bodies. It was an exercise in futility because we knew that Gideonse controlled the process and that he had already approved a new newspaper with a handpicked staff. We took our case to the public. New York City newspapers printed our story and college newspapers warned of the growing danger of repression on campus. We raised enough money to publish our own new newspaper, sponsored by various student organizations, off campus.

It was called *Campus News*, and it published its first issue in late October, only a couple of weeks after the demise of the *Vanguard*. After the administration threatened to ban the sponsoring groups on grounds that they did not have publishing clauses in their charter, all except Students for Democratic Action (which did have a publishing clause) withdrew their support. But we were running out of money anyway and at the end of the year, after a dozen issues, we had to fold *Campus News*.

The Gideonse administration decided also to make an example of me by labeling me, along with Sy Landy, leader of Students for Democratic Action (an affiliate of Americans for Democratic Action), a "bad campus citizen," an appellation that denied me a listing in *Who's Who in American Colleges and Universities* and any other extracurricular honors that might come my way. The disgrace was to be made part of my permanent record. Meanwhile I found myself for a brief period in demand as a speaker. Among the groups that called on me were the various communist sects that dotted the New York scene in that era— Stalinists, Trotskyites, Schactmanites (a rival wing to Trotsky's in the Socialist Workers Party led by Max Schactman), and others. While I was unschooled in the arcane politics of these organizations, it soon became apparent that I was in demand not for my views but as a victim. I was to be the latest poster child for the message that capitalism was corrupt. I rejected the role and learned a lesson that proved useful in later years: to beware of people who would use the misfortunes of others for their own purposes.

After the charter of Vanguard *was revoked, there followed a lively period of protest, with people on all sides of the controversy expressing their views.*

One day, a group of conservatives gathered outside the college president's office to show their approval of the banning of the newspaper. Soon, the college's security team arrived and ordered the group to disperse.

"But you don't understand," one of the demonstrators protested, "we're the anticommunists." The head of the security team replied, "I don't care what kind of communist you are."

Eventually, the controversy subsided. Our appeals were rejected by the Gideonse administration. I graduated in December 1952. After law school, when I passed the Bar and had to face the Committee on Character and Fitness, I dutifully reported that I had been disciplined as a college student. The Bar examiner told me that whatever had been in my record was no longer there.

Most likely it was serendipity that brought me into circumstances in which, at the tender age of nineteen, my career was threatened with ruination. But I also can detect some aspects of my upbringing that may have contributed to and also influenced my direction. In many respects, my life was similar to that of many young people from immigrant families growing up in New York City in the '30s and '40s. But as with anyone else, there were some interesting wrinkles.

My parents were members of large Jewish families that had emigrated to the United States from Lithuania early in the twentieth century. They were fleeing persecution and arrived without resources. My mother was the youngest of eight brothers and sisters and my father the second youngest of six. He was an infant when his family arrived and my mother was not yet a teenager. That helped make them the most assimilated in their respective families, speaking without an accent and adapting fairly easily to American ways. My father became the first in his family to graduate college, receiving a degree in civil engineering from Brooklyn Polytechnic Institute, and my mother attended City College in Manhattan for a year.

After they married, while the Taylor clan had settled in the densely populated East New York–Brownsville area of Brooklyn and the Levines (my mother's family) in the Washington Heights area of Manhattan, my parents branched out. They located an apartment in Sheepshead Bay at the southern tip of Brooklyn, a less congested area that had the atmosphere of a fishing village. When I was four, we moved a few miles northwest to a two-family house on the border of Flatbush and Bensonhurst. Italians dominated the Bensonhurst neighborhood and Jews the Flatbush area, with the latter generally more middle class than the former. Some years ago, Marianna Torgovnick, an Italian American who grew up in Bensonhurst, wrote a book entitled *Crossing Ocean Parkway*, in which she said that moving from one side to the other of that broad boulevard was the mark of increased mobility for Italians. My family was on the west—or Italian—side of Ocean Parkway, but our street was integrated. Jews lived on the northern half of East Fourth Street between Avenues T and U, and Italians lived on the south side. We were in the middle of the block, Jews renting from a Sicilian landlord.

Relations between Italian Catholics and European Jews on my block were generally not cordial. On my first day of first grade in 1937 at PS 215, an older group of Italian boys threw me in the bushes and called me a Christ-killer. As I grew older I learned more about anti-Semitism. An avid newspaper reader, I followed the stories about Hitler's rise in Nazi Germany. I listened on the radio to the anti-Semitic rantings of Father Coughlin and I read about the hate campaign in New York of the German-American Bund. Anti-Semitism was also a subject at home. My father felt that his career with the New York City Department of Water Supply, Gas, and Electricity was being thwarted by its discrimination against Jews. Since there were no civil rights laws to protect him, he decided to join the Democratic Club in Crown Heights, a neighborhood we moved to in 1947. The leader was a powerful politician, Irwin Steingut, and one of the captains was Abe Beame, who became mayor of New York in 1974. Somehow the barriers my father faced were removed and he moved up the ladder, eventually becoming the commissioner of Water Supply for Brooklyn.

My early school career was also marked by decisions my teachers made, when I was in first and second grades, to skip or push me ahead a semester. The decisions were based on the results of the then prevalent IQ tests which were supposed to measure aptitude. I found these sudden changes profoundly unsettling and for a couple of years I generally arrived at school with an upset stomach (a condition for which my fourth grade teacher prescribed cocoa, which helped). In retrospect, I think that for all the difficulties it posed at the time, my skipping ahead was not necessarily a bad thing. It made me feel "different," but different was not bad because it altered my perspective and overturned any notion that there were boxes I had to fit into and a progression I had to follow. In speaking with law students in recent years, I have encouraged them to carve their own paths, saying that for a breed that is so assertive in other areas, many have been docile about their careers, too quick to fit themselves into corporate and big-firm models.

Among the consequences of being skipped, however, was that I was behind my classmates in athletic development. This was a serious matter because softball and a variety of street games were a big part of our lives. My father, like many first-generation Americans in New York, was a passionate baseball fan and ranked athletic skill, along with academic achievement, high on his scale of values. Unable to make the grade, I adapted by organizing my own softball team—the Stars Social Athletic Club—of which I became the manager, statistician, and right fielder. Although I did not consciously plan it that way, the club brought together the sometimes warring factions of Jews and Italian Catholics in the neighborhood. Jiusto (Joe) Merendino, Albert Piasio, Heschy Mandelbaum, and Bennett Sachs were all starters and we took particular pleasure in defeating the Vikings, an all-Jewish team from a more affluent area a few blocks away. And our interreligious group managed to get along fine. That may have been my first civil rights endeavor.

My father's love for baseball influenced me in other ways. He took me to Ebbets Field to see my first Brooklyn Dodgers baseball game when I was six, and we returned time and again. When I couldn't be there in person, I listened on the radio to Red Barber doing the play-by-play. His fluency and mastery of an original kind of Southern vernacular convinced me that I wanted to be a sports broadcaster or journalist.

I joined the staff of the student newspaper when I entered Abraham Lincoln High School. In 1947 I was the 15-year-old sports editor of the *Lincoln Log* when Jackie Robinson broke the color barrier by signing with the Dodgers. I wrote him a letter asking for an interview and he wrote back telling me that I should come to the clubhouse after a game and that he would talk to me. When I appeared a few days later with the letter, the guard at the clubhouse gate ordered me and my schoolmate to leave. We waited on Bedford Avenue for Robinson and when he came out I said, "Mr. Robinson, they wouldn't let us in to interview you." He replied, "That's okay, kid, come back next week and I'll have it fixed." And then he jumped into a cab. I never did get into the clubhouse and I thought for years that if I were a real journalist I would have gotten into that cab with him and done the interview there and then. But I was only fifteen and didn't have that kind of moxie.

I did, however, follow Robinson's career and learned in a concrete way about racial prejudice. I read about his going south for spring training and being unable to stay with white players at the team's motel or to eat in the same restaurants. Some of his teammates voiced their resistance to his presence on the team. When the season started, Robinson faced vicious verbal abuse from opposing teams, particularly the Philadelphia Phillies, which was led by a racist manager, Ben Chapman, and the St. Louis Cardinals, whose catcher Joe Garagiola aimed racial slurs at Robinson. Then there were the catcalls from the stands and the death threats in the mail.

Robinson absorbed all the insults and threats stoically and with great dignity although it was clear that normally he was not a passive person. Ultimately he did as much for civil rights and for ameliorating racial prejudice as anyone of that era, if not more. He was the epitome of the Hemingway definition of courage—grace under pressure. And for me, living in New York City miles away from Harlem and with virtually no interaction with African Americans, Jackie Robinson provided my only civil rights education. His experience was the base of my knowledge of the black experience when I joined the NAACP Legal Defense Fund seven years later.

Even as I entered Brooklyn College I think I was aware that I was not destined to be the next Red Barber or Red Smith. Growing up as a Depression baby in the '30s and into the '40s, the dominant figure in my world was Franklin Delano Roosevelt. His New Deal was living proof that government could be an affirmative force for good, to empower people to empower themselves. We listened to Roosevelt's fireside chats, and talked about his administration at home. We cried when he died. I think I knew then that I wanted to enlist in whatever crusade might follow the New Deal.

It also became increasingly clear that law would be the instrument for me to try to realize my ambitions. In fact, there is some evidence that I was programmed at an early age to enter the legal profession. A favorite family story had me misbehaving in a restaurant at age three or four. When my father chided me to "be a gentleman" I allegedly replied, "I don't want to be a gentleman, I want to be a lawyer." Many years later when my father was literally on his deathbed, he told me for the first time that, while he was not dissatisfied with his career as a municipal engineer, his secret ambition had been to be a lawyer.

The *Vanguard* story has reverberated periodically throughout my life. First and foremost, it brought me together with the woman who would become my wife. Harriett Rosen was a freshman at Brooklyn College in October 1950 when the newspaper's charter was revoked. She had been an editor of her high school newspaper and, being unaware of the issues surrounding the revocation, she joined the staff of the *Kingsman*, the newspaper the administration assembled to replace the *Vanguard*. We met when she came to interview me about how it felt to be labeled a bad campus citizen and stripped of student honors. She decided she was on the wrong side of the controversy and quit the paper even though, by virtue of the fact that she was the only staff member who had any journalistic skills, she had been named managing editor.

Immediately attracted to each other, we became a couple and were married in June 1954 after I graduated from law school. All through our forty-three-year marriage—which ended with Harriett's death in 1997—we supported each other's hopes and ambitions. I encouraged her to apply to law school at a time when few women were lawyers and people close to her frowned on the idea. She never questioned, and indeed supported, my decision to carve out an unconventional career in public-interest law even though my moves were sometimes economically risky. Our friends viewed our marriage as among the happiest they knew, and they were right.

Later on, the *Vanguard* episode had other interesting repercussions—in the '60s, when I was a candidate for staff director of the U.S. Commission on Civil Rights; in the '70s, when I ran into Harry Gideonse in the course of a job search; in the '80s, when I met his son while I was prosecuting a case in Cincinnati; and in 2001, when Brooklyn College issued to me an unexpected but welcome invitation.

In retrospect I believe that the *Vanguard* experience prepared me for life's struggles. During the '60s when I was directing the Civil Rights Commission's investigations in the South, I came to know some of the young people who participated in the Mississippi Summer or who were civil rights workers in other places. Some came away from the experience stronger and more determined. Others were embittered, I think in part because they sought to change the world before they had any real idea of how difficult it would be.

At Brooklyn College we got a chance to test our mettle in a lower-stakes endeavor where people's lives were not on the line. Still, I think we were pretty bold, particularly as children of the Depression who were taking some economic risks in defying those who sought to punish political nonconformity. Maybe we were influenced by the presence on campus of World War II veterans, many of whom had taken far greater risks. Probably it was because we were all young and we had each other. Among allies, it felt good to be fighting for a cause that was larger than myself and despite all the turmoil, I was eager to do it again.

Working for Thurgood and Bob

Brown v. Board of Education

I n December 1954, I landed the job that would shape my entire professional career. In May of that year, the Supreme Court had decided unanimously in *Brown v. Board of Education* that laws and policies that called for racial segregation of public schools violated the equal protection guarantees of the United States Constitution. The decision mandated a huge change in the status of black citizens. It was and is rightly regarded as the most important Supreme Court decision of the last century.

A few weeks after the May 17 decision, I graduated from law school, and in June, Harriett and I were married. Because I had expected to be drafted into the army immediately, I had not engaged in any kind of job search. But my entry into the army was deferred. So I found myself on the job market without any preparation. I took a short-term job with the Corporation Counsel of the City of New York—then the largest law office in the world—which handled all of the city's legal business. The work was interesting in some respects. I became the most junior member of the city's legal team in defending against a big lawsuit brought by several printing plants on the west side of Manhattan. The plants had suffered damage when the ground settled after the City pumped water out of nearby excavations in order to build the Brookly-Battery Tunnel. I learned a fair amount from the skilled lawyers on both sides. But I hoped for a job more suited to my interest in social justice.

In the late fall, Jack Greenberg, who had argued one of the *Brown* cases, came to Columbia Law School to discuss the victory with students. Harriett, then a third-year student, attended and after the presentation approached Greenberg and asked if there might be any jobs for lawyers available in his office. He said that the NAACP Legal Defense Fund had a one-year position for a new lawyer and that the position might still be open.

The next day, I went tearing down to the Legal Defense Fund headquarters on West Forty-Third Street in Manhattan. Their offices turned out to be extremely modest. I was armed with a résumé and a letter of recommendation from Charles Black, a professor of constitutional law at Columbia who had been a central figure in helping to draft the brief in the *Brown* case. I knew Charles because he had been married earlier that year to Barbara Aronstein, Harriett's best friend from Brooklyn College and a fellow student at Columbia.

After interviews with the senior lawyers I was told that the job was mine, and I accepted it on the spot. I was shown to my office, which had on the door a plaque reading "Prince Hall Masons Fellow." This signified that the position was created with the financial support of Charles Wesley Dobbs, a wealthy Atlanta businessman and Mason (the father of Mattiwilda Dobbs, who in 1956 became the first black soprano to sing at the Metropolitan Opera).

I was entering a new world for which my education at Yale Law School had prepared me only partially. Yale had long been my school of choice because of its reputation gained in the '30s and '40s as the place for people who were dedicated to public service and social change. Its faculty in that era included William O. Douglas, who later ascended to the Supreme Court; Robert Hutchins, the educational innovator who became dean of Yale Law School and president of the University of Chicago at 30; Thurman Arnold, the Roosevelt adviser on antitrust policy and perceptive analyst of capitalism; Judge Jerome Frank, who helped found the progressive philosophy of legal realism, and other public thinkers and civic doers. By the time I arrived, these figures had been succeeded by other teachers who helped maintain the school's reputation.

I found that I had little interest in the commercial and tax courses in the curriculum. Rather, what engaged my attention were substantive courses in civil rights, international law, judicial philosophy, and other offerings like evidence and procedure that had their own internal logic.

Yale was also helpful by opening a wider world to me. This was my first experience in living away from home and encountering people who were not New Yorkers. There was a fairly large contingent of sons of privilege (women numbered only ten in a class of almost two hundred). Most of this contingent, along with some others, were destined for careers at large law firms or in business. But there were still others who had different ideas about their futures. One who immediately captured my attention was Allard Lowenstein, a New Yorker who, while an undergraduate student at the University of North Carolina, had become president of the National Student Association. He left the impression of a whirling political dervish wherever he went. When I arrived as a transfer student at Yale in September 1952, having spent the January 1952 semester at New York University Law School, one of the first events I attended was a speech by Eleanor Roosevelt that Allard had arranged in the midst of the Eisenhower-Stevenson election campaign.

In later years, Allard went off on a mission to visit members of the outlawed African National Congress, who were followers of Nelson Mandela. The result of his visit was a petition to the United Nations and a book, *Brutal Mandate*, detailing the horrors of apartheid, published in 1962. Later trips included underground visits to Spain to help those planning to establish democracy after Franco. Only rarely was Allard to be found in class in New Haven; yet he maintained his good standing at the law school. His freestyle advocacy gave me an alternative model to the more structured process being taught in our classes.

Yale did instill in me something of the fabled ability to "think like a lawyer." This meant to me the duty to scrutinize facts carefully and to examine all sides of an argument, if only to be prepared to counter positions different from my own. On the other hand, almost all the case books and materials we studied were drawn from appellate decisions rather than the trial courts which had actually been the battlefields for competing facts.

And in those days there were few legal clinics where a student could gain practical experience. My one brief stint was at the Legal Aid Society where I was able to meet real people with real problems.

Things were different when I got to the Legal Defense Fund. While I did not deal directly with clients, the lawyers I worked with were bonded with the people they represented. Like their clients, they had engaged in a lifelong struggle for equal opportunity while living and breathing the stifling air of segregation and discrimination. Thurgood Marshall was chief counsel, having worked since the 1930s with his mentor Charles Houston to build the Legal Defense Fund. The fund pursued litigation challenging the legalized caste system that southern States had imposed after the end of Reconstruction and that with only a few exceptions had been approved by the federal courts until the end of the 1940s. Thurgood had grown up in Maryland in an era when lynchings were not uncommon and, when he took on the civil rights work of the Fund, he often traveled to the most dangerous areas of the Deep South to gather facts and line up clients. Marshall had only a handful of lawyers in the New York office. His chief deputy was Robert Carter, my day-to-day boss. When I joined the Fund, Bob was pushing hard on cases to take full advantage of the victory in *Brown* a few months earlier. The other staff lawyers were Jack Greenberg, who later succeeded Marshall as head of the Fund when Thurgood was named as a federal appellate judge; Constance Baker Motley, who became a federal district judge in New York, joining Bob Carter as a colleague on the bench; and Elwood Chisholm, who had taught at Howard Law School.

This small band of lawyers was able to have a great impact in part because of a network of cooperating lawyers who worked with the Fund throughout the South and in a few other locales. For instance, Virginia was one of the four cases challenging segregation that the

Supreme Court accepted and consolidated as the *Brown* case. Much of the trial work was done by Spottswood Robinson and Oliver Hill, law partners in Richmond. Robinson, who had the best academic record in the history of Howard Law School, provided much of the intellectual spark for Virginia and other cases while Hill, also a high-achieving classmate of Thurgood's at Howard Law School, did much of the trial work. In Delaware (another of the *Brown* cases), the cooperating lawyer was Louis Redding, who was the first Negro admitted to the practice of law in the state in 1929. Redding expressed himself precisely, often eloquently, and he came through to everyone he met as a person of great dignity. In Washington, D.C., the site of *Bolling v. Sharpe*, the companion case to *Brown*, the legal team was headed by James M. Nabrit, Jr, later to become dean of Howard Law School and president of the university. Nabrit, a passionate advocate who had struggled against ugly discrimination in his native Texas, took over the D.C. case when Charley Houston died. Nabrit insisted that nothing less than full desegregation would be an adequate remedy.

When I arrived in December 1954, Bob Carter immediately put me to work on legal initiatives to expand *Brown's* prohibition of segregation laws and policies. My first assignment was to put together research for an NAACP petition to the Interstate Commerce Commission, seeking rules that would bar racial segregation not only in the terminals of interstate rail carriers but in the leased restaurants in the terminals as well. We relied on broad language in the Interstate Commerce Act banning "any undue or unreasonable prejudice or any disadvantage in any respect whatsoever." Although we won a substantial legal victory in 1955, it was not until the bloody violence against the Freedom Riders in 1961, almost a decade later, and the resulting litigation in the Supreme Court that segregation in rail and bus terminals was finally ended.

Next, I went to work on a series of charges to be filed with the National Labor Relations Board against oil companies in Texas, Louisiana, and Arkansas. As I read through the dozens of affidavits of Negro workers compiled by Herb Hill, the NAACP's labor secretary, I began to understand the frustration and anger the workers must have felt. These were people who regardless of experience were assigned unskilled, menial jobs when they were hired. They were denied entry into apprentice job training programs. Even when they came to perform more skilled work, they were kept in the lowest job categories and paid minimum wages. If they joined a union, they were assigned to a separate, colored local, an appendage to the main union, which provided them no representation. Many had coped with these injustices for a decade or more. As I worked, I wondered about the outrage these workers must have felt and about the toll that such discrimination must have taken on them and their families as they were denied the opportunity to have their labors rewarded with even a modest wage and fair treatment.

Here again, we were relying on a law—the National Labor Relations Act—that called for nondiscrimination against workers but that did not address racial practices specifically. It would be almost a decade before the president and Congress took decisive action against job discrimination.

As I worked on these and other matters in the winter of 1954, the major looming question was what rules the Supreme Court would adopt in providing a remedy for the racial segregation of public schools that it had outlawed in the first *Brown* decision. When Earl Warren came to the Court as chief justice in October 1953, he performed a miracle, persuading his deeply divided colleagues to come together in the unanimous *Brown* opinion. But the miracle came at a price. Warren, a superb politician, decided that it would not be wise to burden the Southern states with the invidious intent of the systems of segregation they had maintained for half a century nor with the bonds in which black people were held. Instead, his opinion focused on the harm that racial isolation did to black children, citing social science evidence to support the conclusion that segregation "harmed their minds and hearts in ways unlikely ever to be undone." Beneath the surface, the opinion seemed to be a plea to southerners, saying, "We know we are asking you to change a whole way of life, but we are forced to do it because the lives and futures of little children are at stake." Instead of evoking understanding, the opinion was challenged by Southern leaders as based not on law but on mushy social science.

Most tangibly, the price Chief Justice Warren paid for a united court was the decision to postpone the question of remedy for a year and to call on the parties to file new briefs. As the Legal Defense Fund mobilized to prepare reply briefs answering the court's questions about remedy, my task was to read all of the briefs filed by the state defendants and the other briefs filed by states as friends of the court, and to summarize their arguments. I still have the charts that I prepared then and I am struck with how blatantly racist some of the claims were. For example, Texas, Maryland, North Carolina, and Florida said that the jobs of Negro teachers would be jeopardized because it would be "impractical" to use them in mixed classes; the latter two states said that intelligence tests show that white children have much higher achievement than Negroes and that integration would lower school standards; Florida said that integration would cause health problems because of the greater incidence of disease among Negroes. Virginia said that, in deciding on an assignment system, the differing health and morals of the races ought to be considered.

My friend Charles Black summed up these Southern arguments by neatly likening them to the "defendant who killed his father and mother and came to court pleading for mercy because he was an orphan."

To prepare for oral argument, Thurgood, as he often did in important cases, convened his "kitchen cabinet." It included the key lawyers in the cases—Carter, Greenberg, Motley, Robinson, Hill, Redding, and Nabrit.

There were others present, including Bill Coleman, an honors graduate of Harvard Law School and the first African American to serve as a law clerk for a Supreme Court justice (in this case Felix Frankfurter). William (Bob) Ming was full professor at the University of Chicago Law School and a respected theoretician.

While there was a clear objective for this and similar meetings, there was no set agenda. The sessions were freewheeling, high spirited, and often raucous. Ming, who seemed to produce an idea a minute, might go off on a rhetorical flight, with Coleman or Robinson following up with a sober analysis of the arguments. Nabrit brought passion as well as practical wisdom to the table, reminding Thurgood to "wrap himself in the American flag" as he closed his presentation. Thurgood said little; I wondered what he was thinking. Later, I discovered that he had carefully sifted through the avalanche of conversation to identify the three or four points that would be most useful to him in the argument and the best ways to answer the most challenging questions he might face.

Gradually it dawned on me that I had lucked into a convocation of some of the best legal minds and most accomplished advocates in the nation.

In addition, while most did not wear their hearts on their sleeves or project the intensity of some latter-day public-interest lawyers with whom I would work, they had all been tested in the crucible of racism and had a clear personal vision of the evil they were fighting.

For example, Bill Coleman in many ways was among the most measured and soft-spoken members of the group. By 1990 he had become senior partner in a major law firm and a member of the boards of directors of several large corporations after having served as secretary of transportation under President Ford. The major civil rights issue pending in Congress at the time was legislation to restore the effectiveness of the fair employment laws that a conservative majority of the Supreme Court had undermined in a series of decisions. Bill Coleman and I paid a visit to Senator John Danforth (R) of Missouri, whose support was key to reaching a favorable outcome. Danforth was accompanied by a young aide who was his legislative chief of staff. At one point, the aide said something that seemed to downgrade the importance of having strong fair employment laws. Coleman responded quietly. Directing his gaze at the young aide, he gave a brief personal history, saying that after graduating magna cum laude from Harvard Law School as an editor of the law review and serving as Justice Frankfurter's law clerk, he could not obtain a job with any of the major law firms in his home town of Philadelphia. He noted that a partner in one of these major firms was the aide's father.

While times had changed, Coleman said, protections were still needed against this kind of biased and hurtful treatment. The aide looked rueful and Senator Danforth became a valuable ally in the successful campaign to enact the Civil Rights Act of 1991.

Massive Resistance and Little Rock

In the spring of 1955, the Court issued its remedy decision in *Brown*. While there was some good news tucked away in the opinion—notably, that states were required to completely dismantle their racially dual education systems and replace them with "unitary" systems—the major news was very disappointing. Public authorities were required to desegregate their schools "with all deliberate speed," a vague formulation that was to be given content by each individual district judge, meaning that courts would be faced with pressures for delay in every community.

The Court's decision was accompanied by more bad news. President Eisenhower refused to say what he thought about the Court's mandate to end segregation and embraced a brand of social Darwinism by saying that "the law could not change the hearts and minds of men." In Congress, the only organized effort was the drafting of the Southern Manifesto by elected officials of the Old South—a document that challenged the authority of the Supreme Court to interpret the Constitution and called for nullification of the desegregation decisions. Into the vacuum created by these abdications of responsibility, Southern governors and legislators leaped. Led by Virginia state legislators, they fashioned a strategy of massive resistance. One part of the strategy was designed to delay and thwart desegregation orders, by requiring black students to overcome a series of administrative hurdles in order to gain entry to new schools, by allowing state money to support private segregation academies, and by providing for the closing of public schools if courts issued final desegregation orders. The second part of the strategy was to launch a direct attack on the NAACP, seeking to intimidate the organization by demanding membership lists and tax information, and threatening lawyers with criminal prosecutions or disbarment for stirring up litigation.

After these developments, much of the heady atmosphere created by *Brown* evaporated. From then on, work at the Legal Defense Fund became a combination of trying to implement and extend the decision, and to ward off the attacks on the NAACP, its sister organization. I found myself becoming familiar with such phrases as "barratry, champerty, and maintenance" and "running and capping"—all archaic concepts of lawyer misbehavior that Southern politicians were dusting off to disable the NAACP and its lawyers. Ultimately, in these cases the Supreme Court ringingly affirmed the right of public-interest lawyers and their clients to bring test cases to the courts.

All the while, I was learning from Thurgood and Bob how to be an advocate. Bob had a creative mind and liked to push the envelope. It was he more than anyone who pioneered the use of social science evidence. In *Brown*, psychologist Kenneth Clark testified about the results of his "doll tests" in which African American children consistently expressed positive views about white dolls and negative views about black dolls, supporting the conclusion that segregation led to low self-esteem. The use of such social science evidence became standard in many types of public-interest litigation. At the same time, Carter organized and managed the case docket, pushing hard to take full advantage of the 1954 victory.

Thurgood had a deceptively folksy manner. He loved to tell stories and jokes, and we seemed to develop an affinity because I appreciated his stories and liked to tell my own. He was at times raucous and crude in his manner. Years later when I asked Bob Carter what he thought about a television docudrama in which Thurgood was played by Sidney Poitier, he paused a moment and replied, "Sidney Poitier was Thurgood as we all wished him to be." Thurgood also liked to loosen up for oral arguments with a few drinks. It had become traditional to do a "dry run" of an argument at Howard University Law School, with lawyers assuming the role of justices and asking challenging questions. After one such session, we repaired the night before argument to Thurgood's suite at the old Park Sheraton in Washington. A half dozen of us talked about the case for hours while Thurgood consumed most of the contents of a bottle of Jack Daniels. Somehow he was fully alert and ready for argument the next morning.

Thurgood was also a skillful politician. He had a friendly, joshing manner with lawyers representing the other side. Even though he detested the positions they were advocating, he apparently had decided that nothing was to be gained by dealing with them as enemies. I thought at times that if he had chosen, Thurgood could have been elected to public office.

Underneath all this, Thurgood was a superb advocate. He used the sessions with his kitchen cabinet to decide on his basic arguments and on how to handle potentially difficult questions. He had the critical skill that the great oral advocates I've known have all possessed—the ability to translate complex problems into simple terms without distorting or reducing their content. He was able to relate to and even bond with Supreme Court justices. They had learned that he would be well prepared and that, without histrionics, he would describe the plight of his clients in ways that made them real people for the justices.

All through 1955 and the first half of 1956, I continued to write briefs in a wide variety of cases. When my one-year internship concluded, I became a regular staff member. Although my work was in New York, I occasionally attended meetings around the country. In April 1955, NAACP leaders gathered in Atlanta to express their determination to carry through with the effort to desegregate. I flew down to the meeting with Frank Reeves, a Howard Law School professor and black civil rights lawyer who later became commissioner of the District of Columbia. We had heard that, despite rigid segregation in almost all hotels in Atlanta, there was one Holiday Inn that accepted black patrons. We obtained directions at the airport and took off in our rented car. The trouble was, we were directed to a different Holiday Inn and wound up in Hapeville, a rural outpost in the metropolitan area. When we arrived, a huge Confederate flag hung in the lobby told us that we were in the wrong place. The angry glares of an assortment of white men hanging around the lobby confirmed this. We took off in a hurry. Some months later, Frank and I were returning by auto from a meeting in Virginia. We decided to stop in northern Virginia at one of the then-new fast food joints for something to eat. We ordered from the car and in a few minutes a waitress appeared carrying our order. When she saw Frank in the car she turned on her heel and took the trays back to the restaurant. We briefly discussed repeating our adventure at other fast food places but decided it wouldn't be a good use of our time.

In February 1956, the NAACP invited Martin Luther King Jr. to speak at its annual board meeting to be held in New York. It would be a small affair of about fifty board members and staff. King had recently emerged on the scene as the leader of the successful Montgomery bus boycott. But the NAACP eyed him warily as a potential rival for leadership and decided to use the invitation to establish contact. As the most junior member of the legal staff, I was asked to meet King at LaGuardia Airport in a limousine and escort him to the meeting. My neighbors on West Ninety-second Street in Manhattan gawked as the limousine pulled up to my house. I don't recall anything of note about my conversation on the way in except that he was self-possessed and friendly. Long after the event it struck me that, at the age of twenty-four, I had met a man who was destined to change the face of America and who was already a leader at the age of twenty-eight. Thurgood took a less benign view of King. He believed that, with his direct action movement, King just made a mess and that it fell to Thurgood and his staff to clean it up. I have to think, however, that in his heart Thurgood had come to know that legal victories were not enough and that it required the leadership of a King to get black people to take ownership of the *Brown* decision and strive to make it a reality. In the dozen years that King lived after our first encounter—years in which he changed the face of the nation—we met on several occasions, and he always expressed appreciation for the work others and I were doing at the U.S. Commission on Civil Rights, which was one small piece of the effort to alter American attitudes about race.

In July, 1956, my draft notice came from the army and I was sent to Fort Hood, Texas, for basic training with the Fourth Armored Division. The temperature in central Texas was over one hundred degrees practically every day and the area was a wasteland. Once when I was on a detail, the supply sergeant told me that I had just received a package "from the States." It certainly felt like we were not in our own country. But when basic training was concluded, I was sent (thirty pounds lighter) to an assignment some of my journalist friends had held in prior years, with the Recruiting Publicity Center at Governors Island, New York City. My work at the center, largely consisting of writing ad copy to entice young men to enlist in the army, was less than demanding and I found I could leave by four p.m., catch the ferry into Manhattan, and then spend the next several hours each day at my work for the Legal Defense Fund.

My situation permitted me one more frolic and detour. Quiz shows had become the rage and several friends encouraged me to seek to become a contestant on the most rigorous one, *Twenty-One*. I took the test and was accepted, becoming a standby on *Twenty-One* and a contestant on a sister show, *Tic Tac Dough*. There I won seven thousand dollars before deciding on the advice of Harriett to take the money and run. The show was fun, enabling me to display my mastery of such trivia as the pen name of Charles Dickens (Boz), the nom de plume of Amandine Dupin (George Sand), and the name of a popular 1930s tune ("Jeepers Creepers"), On the other hand, to my embarrassment as a lawyer. I froze when asked the first five words of the preamble to the Constitution, being able to recall only the first five words of the Declaration of Independence. My winnings helped supplement my low yearly salary at the Legal Defense Fund (four thousand dollars) and my meager army pay. The windfall was especially welcome since our first child, Lauren, had been born only a couple of months earlier and Harriett was still on unpaid maternity leave from her job with a labor-law firm. But I was also ready to quit the show, in part, because I thought I was being cast in a role—the humble and lowly army private in uniform—to encourage the audience to think that anyone could win.

When I informed Jack Barry, *Tic Tac Dough*'s host, of my decision he was very upset. It was ratings week and the show's producers had a considerable investment in me because I was now an identifiable figure to their audience. If I stayed, Barry said, I would be guaranteed that only half my winnings would be at stake, instead of all of them. I refused. That day I received a call at the base from a producer asking me to talk to Dan Enright, the chief producer of the show, who would make me a better offer. I assumed that he would propose to give me answers. Before they could "improve" their offer, I again said no to continuing. I said that it would be impossible for me to say anything else because acceptance of any inducements could lead to my losing my license to practice law, for unethical behavior.

My participation on the show did earn me an appearance before a grand jury when the quiz show scandal broke months later. There I was told by the grand jury foreman that at least on *Tic Tac Dough*, I had won more money than anyone who was not being supplied with answers. I never did figure out the mindset of people of stature who did take answers. When I was a standby on *Twenty-One*, the other standby was a professor at Columbia University. As we stood in the wings, we tried to answer the questions being put to the contestants. I found the questions difficult and missed several. She answered all of them. Later she went on the show and won more money than any previous contestant—including Charles van Doren, who was famously fed answers—after which it was revealed that she had also been given answers. Since I doubted that she had been fed answers as a standby, I never understood why she would not trust in her own abilities when she became a contestant.

When I returned to the Legal Defense Fund, I discovered that things had changed. The Internal Revenue Service had been putting pressure on the Fund. Since its sister organization, the National Association for the Advancement of Colored People (NAACP), engaged in legislative lobbying, it was not eligible for tax-exempt status. If the Fund was deemed too closely tied to the NAACP, it could lose its tax-exempt status, too. The solution was to separate the organizations. Thurgood, who had been counsel for the NAACP as well as director-counsel for the Fund, stepped down from the former position, and Bob Carter became general counsel of the NAACP. I found that the schism was more than formal. Thurgood and Bob had ended their friendship, and other lawyers on Thurgood's staff suggested that I line up with Thurgood and terminate my work and friendship with Bob. I refused to do so and walked a tightrope to keep up my relationship with both.

On the policy side, Bob, always searching for new frontiers, sought to expand litigation to attack school segregation in the North. Relying on the Supreme Court's implication that segregation caused harm even if not deliberately imposed, he appeared not to appreciate fully the legal difficulties in making the case in Northern states where there were no current segregation statutes. But Thurgood had a more practical political objection. He thought it would not make sense to open a second front in a war in which there was still major resistance on the first front. If suits were brought in the North, some white folks who had been supportive of civil rights would begin to focus on the implications for their own lives and withdraw their support. This was the substantive element of the breach, but I gathered there were other elements as well. Bob and Thurgood did not reconcile until the 1980s. Julius Chambers, a successor to Thurgood at the Fund, planned a reception to honor Bob that was in the nature of an olive branch. Bob was clearly touched but, not able to fully suppress his acerbic wit, he said in his speech that "Now I know what it feels like to be rehabilitated."

The high point in my career at the Fund came right after I returned to the Fund full-time on the completion of my army stint. I was put to work immediately on the Little Rock school case. In 1957, the massive resistance tactics of Arkansas governor Orval Faubus had created a confrontation at Central High School, where a court had ordered desegregation for the first time. President Eisenhower was forced to deploy federal troops to ensure that the court's order would be obeyed and that the nine black students would gain entry to their classes. In 1958, however, as resistance continued, the school board decided to suspend desegregation during the next school year. While the Supreme

Court had said in 1955 that delays based on community resistance would not be countenanced, such delays were occurring in many places, such as Richmond, Virginia; Atlanta, Georgia; New Orleans, Louisiana; and Jackson, Mississippi. Little Rock, Arkansas, posed the clearest challenge to the Court's authority.

In the summer of 1958, the issue came to a head and the Supreme Court decided to convene an extraordinary summer session to address the crisis the case posed. (There have been only a handful of summer sessions in the Court's history.) The oral argument was scheduled for August 28, 1958, and, as I entered the Court with Thurgood, Bill Coleman, and Jack Greenberg, I think we all had the sense of history being made. Thurgood made a strong argument followed by an eloquent statement from J. Lee Rankin, the United States solicitor general. Rankin said in part: "If you teach these children in Little Rock or any other place that as soon as you get some force and violence, the courts of law in this country are going to bow to it, they have no power to deal with it, they will give way to it, will change everything to accommodate that, I think you destroy the whole educational process then and there."

The oral argument had been scheduled so rapidly that there was not enough time to follow the usual procedure of submitting briefs before argument. Afterward it fell to me to draft the Fund's brief in a few days. The basic question was whether the Rule of Law would be upheld or whether the Constitution's protections as interpreted by the Supreme Court could be nullified by violent local resistance. I put together a brief history of how the Court had handled previous crises and a statement of why it was crucial to the integrity of our constitutional system that the Rule of Law be upheld in this case. With input from other lawyers and relatively minor editing, the brief was approved for submission and I took the train to Washington to file the copies with the Clerk's office. In September, the Court upheld our position with the unequivocal statement that "the constitutional rights of respondents are not to be sacrificed or yielded to the violence and disorder which have followed upon the actions of the Governor and the Legislature. . . ." Not only was the decision unanimous, each justice signed his name to the opinion, an unprecedented action. There was still much strife to follow, but the Little Rock decision made it clear finally that *Brown* was the law of the land and would have to be obeyed.

In the years after I left the NAACP in 1958, I maintained my friendship with Bob, but I saw Thurgood only sporadically, and in his later years on the Supreme Court I saw him hardly at all. My friend Wiley Branton, the Little Rock lawyer who was one of the few people to see Thurgood regularly, reported that he had become embittered.

I got some inkling of this in the '80s. At a time when there were many events celebrating the bicentennial of the Constitution, Thurgood had made a powerful speech to the American Bar Association in Hawaii, arguing that the original Constitution was defective because it countenanced slavery and that we did not have a Constitution we could be proud of until adoption of the post–Civil War Amendments. Not long thereafter I was helping plan a commemoration for lawyers and judges and civil rights advocates on the adoption of the Fifteenth Amendment, which was intended to guarantee black people the right to vote. I thought Thurgood would be the ideal keynote speaker and sent him an invitation, asking Wiley to put in a good word. A couple of weeks later, my assistant pulled me out of a meeting, telling me Justice Marshall was on the phone. I said hello and he roared back at me, "Why in the hell should I do that?" I thought quickly. "Because your speech to the Bar in Hawaii was so powerful and this would be a great audience to hear your message." "I did it once, I don't need to do it again," he said, ending the conversation.

In the 1970s, two 5–4 decisions of the Court—one, written by Justice Powell, countenancing major disparities in state school financing that worked to the disadvantage of minority and poor children and the other, written by Chief Justice Burger, all but closing the door to metropolitan school desegregation remedies (the only kind that would work in segregated cities), dealt a crushing blow to the quest for equal educational opportunity. Thurgood's dissents were strong and eloquent, but decidedly in the minority.

It may have been particularly galling to Thurgood, having reached a position of great influence, to find that he could no longer preserve the victories he had achieved as an advocate. With Reagan's appointments to the Court in the '80s things only got worse. In 1992, after Thurgood had resigned and Clarence Thomas was narrowly confirmed to be his successor, Thurgood's longtime assistant, Alice Stovall, called to ask whether I would like to have lunch with him in the office he still maintained at the Supreme Court. I leaped at the opportunity. Our lunch was mainly nonpolitical; we swapped stories and talked of the old days. But toward the end Thurgood leaned toward me and said in a conspiratorial tone, "Do you know what they told me about Clarence Thomas?" No, I said. He said, "There were ten Negroes in his class at Yale Law School and he ranked number ten."

The comment illustrates one aspect of Thurgood's character. He was a firm believer in the merit principle. His opposition to Thomas was based not just on the latter's anti–civil rights positions ("a black snake is no better than a white snake," he had said) but on his conviction that Thomas simply did not have the intellectual qualifications for the position. Thurgood's bitterness, it seems to me, also stemmed from another conservative part of his character—his almost religious faith in the power of the law. That faith helped sustain his belief that law could be the instrument for overcoming entrenched racism in this country. When Potter Stewart, the swing vote on the Court, shrank in the Detroit case from approving the only school desegregation remedy that would work, Thurgood wrote in dissent that "today's decision I fear is more a product of perceived political realities than of the application of neutral principles of law."

He was right, of course, but I remain sad that he felt so alienated. Certainly the struggle for equality today is being thwarted on many fronts. And I find irony in Thurgood's name being etched on so many schools that remain racially isolated. But this nation is a different and much better place because of his heroic efforts. And I wish he could have allowed himself to savor his contributions and accomplishments.

A Little Democracy

When one dips one's hand into the federal treasury, a little democracy necessarily clings to whatever is withdrawn.
—A California judge commenting on the obligation not to use federal funds in a discriminatory manner, in *Ming v. Horgan* (1958)

While working on the Little Rock case had been the culmination of a dream, by the end of 1958 I was ready to strike out on a new path, one where I might see more of the world than the inside of a book-lined law office. As one inspired by the New Deal, I was drawn to Washington, D.C. The White House was then occupied by a Republican, so working on legislative matters seemed the next best thing.

One of the members of Thurgood's expanded kitchen cabinet was Joe Rauh. Joe had worked in the New Deal after serving as a Supreme Court clerk to Justice Benjamin Cardozo and then to Justice Felix Frankfurter. After his stint in the New Deal, working to implement the Lend-Lease program to help the British and the war mobilization effort, and service in the South Pacific in World War II, Joe struck out on his own as a lawyer. By the '50s he had become a powerful voice for civil rights and civil liberties, and a political force in Washington. At the 1948 Democratic Convention, Joe had helped Hubert Humphrey craft his extraordinary speech urging Democrats to "get out of the shadow of states' rights and walk forthrightly into the bright sunshine of civil rights." This was the message that led to the immediate walkout of Strom Thurmond and the Dixiecrats but ultimately to the rebirth of the Democrats as the party of civil rights.

After the war, Joe had worked with a group of young liberals—Jim Loeb, a journalist who later became an ambassador during the Kennedy administration, economist Bob Nathan, labor leader Walter Reuther, and others—to establish Americans for Democratic Action. The organization, designed as a progressive force in American life, would oppose the influence of communism both at home and abroad without repressing civil liberties. When I learned that ADA was looking for a lobbyist on domestic affairs, I applied. In 1957, Joe and Clarence Mitchell, chief lobbyist for the NAACP, had led a coalition of civil rights, labor, and civic groups in pushing for enactment of the first civil rights legislation since the end of Reconstruction. A bill passed, but it was a rather pale shadow of the law that was sought, notable largely for authorizing the attorney general to bring voting rights cases and for establishing a bipartisan, independent Commission on Civil Rights to find facts about denials of equal protection and voting.

It was into this environment I stepped upon joining ADA. Again I was becoming part of a boutique operation with a big agenda. The ADA staff in Washington consisted of a director, a political director, a field representative, a communications person, an expert on foreign policy issues, and me. I soon discovered that I was expected to become knowledgeable (if not expert) about a very wide array of public issues. Looking back, I realize that, over the course of the two and a half years I worked for ADA, I testified before Congress about a dozen times, covering such issues as the foreign aid appropriation, congressional reapportionment, and trafficking in television licenses. On other occasions, I helped experts prepare testimony on such topics as the bill that became Medicare, housing for low-income people, increases in the minimum wage, and the like. These days, it would be almost unthinkable for any one organization, particularly one the size of ADA, to cover such a wide spectrum of issues. With the growth of specialized groups dealing with the environment, energy, budget policy, and other subjects, the role of ADA and other broad-ranging organizations has declined. No longer is it necessary for someone who wants to reform, for example, communications policy, to turn to ADA as the vehicle for his concerns, when a more specialized and focused group working on telecommunications issues is available.

Working on Capitol Hill for ADA was a great learning experience, just as being a lawyer for the Legal Defense Fund had been. I learned how to prepare written testimony and to deliver it before congressional committees, to lobby and rally the liberal forces by speaking around the country, to write a monthly legislative newsletter, and to moderate discussions on radio stations that aired public service broadcasts.

Two sets of issues dominated during the time I spent at ADA. One concerned the considerable vestiges of the McCarthy era. Although the senator from Wisconsin left the Senate in disgrace and died in 1957, the repressive atmosphere he had helped to create still existed in 1959 and was reflected in a host of bills in Congress seeking, for example, to deny passports to people with suspect views (like playwright Arthur Miller and Nobel Prize–winning scientist Linus Pauling) and to allow the summary suspension and dismissal of federal employees, even those in nonsensitive positions, on grounds of national security. Where the Supreme Court had protected the right to travel or to be accorded due process of law, the sponsors of repressive legislation were ready to override the Court or to repeal its jurisdiction over the matter. Some of the discussion at the hearings was almost comical. I remember once being in the company of a historian on a panel in the House discussing passport legislation. The historian repeatedly quoted Jefferson to illustrate how the bill violated Jeffersonian ideals. Finally, the chairman of the committee, a congressman from Tennessee, exploded. "If Jefferson were alive today," he said, "he'd be turning over in his grave."

Fortunately, I discovered that it is often much easier to prevent bad legislation from becoming law than it is to secure the enactment of good legislation. Although support for anti–civil liberties bills was still significant by 1959 and 1960, much of the steam had gone out of the movement and alert advocates and progressive legislators were able to stymie efforts to move the bills into law.

In civil rights, however, the problem was quite the opposite. In the House, the Rules Committee was the traffic cop for all bills, and it was presided over by Howard Smith of Virginia, who would use a variety of tactics including leaving town if a civil rights bill was presented to his committee. In the Senate, the existence of a one-party South, along with the seniority system, meant that all of the key committees were chaired by Democratic mandarins who could thwart bills to advance equality or ameliorate poverty. Civil rights advocates were intent on obtaining a new law that would strengthen the timid 1957 Act. Even in voting, the one area in which the 1957 Act had provided a seemingly effective remedy, little was being accomplished because Southern federal judges, many of whom reflected the racial attitudes of the communities in which they served, let dilatory tactics thwart suits filed by the federal government. In 1959, the Civil Rights Commission recommended creating a system of federal voting registrars to enroll Negro applicants where state and local officials continued to reject them, and civil rights advocates sought to have that recommendation written into law.

I got a taste of what lobbying on civil rights would be like when in 1959 I accompanied Joe Rauh and Clarence Mitchell to a meeting with Illinois Senator Everett Dirksen, whose status as a Republican leader made his support crucial. After a few preliminaries, Dirksen spoke. Addressing himself to Clarence Mitchell, he said, "Clarence, as you know, I voted with you on the 1957 Act, but that vote brought me no support from the NAACP or from Negro citizens in my district. I don't see any reason to support you this time." Wow, I thought. I knew that such political calculations were a dominating factor in the legislative process, but I had no idea that it was so crass and out in the open.

Dirksen's response proved to be an accurate predictor of the mood in Congress. Despite the growing salience of civil rights as a legislative and political issue, there simply was not enough drive or momentum to overcome the well-organized resistance. The Civil Rights Act of 1960 turned out to be one of the more forgettable pieces of legislation in history. It did provide an administrative process ("voting referees"). But the process could only be activated at the end of a lawsuit that had to be filed in federal court. It did nothing to deal with the overriding problem of delay in according minority citizens their right to vote.

While we had little to show for our efforts, working in that campaign and other legislative endeavors was a personally rewarding experience. It brought me into contact with an extraordinary group of progressive legislators, among them Hubert Humphrey, Paul Douglas, and Jacob Javits, all of whom were eloquent voices for economic and social justice. While there are many fine senators and representatives today and while Ted Kennedy remains the most dominant and effective legislator of the last half century, I think it is something more than the haze of nostalgia that leads me to conclude that the '50s and '60s were an era of excellence that we have not seen since. The infection of the political process with money from well-heeled contributors, incessant polling, and simplistic sound bites makes the emergence of quality leadership far more difficult now.

On the other hand, there were congressional practices then whose passing will not be regretted. Many legislative hearings were held in secret, with the public excluded from attendance. I remember testifying once on foreign aid before the House Foreign Affairs Appropriations Subcommittee. The hearing was held in the Capitol in a room with slatted wooden doors and tables covered in green felt, that reminded me of a billiards parlor. The chair of the committee was Otto Passman, a "good ol' boy" from Louisiana, who demonstrated his contempt for me and my organization by reading a newspaper during my testimony. At the same time, there were offensive displays by legislators that were not fit for public consumption. My attendance at evening sessions of the House or Senate not infrequently treated me to a rambling, incoherent speech by a legislator who was totally in his cups. With the advent of C-SPAN such performances have not disappeared totally, but they are rarer.

One senator I did not meet was Lyndon Johnson, the majority leader since 1955. Johnson was anathema to civil rights and liberal organizations, reviled as the person responsible for having diluted the Civil Rights Act of 1957. We regarded as spurious the argument that Johnson had helped make possible the first civil rights legislation since Reconstruction. Johnson had never declared support for the Supreme

Court's desegregation decision and his general stance on race resembled that of his Southern colleagues.

One person I did come to know was Harry McPherson, a young Texas lawyer and a key legislative aide to Johnson. Despite our very differing roles, we seemed to share common values and political ideals. In early 1960, talk was emanating from the Johnson camp of a possible run for the presidency, based largely on Johnson's meteoric rise as majority leader. Harry and I had lunch and he told me that he thought Johnson would be a great president on domestic issues. But at the same time Harry worried about how Johnson would perform on foreign policy. While at the time I rejected Harry's praise of Johnson, I came to think later that those were the most prescient words I had ever heard uttered in all my years in D.C.

In the summer it was my job as ADA legislative representative to present the organization's positions to the Republican and Democratic national conventions. At the Republican convention I felt like Alice in Wonderland as I heard Barry Goldwater explain to the delegates that the Supreme Court was wrong in *Brown* because you could read the whole Constitution and never find the word "education." At the Democratic convention in Los Angeles my friend and ADA colleague, Richard Sachs, had managed to get friends of his to lend him a house in the Hollywood Hills with a swimming pool to which we could repair after a hard day's lobbying at the convention.

Our idyll came to an end when it was announced that Jack Kennedy as the presidential nominee had decided that Lyndon Johnson would be his running mate. Richard and I managed to wangle our way onto the floor of the convention in time to hear Joe Rauh make an impassioned public plea to the candidate. "Please, for God's sake, Jack, don't do it." Meanwhile in the scene of confusion that followed, I ran into Senator Bill Proxmire of Wisconsin and Representative Jim O'Hara of Michigan, both staunch Johnson opponents. They were celebrating. With Johnson as vice president, they reasoned, "We'll never have to worry about him again." Those were possibly the *least* prophetic words I have heard in my years in politics.

Hubert Humphrey had been ADA's hero in the primaries, but once he was defeated, the organization turned quickly to Jack Kennedy, eschewing advocacy of a third Adlai Stevenson campaign, which seemed a likely loser. While I was less than enchanted with Kennedy's credentials as a liberal, one aspect of his campaign captured my interest completely. That was the organization of a group of Kennedy supporters to develop a program for enforcement of civil rights through executive action and to make it a central part of the campaign, designed to attract the votes of black people and white progressives. The theme of the civil rights program was that, while legislation was needed, there was much the president could do to enforce civil rights even without new laws.

Since 1957, I had pursued research that led me to a similar set of beliefs. The president, I thought, could draw upon his constitutional power to "take care that the laws be faithfully executed" to ensure that constitutional rights declared by the Supreme Court were enforced even if Congress had not ratified those rights through legislation. This executive authority could include issuing executive orders with-drawing federal funds from institutions that continued to engage in racial discrimination. It might also include the ability to send the attorney general into court to enforce rights declared in Supreme Court decisions, authority that had been unsuccessfully sought in Congress.

I signed up to work with this aspect of the Kennedy campaign. At the end of October we staged a national conference on constitutional rights in New York City attended by four hundred enthusiastic civil rights and community leaders from forty-two states. Kennedy spoke on the importance of executive leadership, saying there were many things that "can be done by a stroke of the presidential pen," including an executive order for equal opportunity in housing. Afterward, I helped draft a report from Hubert Humphrey, chairman of the confer-ence, addressed to candidate Kennedy, describing the main recom-mendations for a program of executive action.

We were elated by Kennedy's electoral victory over Richard Nixon. John Silard, Joe Rauh's law partner, organized a seven-course celebratory dinner for Kennedy civil rights supporters at the Peking Restaurant in downtown D.C. John had written a campaign speech for Kennedy, calculating the chances that a Negro baby born then had—compared with a white baby—of graduating high school, going to college, enjoying good health, living a long life. The disparities in every category were striking, and Kennedy continued to use them in speeches after he became president. Even those of us who were habitually skeptical could not help but be invigorated by the youthful energy of Kennedy and his retinue.

Redeeming the campaign promises proved to be another matter. The idea had been for Kennedy to establish an office on civil rights in the White House to serve as the hub of a new program that would involve every federal agency in executive action. But when the victory turned out to be so narrow, Kennedy's closest aides had second thoughts. Such an office so closely associated with the president might damage his relations with key Southern legislators. And Richard Neustadt, a political science professor who was a Kennedy adviser, counseled against the creation of subject matter groups in the White House as conflicting with cabinet functions.

Instead, it was decided to appoint a special assistant for civil rights—Harris Wofford, who had worked at the Civil Rights Commission and had played a key role in the campaign—and to establish an interdepartmental committee composed of appointees at the assistant secretary level or above to plan a program of executive action. I was asked to serve as the secretariat for Wofford and the committee, but to carry out my duties from the post of special assistant to the staff director of the U.S. Civil Rights Commission rather than in the White House. Although the structure was cumbersome, we were optimistic.

President Kennedy set a new civil rights tone for his administration. When he pointed out that there were no servicemen of color in the Coast Guard contingent that marched in the inauguration day parade, he sent a message to all government agencies to look to their hiring practices. He spoke up in support of the Supreme Court's *Brown* decision, something his predecessor had resolutely refused to do.

The new interdepartmental committee—dubbed the Subcabinet Committee on Civil Rights—met monthly, usually in the Roosevelt Room at the White House. Many of the discussions focused on the need to actively recruit people of color for federal positions. Within nine months the administration had compiled a creditable record. Thurgood Marshall was nominated to the Court of Appeals for the Second Circuit; Cecil Poole, a young prosecutor, became the first black U.S. attorney; Bob Weaver, a veteran housing expert, was named administrator of the Housing and Home Finance Agency; and several other men of color were named to ambassadorships and subcabinet positions. The concern about minority employment extended throughout the ranks of federal agencies. The Civil Service Commission conducted a tour of twenty-four Southern black colleges to recruit employees. A few months later, the Treasury Department reported to me that the treasury secretary's office had employed four Negro secretaries, the first people of color to work in that office, and that at the Internal Revenue Service office in Atlanta, six Negro key-punch operators were scheduled to report for duty—a mark of how exclusionary the federal government had been.

At the same time, the subcabinet group was pondering ways to have federal officials set a standard and make a statement by their own conduct. So, Secretary of Labor Arthur Goldberg issued an order forbidding Labor Department employees from attending meetings at segregated hotels. The impact was to cancel the participation of federal employees in the state conference of employment security agencies being held in Atlanta. The president issued a directive in April 1961 stating that no federal agency could permit its "name, sponsorship, facilities, or activity" to be used in connection with any employee recreational group that practiced discrimination.

Some of these efforts involved funny or peculiar twists. It was not too difficult for the government to bar cafeterias or restaurants in federal buildings from segregating or excluding black employees—a common practice in those days. But what about such dining facilities when they were located in buildings where the federal government occupied only leased space? That seemed a more complicated legal problem, so I was dispatched along with my associate Pete Libassi to try to solve the problem by jawboning with representatives of the building owners. We went to see a lawyer in New York City who represented several owners of buildings in the South where the federal government leased space and where on-site cafeterias excluded blacks. This lawyer had frequent dealings with people from the federal government, particularly housing officials, and said at the outset of the conversation that he would be glad to see what he could do for us. He listened as we explained the problem and then was quiet for a few moments. Finally, he said, "If you guys were from the FHA [the Federal Housing Administration], I'd know what to do with you," accompanying his statement with a gesture rubbing his thumb across his other fingers to suggest the exchange of money. "But you are a different kettle of fish; I don't know what to do with you." We were startled a bit by the directness of his response. It was a while before we got cafeterias in his buildings desegregated.

Another problem was brought to the subcabinet group by Pedro Sanjuan, a young aide at the State Department. Black ambassadors from newly independent African nations were encountering discrimination when they sought service in restaurants on Route 40 between Washington and Baltimore. This, too, seemed a problem susceptible to jawboning, and Harris Wofford and State Department representatives undertook to persuade restaurant owners to abandon their discriminatory practices. At one point someone suggested that the problem might be more easily solved if the diplomats would wear traditional dress—dashikis or turbans—when they drove along Route 40. But that idea was scotched after a couple of black journalists from Baltimore donned such robes to seek service. And it seemed to miss the point that American foreign policy was ill served by discrimination against any black person regardless of nationality. President Kennedy, who favored conflict avoidance, suggested to the State Department that it encourage black ambassadors to fly rather than take Route 40, which he said was "a hell of a road." Eventually the restaurant owners saw the light and in 1964 Congress made discrimination in public accommodations unlawful.

Race is the issue that clouds our minds. Assumptions about race often evoke reactions that are interesting and sometimes funny. Here are a few illustrations.

Wiley Branton was the best storyteller I ever knew. I first met Wiley in 1956, when he was representing the black children in the Little Rock school desegregation case and I was doing research and writing briefs in the litigation. Wiley had a down-home manner, a fine legal mind, a cherubic face, and a Mediterranean olive complexion that often led people to assume mistakenly that he was white.

One of Wiley's stories had to do with a phone call he received from a friend named George who had been a high school classmate in a segregated school in their hometown of Pine Bluff, Arkansas. George was in trouble with the law in a city in the panhandle of Florida, where a complaint had been filed against him on a minor matter. But as a black man in a white town facing a criminal charge, he had to take it seriously, so he called Wiley. Wiley called the legal authorities to notify them he would be representing George and suggested in his call that George was a kind of retainer for the Branton family and that he, Wiley, was providing his legal services as an act of noblesse oblige. When Wiley arrived in Florida, he was warmly received. Within a few days, the district attorney asked him to address the local bar association and the sheriff invited him to go duck hunting. In short order the charges were dropped.

Wiley and George decided it would be prudent to leave Florida immediately. As they drove toward the state line, they needed to make a rest stop at a gas station. As Wiley recounts it, George got out of the car first and asked the attendant where the men's room was and was told that none was available but that he could go to the back of the building. Wiley got out of the car and made the same inquiry and was told, "right this way, sir." Wiley said he got to the men's room and, "I heard old George splashing up against the wall outside and the absurdity of it all just struck me. So I leaned out the window and shouted to George, 'Niggah, niggah, niggah.'

Carl Holman was a journalist for black newspapers, a poet, and for several years my colleague at the U.S. Commission on Civil Rights. He told me once of having been invited to speak at a historically black public university in the South. At least through the 1960s these institutions, while nominally headed by black presidents, were under the thumb of white officialdom and observed all of the local customs. So Carl's invitation was unusual. He told of having arrived by plane at a Southern airport late at night and entering into a nearly deserted waiting room. There, a young black man was peering around the room evidently looking for the person he was to meet. Carl finally approached him and inquired if he was waiting for Mr. Holman. The young man looked stricken but acknowledged that this was his mission. They got into the young man's car and drove for a while in silence. Finally the young man said, "I'm supposed to meet Whitney Young next week. Will he be colored, too?"

In Wiley's adventure, it is clear that things might not have gone nearly as well for his friend George if the Florida authorities had concluded that Wiley was a black man. In Carl Holman's case, the student who came to meet him was challenged perhaps for the first time to think about the roles that African Americans play in this society.

Of course, ethnic or religious differences other than race can cause confusion, too. When I was hired by the NAACP Legal Defense Fund at the end of 1954, I became part of a professional staff of eight headed by Thurgood Marshall and Bob Carter. Those who were not away on cases often lunched together near the office. One day at lunch, after I had been there for three or four months, one of my companions said the group had a confession to make. They had thought because of my name and appearance that in hiring me the Fund had captured its first WASP (I had to explain that the original family name was Chiat, but that according to family legend it was changed to Taylor when my grandparents arrived at Ellis Island, chiat being Hebrew for "tailor.") My colleagues said they had been very disappointed to learn that I was Jewish. Jews they had, but they had never had a white Protestant.

More than thirty years later, at a time when tensions between blacks *and Jews were high, a liberal philanthropist arranged a meeting between members of each group who had worked in civil rights to promote an atmosphere of reconciliation. This was not to be a discussion of divisive issues, our convener told us, but a time to tell stories and share reminiscences. I told my Legal Defense Fund story, figuring that it was as good an illustration as any of the close historic ties between blacks and Jews. It was well received.*

Afterward, I was approached by Oliver Hill, a veteran lawyer from Richmond who had been part of the team who tried the Virginia part of the Brown case. Oliver and I had worked together and become friends in the '50s. Now he told me earnestly that he appreciated my story, but he added, "You know, during those days I thought the same thing as the other folks, but now that you are older and your face has changed, I can see it."

The First Days of Affirmative Action

Some issues ran deeper. One of the accomplishments of the early months of the administration was President Kennedy's issuance of a new executive order prohibiting discrimination in employment by companies that received federal contracts. The policy in this area had an interesting lineage. Just before the entry of the United States into World War II, A. Philip Randolph, the pioneering black labor leader who headed up the union representing Pullman car workers, called on President Roosevelt to take action against employment discrimination and threatened a mass civil rights march on Washington if the government was unresponsive. With the intervention of Mrs. Roosevelt, the administration issued an order barring discrimination against Negro workers in defense plants. After the war was over, President Truman and then President Eisenhower promulgated new executive orders continuing the policy.

The new Kennedy order strengthened the authority of the committee designated to enforce its provisions, decreasing the likelihood that individual government agencies, anxious to get their contract work done, would turn a blind eye to discrimination. The order also bolstered sanctions that included terminating contracts and barring a discriminating contractor from further contracts. Most intriguing was a new phrase, not found elsewhere in federal laws or policies, which required contractors to "take affirmative action" to bring about compliance.

The idea came from John Feild, who had directed the Michigan State Civil Rights Commission and who had been recruited to head the new government contracts committee. At an early meeting of a small ad hoc group that Harris Wofford had organized to plan strategy on a weekly basis, John explained that his experience in Michigan had taught him that you could not expect that tangible results would be achieved just by ordering employers to terminate long-entrenched practices of discrimination. "Just taking down the signs that say 'no Negroes need apply' won't do it. You need to have affirmative outreach." In the early days, that meant advertising in Negro newspapers, launching recruiting visits to black colleges, and getting black people into apprenticeship and other training programs. (Later it was found that in some areas such as the building trades, where exclusionary practices were deeply embedded in the culture, these measures were not enough. First Lyndon Johnson and then Richard Nixon adopted plans to set numerical goals and timetables, beginning what has become the forty-year struggle over the policy of affirmative action.)

Using these new tools to try to change employment patterns proved slow going, and matters were made more difficult by a public relations effort that Lyndon Johnson organized to encourage businesses to commit themselves to fair employment. Dubbed "Plans for Progress," it was led by Bobby Troutman, an Atlanta entrepreneur who had been a longtime friend of President Kennedy. The idea was that large contractors would sign a general agreement with the government that all their job practices would be nondiscriminatory. The signing would be accompanied by a photo opportunity with the vice president and as much media hoopla as could be mustered. The trouble, though, was that there was no serious implementation or followthrough. A couple of years later, a study revealed that, taken as a whole, the civil rights records of the companies that signed were not even as good as those of comparable companies that were not government contractors and had no obligations under the executive order. By that time, Troutman, whose aggressive ways and P. T. Barnum style had offended many people, had quit and the program was in mothballs.

A Stroke of the Pen

If creating equal job opportunity posed problems, dealing with government's long history in subsidizing racial discrimination in housing was even tougher. As I studied the subject I realized how deeply implicated the federal government had been in creating the racially isolated housing patterns that marked most of the nation. In the 1930s when the public housing program was begun under the New Deal to provide shelter for the poorest people, a policy of "racial equity" was established, but this did not prohibit the rigid segregation of housing projects—some for whites, some for blacks—in every part of the country. No progress was made in ending this segregation until after the *Brown* decision, when challenges to segregation were brought in Detroit and elsewhere. By this time, the sites selected for public housing were so often located in black neighborhoods that it was difficult to dislodge segregation.

Even more far-reaching in its impact was the housing legislation adopted by Congress in 1934 to counteract the effects of the Depression. The idea was to help people avert the loss of their homes and to acquire new ones through low down payments and subsidized mortgages. Eventually, the program aided the spurt in home building after World War II that led to burgeoning suburbs throughout the nation. The trouble was that, while all this was happening, the official policy of the United States government was to promote racial segregation and exclusion. The government shared the private housing industry's belief that property values suffered when residents of a neighborhood were not homogeneous. So the Federal Housing Administration issued an underwriting manual in 1938 declaring that "if a neighborhood is to retain stability, it is necessary that properties continue to be occupied by the same social and racial groups." To make its views operational,

FHA recommended the use of racially restrictive covenants to ensure against the mingling of "inharmonious racial groups," helpfully including a model covenant that would make the owners of FHA-insured homes liable to a lawsuit if they sold their homes to someone of another race.

By the end of the '40s, the Supreme Court had ruled the enforcement of racially restrictive covenants unlawful, and the FHA policies were officially off the books. But the damage had been done. Millions of white people had used the low down payment, low interest provision of federal law to acquire suburban homes, and they began to acquire equity that would contribute significantly to their personal wealth. African Americans were not just segregated but effectively excluded from the new housing opportunities in suburbia. While African Americans constituted more than 10 percent of the population, fewer than 2 percent were beneficiaries of government-subsidized mortgages.

We sought an executive order that would ensure that institutions, banks, and savings and loan associations that received federal benefits like insurance on deposits or subsidized mortgages would not discriminate on the basis of race. It was clear, given the almost complete exclusion from the suburbs of people of color, that an order would have to be as comprehensive as possible to make any real dent in the problem.

For more than a year, every time the question of issuing an executive order was raised in policy sessions, it was deferred. Recalling Kennedy's campaign promise to end discrimination in housing with a stroke of the pen, many people began sending pens to the White House. According to Harris Wofford, Kennedy tartly said all the pens should be sent to Wofford for talking him into making this rash pledge.

Finally, in the spring of 1962, Lee White, who had taken over Wofford's civil rights duties at the White House, asked me to canvass all the federal agencies that had housing responsibilities to get their recommendations on the scope of an executive order. Along with Pete Libassi, I conducted a series of interviews with people at the Federal

Housing Administration, the Veterans Administration, the Justice Department, and other agencies. People held a wide range of views. Some wanted a strong and comprehensive order. Others, particularly in the FHA, saw things through the lens of the housing industry and wanted to spare them the difficulties involved in ending longstanding discriminatory practices.

We encountered the greatest resistance to a broad order at the Department of Justice. The issue was whether an executive order could require that nondiscrimination be enforced by the agencies that regulate financial institutions—agencies like the Federal Reserve, the Federal Home Loan Bank Board, the Comptroller of the Currency, and the Federal Deposit Insurance Corporation. These were viewed by some as "independent agencies" beyond the authority of the president to command because they were not part of the executive branch. The Office of Legal Counsel, a unit of the Department of Justice that prepares opinions for the president on executive authority, determined that President Kennedy lacked legal authority to include the financial agencies in his executive order. The Civil Rights Division, another unit of Justice, argued to the contrary and we supported that view with memos of our own as legal staff of the subcabinet committee.

One day in early summer we all gathered in the office of Attorney General Robert Kennedy so that he would have the benefit of knowing both sides of the debate before making a recommendation to the president. Norbert Schlei, assistant attorney general in charge of the Office of Legal Counsel and a contemporary of mine at Yale Law School, made an argument replete with legal citations that the president lacked the necessary legal authority.

Bobby Kennedy interrupted him, asking an aide to bring in a list of the officers and directors of all of the agencies with the dates that their terms were due to expire. Once the list was presented to him, he perused it, seeking the date when a majority of the terms of office expired and the president could make new appointments. When he completed his analysis, he said, "Well, I see that the Home Loan Bank Board is 'independent' only until 1963," implying that the president could then appoint new members committed to a fair housing mandate. Then he noted that Earl Cocke Sr. was head of the FDIC and mused, "Doesn't he have a son who works for us?"

I found myself transfixed by the attorney general's approach. This was not in any political science textbook I had read in college or anything I had studied in law school about the separation of powers. Instead it described the world of realpolitik. In the end, however, the administration's simple political calculations about the likely support and opposition to a strong order trumped the legal arguments and the attorney general's reflections on how the president could use his power. Indeed, as the writings of Ted Sorenson and Arthur Schlesinger have confirmed, the administration waited until November 20, 1962, after the midterm congressional elections, to issue the executive order and released the news during a moment when it would attract the least attention. The order itself covered only federally assisted transactions that took place after the date of its issuance and placed no duties on the banking regulatory agencies. Thus, even if vigorously enforced, it could have no significant impact on racial residential patterns. A few years later, in the wake of the assassination of Martin Luther King Jr., Congress passed the Civil Rights Act of 1968, giving citizens the right to go to court to obtain damages or injunctions when they suffered discrimination in seeking housing. But that act, too, was weak in its enforcement provisions. In the 1970s we sought other remedies for discrimination in mortgage lending, through Congress and the courts. While we enjoyed more success then, the rigid residential segregation that persists in some parts of the nation remains one of the greatest obstacles to equal opportunity.

By June 1963, the civil rights struggle had heated up to the point that the Kennedy administration decided it would be wise to submit to Congress a civil rights bill with real substance. It did so on June 19, proposing a bill to authorize the attorney general to file suits in federal court to end school segregation and calling for the abolition of discrimination in places of public accommodation. But the bill stopped short of advocating a right to fair treatment in the workplace. And the administration remained equivocal on enforceable action to ban discrimination in the use of federal funds.

In ringing terms he had used on other occasions, the president said:

> Simple justice requires that public funds, to which all taxpayers of all races contribute, not be spent in any fashion which encourages, subsidizes, or results in racial discrimination.

Yet having said this, he asked Congress only for a statement that the executive branch had authority to deal with such discrimination, not that it had an obligation to do so through withholding money from recipients of federal funds that continued to engage in discriminatory practices.

The '64 Act

In the fall of 1963 I received a call from Senator Humphrey's office, asking me to meet with his legislative director, John Stewart, and Senator Javits's chief legislative aide, Steve Kurzman. Both were talented lawyers and legislative analysts. When we met, they told me that both senators were thinking of proposing a strong provision on federal funding that would require mandatory action against recipients that persisted in discrimination. To start the process moving, they wanted to draft a letter from their senators to the administration and every federal agency asking them what discriminatory practices existed in their grant programs at that time, whether they believed they had enough authority to deal with them, and what additional authority they needed from Congress to do the job.

What Kurzman and Stewart wanted from me was help in drafting the letters, as they considered me to be expert in this area. It took about ten days for me to put everything together, after which the senators sent the letters to the administration. About a week later, I got a call from Lee White, the chief White House aide on civil rights. "We have received letters from Senators Humphrey and Javits asking questions about federal funding and discrimination, and you are the only person who knows enough to answer them," he said. "Please take on this assignment," he added.

Thus I had the surprising opportunity to answer my own letter, writing in the name of the Kennedy administration to reply to the questions of two prominent senators that had been drafted by me. I had been in a similar situation in 1961. Harris Wofford got the idea that it would be good to have a report from the Civil Rights Commission reviewing progress made since Lincoln's Emancipation Proclamation, the centennial of which was coming up in January 1963. Harris asked me to draft a letter to the commission from the president asking that it undertake the project. The commission was receptive to the idea but thought the administration should make available special funds for the study. So I drafted a letter for John Hannah, chairman of the commission, asking for the funds. Top officials of the administration decided that funds could not be made available. So I drafted another letter from President Kennedy declining the request for funds but hoping the commission would undertake the report anyway. It did so.

But this new version of "I'm gonna sit right down and write myself a letter" had potentially more far-reaching consequences. During the weeks that followed Lee White's assignment, I contacted federal agencies throughout the government, asking them about practices of discrimination by their grantees, and whether they believed they had the legal authority to deny grants to discriminators, or whether legislation would be necessary before they could do so. In doing this, I compiled a large list of discriminatory practices throughout American society— segregation in hospitals that received funds under the federal Hill Burton law; exclusion of black people from federally sponsored employment training and apprenticeship programs; the continuation of segregation and discrimination in public schools—all assisted by federal funds. I had to swallow hard in dealing with the question of executive authority. Although I believed that the president had ample authority to issue executive orders and directives to bar discrimination in the use of federal funds, it was clear by now that many top federal officials held different views, whether based on the law or political considerations. Ironically, the administration's position that it had limited authority actually strengthened the case for legislation. By January 1964, all agencies had completed their responses except the Department of Health, Education, and Welfare (HEW) and the Department of the Interior. At a subcabinet meeting, Lee White asked me to help expedite these replies.

By this time, public support for strong civil rights legislation had grown enormously in the wake of President Kennedy's assassination and his successor's call for a strong law. The two major additions in the House's pending legislation were a fair employment practices provision and a strengthened version of Title VI, the provision to withhold federal funds from institutions that practiced discrimination. As one example of the failure of civil rights opponents to understand the changing terrain, Howard Smith of Virginia, the chair of the Rules Committee, allowed an amendment to the fair employment section providing a remedy for sex discrimination. He thought the new provision would surely kill the bill. Instead it passed handily.

In the Senate, Richard Russell of Georgia was the leader of the opposition and was widely regarded by friend and foe as a superb tactician. But Russell focused almost all his energy on the fair employment section, while Senators Humphrey, Javits, and others were using the record we had compiled to make the case for Title VI, potentially a stronger tool in eradicating discrimination. In the end, Title VI and the rest of the law passed by a wide margin.

With the perspective of almost forty years of experience, it has become clear how central the enactment of Title VI was in protecting the rights of all Americans. Perhaps the most dramatic illustration of this came shortly after passage. For a decade after the Supreme Court's decision in *Brown*, Southern resistance had kept public schools rigidly segregated, with only about two percent of Negro children in the Old South attending schools with whites. A year after passage of the 1964 act, Congress passed the Elementary and Secondary Education Act, providing for the first time substantial federal aid to public education.

The funding was terribly important to school districts, and Lyndon Johnson, in an act of courage, told HEW secretary John Gardner that he was free to withhold federal funds from districts that would not desegregate their schools. Although the opponents of Title VI had claimed that Southern officials would spurn federal funds and that children would suffer the consequences, that is not what happened. Faced with losing the money, most school districts decided to obey the law. By the end of the decade, with Title VI and Justice Department lawsuits, more than half of black children were attending desegregated public schools.

Title VI also helped end a debate about whether rules against discrimination should apply only to government or to other important institutions in our society. Those who took the government-only position pointed to the fact that the Fourteenth Amendment commanded only that "no state" should deny to people the equal protection of the laws. But with the growing involvement of government in what once had been thought to be private institutions—hospitals and private colleges, for example—making a principled distinction became harder. In the end it was recognized that race should not bar anyone from having access to all of American society's important institutions. And that recognition signaled an end to segregated waiting rooms and hospital wards and to so many other racial anomalies that prevailed before the 1960s.

Title VI also served as the model for similar legislation enacted in the 1970s to protect other groups from discrimination. Title IX of the Education Amendments of 1972 required that federal grants to educational institutions be conditioned on the elimination of sex discrimination. Title IX, although best known for ushering in a revolution in women's participation in athletics, also opened the way for breaking down barriers in academia that relegated women to stereotyped roles. The law is now so rooted in our society that when the second Bush administration tried to water down the regulations, a public outcry forced it to back down. So, too, enactment of Section 504 of the Vocational Rehabilitation Act was one of the first steps to require major institutions to offer equal opportunity in jobs and services to people with disabilities. The law not only changed practices but helped break down the stereotype that people with disabilities could not be full participants in the life of the nation.

Finally, Title VI as it has been interpreted and administered over the last forty years has provided a lever for ending many needless practices that hurt minorities even if they were not intended to discriminate. When Title VI was enacted, it required that the president and all federal departments and agencies adopt regulations to implement the law. I was on the team that helped draft the regulations. Again, I profited from the experience of some of my friends and colleagues who had worked with state civil rights agencies. Proving that practices that harmed people of color were motivated by invidious racial intent was often difficult, they said, particularly as such blatant bias became less and less acceptable in polite company. Rather, they argued that it should be sufficient to establish that the practice worked to the disadvantage of minorities and could not be justified as necessary to the operations of the institution. With that reasoning, Pete Libassi and I were able to insert into the regulations a provision that said fund recipients may not "utilize criteria or methods of administration which have the effect of subjecting individuals to discrimination because of race, color, or national origin."

We did not realize at the time how important that brief sentence would turn out to be. As the Supreme Court became more conservative in the 1970s, a majority began to insist that, in order to prove a violation of the Fourteenth Amendment, a showing of invidious intent was necessary. Because Title VI was viewed as a reflection of the Fourteenth Amendment it, too, was interpreted as requiring a demonstration of intent. But the Court also said that it was legally appropriate for the Title VI regulations to go beyond the statute and bar practices that had a discriminatory effect, regardless of what was known about their intentions.

The importance of what came to be called the "disparate impact" standard can be seen in the fact it remains a battleground. For the last thirty years, I and others have been fighting with Senator Orrin Hatch to stave off his efforts to repeal the disparate impact standard as it is reflected in civil rights laws and regulations. In 2001 Supreme Court Justice Antonin Scalia wrote an opinion holding that, while victims of discrimination have a right to sue in federal court to enforce Title VI, they have no right to sue to enforce the regulations. He also hinted broadly that the regulations could be repealed. The current Bush administration has not repealed the regulations, but neither has it brought proceedings to enforce the law.

And yet Title VI and its companion laws dealing with discrimination based on sex and disability continue to thrive. Title VI has been used to require Los Angeles to redraw its mass transit plans to ensure that poor people of color have better access to public transportation. It has been used to attack the concentration of toxic waste sites in minority neighborhoods. It has been used to ensure that immigrant students with limited English proficiency get language instruction that enables them to succeed in school.

Looking back, I think that in the 1960s I may have been too focused on executive action as the means for making progress in civil rights. My image of the presidency was the model provided by Franklin Roosevelt and the leadership he gave to the country in a time of crisis. In the years since, we have had conspicuous examples of the abuse of executive authority in Nixon's Watergate and Reagan's Iran-Contra. While nothing that we urged in the '60s was at all inappropriate, in the wake of the excesses of the Nixon, Reagan, and Bush administrations, I think I would be more careful in claiming a basis for action that might hint at executive-branch supremacy. And while the Kennedy administration was timid in using the executive authority to protect civil rights, ultimately it was very important to have a policy supported by both Congress and the president. What was sought was so fundamental to establishing a society dedicated to equal justice that it needed the foundation of solid support that could only be given by all three branches of government. Still, we might have made more progress through executive action while working to strengthen the foundation.

Finally, I am even more aware now than I was then of the limited role that my fellow lawyers and I played in the civil rights revolution that took place in the '60s. We did not establish the conditions that made enactment of the laws possible. That happened because of the mass movement led by Dr. King and others, and because of popular revulsion at the violent repression of that movement in the South. We in government and at civil rights legal defense groups were simply the craftsmen. When the opportunity arose for new laws, we tried to identify the ways in which laws could be most helpful in advancing opportunity for people of color. History has shown that, in Title VI, we did pretty well.

CHAPTER FOUR

The Road to Mississippi, 1963-65

Why don't you try Alaska?

—President John F. Kennedy to the U.S. Commission on Civil Rights, February 12, 1963

I f the first two years of the Kennedy administration were marked by treading water and taking small steps forward, 1963 would prove to be far more momentous. It began for me with a celebratory event.

The setting was the White House, February 12, 1963, Lincoln's birthday. The event was a ceremony to mark the centennial of the Emancipation Proclamation issued in January 1863, to be followed by a dinner and reception for about eight hundred civil rights and community leaders and government officials.

Louis Martin, the president's chief adviser on minority affairs, believed the event would enhance Kennedy's standing among blacks and advance the cause of civil rights. Martin was elated because, as he told several of us, "There have never been so many brothers invited to the White House at one time."

Martin had the shambling gait and the clipped speech of a '50s hipster. His invariable greeting to his friends was "Hi, chief." But when you got to know him as I did as a friend and neighbor you learned that he was a deeply thoughtful man and to suspect that the speech patterns were those of an innately shy person seeking to project his ideas. Louis may have been responsible for the election of John F. Kennedy as president in 1960. In those years Democrats did not have the claim on the votes of African Americans that they now possess, and Richard Nixon was competitive among black voters. An experienced journalist and editor of the Chicago Defender, a black newspaper, Louis was recruited by the Kennedy campaign to devise strategies to win black votes. In late October, Louis was working with Harris Wofford on the campaign when Martin Luther King Jr. was arrested and imprisoned in Georgia. The circumstances were such that many feared for King's safety. Although they had no ability to secure King's release, Harris, along with Louis hatched the idea that a friendly telephone call by candidate Kennedy to Coretta King, King's spouse, would be both compassionate and a way to draw public attention to his peril. After Kennedy made the call and Mrs. King welcomed it, Louis and other King advocates undertook to publicize Kennedy's support widely in Negro neighborhoods, getting leaflets out to churches, to bars, and neighborhood establishments in Chicago, and elsewhere. The initiative may well have made the difference in the Illinois vote, which decided the election.

I got to know Louis after the election when Harris Wofford was named a special assistant to the president and assembled an ad hoc group of advisers to meet weekly to discuss civil rights strategy. Louis brought practical judgment to these meetings as well as an offbeat, thought-provoking take on the situation of black people in this country. "I'm always glad to see a brother arrested for robbing a bank rather than for a street mugging," he said at one meeting. "It shows their aspirations are rising."

Louis's major cause was the placement of African Americans in policy-making positions throughout government and, beginning with Kennedy and later as a confidant to Lyndon Johnson and as an assistant to Jimmy Carter, he was very successful, changing the face of the federal government. Louis had a mentoring relationship with younger blacks and his loyalty to them mirrored his deep devotion to his wife Gertrude and their five daughters. When any of us did good work on a cause Louis was interested in, he would thank us by saying, "You're a great American." He was a great American.

The Emancipation Proclamation festivities that Louis had master-minded on February 12 were preceded by a meeting of President

Kennedy with members and a few staffers, including me, of the U.S. Commission on Civil Rights. A year earlier, the president had asked the commission to prepare a history of American race relations since the emancipation, and the Commission was there to present its completed report, entitled "Freedom to the Free."

It was an exciting moment for me. I had participated in many sessions at the White House since joining the commission as special assistant to the staff director in March 1961, but I had never been invited to a meeting with the president. President Kennedy delivered a brief speech noting that "it is the Negroes themselves, by their courage and steadfastness, who have done the most to throw off their bonds. In freeing themselves, Negroes have enlarged the freedoms of all Americans." He concluded by telling the commission that it was making a vital contribution to the completion of the task that Abraham Lincoln had begun a century ago. He then turned to the commission for its comments and concerns.

The commission had one urgent item on its agenda—to hold hearings in Mississippi to question voting registrars and local sheriffs about continuing denials of the right to vote, failures to protect Negro citizens against violence, and discriminatory treatment in the administration of justice. The agency had no enforcement authority and we could only employ our investigative powers to document denials of rights and inform the public. The commission had held hearings in Alabama and Louisiana and had already published reports urging strong federal action to deal with disenfranchisement of Negro citizens in the South.

Our primary need now was to hold hearings in Mississippi. Of all the states of the old Confederacy, Mississippi was the most repressive and racist. While some states, prodded by Supreme Court decisions and recent civil rights laws, were making a modicum of progress in permitting Negroes to register to vote, Mississippi presented a solid wall of resistance. In 1960, only 6 percent of eligible black citizens were registered to vote, far below the proportion in other Deep South states. The state's leading elective official in Congress had been Theodore Bilbo, who said in his reelection campaign in 1946 that he was still a Klansman and threatened to punish "any nigger" who tried to vote. After he left, Bilbo's mantle had been grasped by James O. Eastland, the most vociferous Southern legislator in vowing defiance of the Brown decision.

Bilbo's threats were not idle. As the campaign for voter registration in Mississippi heated up, Gus Courts was shot in Belzoni in 1955 and Herbert Lee murdered in Liberty in 1961, both for leading voter registration efforts. These acts added a specifically political cast to gratuitous racial violence like lynchings and the killing of fourteen-year-old Emmett Till in the '50s. Black sharecroppers in the Delta region were among the most desperately poor people in the country and their economic dependence left them without any ability to assert their civil and political rights. It could be perilous even to be a supporter of rights for black citizens. The state had established a Sovereignty Commission to investigate what it regarded as the subversive activities of people who sought to ameliorate discrimination and, with a few exceptions, newspapers and other media in Mississippi suppressed news that might lead some to question white supremacy. The state had earned the "closed society" appellation given it by historian James Silver in his book of the same name.

So the six civil rights commissioners, a group of moderate educators, lawyers, and academicians whose eyes had been opened by their previous investigations, believed that public hearings in Mississippi were the most important contribution they could make. If the conditions in the state could be exposed and documented, if sheriffs and voting registrars could be required to account for their actions, if the few voices of reason in the state could be given a platform to plead their case, perhaps the American public would support new laws and policies that would be effective in vindicating constitutional rights in the most resistant state.

But it would be risky to hold a hearing without administration support because witnesses would need protection that only the Justice Department could provide, and federal property might be the only place available as the site for a hearing. The Eisenhower White House had given previous efforts the cold shoulder and so far the Kennedy administration had been unresponsive. This meeting with Kennedy presented an opportunity for the commission to make headway.

John Hannah, president of Michigan State University and chairman of the commission, set forward his plea in measured tones. Kennedy replied that Mississippi was a tense place and that he did not think it would be prudent for the commission to go there. An awkward silence followed broken by Robert Rankin, a commission member from North Carolina, who made the off-message observation that perhaps the commission could hold another hearing in Alabama.

Kennedy said, with perhaps the hint of a smile, "Why don't you try Alaska? I understand they have some problems of discrimination there."

I was startled by the seeming flippancy of the response, as were the commissioners. But we were not surprised by the president's negative view of Mississippi hearings. While Kennedy had made presidential action to advance civil rights a central part of his campaign in 1960, the narrowness of his victory led him to take a more cautious approach. He felt that he could not afford to offend Eastland, Richard Russell, and other Southern mandarins who headed the committees that would decide the fate of the administration's other domestic programs. Although he had issued his long-delayed executive order on fair housing in November of 1962 and used federal marshals to secure the admission of James Meredith to the University of Mississippi over violent opposition that autumn, the watchwords of his administration still were "caution" and "avoidance of confrontation wherever possible."

The commission believed it had little choice but to accept the president's verdict. All it could do was to continue to amass information about the violation of rights in Mississippi and to wait for a more propitious day. But the decision chafed. There were continuing reminders of the need for a hearing. Under the law establishing the commission, it was authorized to create advisory committees in each state to assist in its work. In Mississippi, service on the advisory committee was no honorific but an act of courage. I had met the committee in mid-1962 when it scheduled a hearing in Natchez to learn more about voting and other denials of rights in the southwestern part of the state. The members were a group of Mississippi citizens, black and white, mostly professional and business leaders from all parts of the state, who shared a deep concern about the lawless state of affairs. In Natchez we were greeted by a bomb threat. On the advice of an FBI agent who had been designated as our liaison, we canceled the meeting, after which I hastily drove over the state border into Louisiana. The following year, the home of the vice chairman of the advisory committee was bombed and another member of the committee and his wife were jailed on trumped-up charges after their home had been invaded.

In April 1963, about a year after my last trip to Mississippi to meet with the advisory committee, the commission issued a report on Mississippi that reflected the vast frustration its members were feeling with continuing violence in the state, with the lack of federal response and with the limitations the Kennedy administration had placed on commission activity. The report documented the harassment of our advisory committee members, physical attacks on residents and students, and the denial of food to children by Mississippi officials administering the federal surplus food program as a reprisal for voting activities in particular. We also listed the Federal Aviation Administration's grant of $2.2 million for construction of an airport in Jackson, which was made without challenging the airport's plan to build racially separate eating and restroom facilities.

The commission then urged the president to consider using his legal authority to withhold federal funds from the state of Mississippi "until it demonstrates compliance with the Constitution and laws." This was potentially an attention-grabbing proposal, with the commission pointing out that Mississippi received far more in federal assistance than it contributed in taxes. But rather than release it to the press, the commission sent a draft to the White House, where it was greeted with outrage. President Kennedy summoned Berl Bernhard, the commission's staff director, to his office for a tongue-lashing, and White House staff prepared memos denying the commission's factual allegations.

One typical issue was the airport construction. When the commission produced blueprints showing the segregated facilities, the White House countered that these were not in the parts of the airport subsidized by the federal government. In the end it was the White House that decided to go public, advising the media that the commission's proposal to cut off all federal funds was harebrained and radical.

The need for a response to repression continued to grow. During April, protests in Birmingham led to the arrest of Martin Luther King Jr. and his letter from the Birmingham jail responding in compelling moral terms to the urging of local ministers that he slow down his quest for remedies. In May, Sheriff Bull Connor set police dogs and fire hoses on protesters and President Kennedy told Governor George Wallace that he would send federal troops to Alabama if necessary to suppress the violence. In June, Medgar Evers, the NAACP's representative in Mississippi whom I had met a few years earlier when I worked for Thurgood Marshall, was killed by a sniper as he entered his home in Jackson after many other attempts on his life. Evers had been the embodiment of courage in his quiet but determined assertion of the fundamental rights of black Mississippians. All of this was reported on television as well as in the press, and it began to stir the conscience of a public that had been only generally aware of the conflict.

In August, the growing demand for federal action to protect civil rights culminated in the march on Washington. The march was sponsored by major civil rights leaders, orchestrated by Bayard Rustin and electrified by King's "I Have a Dream" speech (when my daughter Lauren, who was then six, heard King voice the words "let freedom ring" from the anthem "America," she said, "Oh, I hope it does"). I have participated in many Washington marches since then, some larger than the 250,000 estimated to have attended the 1963 march, but none has rivaled it in energy and spirit. A scant few months previously, knowledgeable legislators had told me there was little demand for civil rights legislation, as reflected by the lack of mail calling for action.

President Kennedy had sent a bill to the Hill in June, but it was not comprehensive and its prospects for passage were murky. Now things seemed to be changing. On September 15, the conscience of the nation was aroused as never before by the murder of four little girls in the bombing of a Birmingham church.

At that time I was coping with my father's hospitalization in Brooklyn; at age sixty-five he had suffered a serious heart attack. On returning to Washington I discovered I had contracted (probably at the hospital) a case of mononucleosis that laid me low for several weeks. When I came back to work in October, the commission asked me to take on the post of general counsel. For more than two years I had used the commission as a base to work with Harris Wofford and other White House staffers on efforts to secure presidential action that would condition federal funding to states, localities, and private institutions on ending practices of discrimination. We had won some victories but we had also learned the political barriers to implementing antidiscrimination policy solely through executive action. Now the fate of efforts to end federally subsidized discrimination rested with the Congress, where I would do what I could to support what finally became law as Title VI in 1964.

But it also seemed like the time to take on new challenges. In becoming general counsel I would face several—particularly the job of bringing to fruition the commission's effort at last to hold a Mississippi hearing.

I had been in the new job just a month when the assassination of John Kennedy in November turned the world upside down. Until then, even with the violence against civil rights workers, I had been able to think of the nation as a relatively ordered place where issues would be debated and ultimately resolved in stable political forums. Kennedy's death threw that into question. This was compounded by the fact that, in the still-new age of television, we all felt we knew the president and so it was like a death in the family. For two days, I couldn't stop listening to the dirges that played continually on radio and TV. Finally, Harriett told me to turn them off. In the years to come, the numbness I felt when John Kennedy was killed was to be repeated with the assassinations of Martin Luther King Jr. and Robert Kennedy. It was replaced with new pain when Allard Lowenstein was also assassinated in 1980 and when Paul and Sheila Wellstone died violently in an airplane crash in 2002. Allard and the Wellstones were all friends of mine.

In the days that followed the Kennedy assassination, some things became clear. Although John Kennedy was not a civil rights crusader, he was, for most Americans—black and white, the embodiment of decency and the advocate of rational solutions to emotional problems. His death aroused feelings of revulsion against violence and added to the appeal to conscience that had been gaining strength as a result of the killings of civil rights workers and black children. Moreover, Lyndon Johnson, whom liberals like myself had scorned as a wheeler-dealer with no commitment to civil rights, emerged as a powerful advocate of equality, vowing to finish Kennedy's work. Suddenly, if paradoxically, the prospects for passage of a meaningful bill seemed to have brightened.

With my new job, I devoted some time to bolstering the effort to secure passage of what became the Civil Rights Act of 1964 by supplying information and expertise in several areas. The bulk of my efforts, however, were devoted to the investigation in Mississippi. I soon discovered that most of the information collected to that point was either stale or insufficiently documented. We would have to begin anew.

Fortunately, the commission was in a position to recruit, and civil rights had suddenly become a hot area for young lawyers. I helped put together a staff of a half dozen lawyers with diverse backgrounds and skills. Several were Ivy League graduates who had served on their law journals and demonstrated excellent skills in research and writing. Others were fine investigators who had the capacity to win the trust of those from whom we were seeking information. Along with the lawyers, we had journalists skilled in evaluating information and helping determine what was important. Altogether, we were a biracial group with complementary skills, bound together by a common commitment to equal opportunity. This experience in building the commission's staff showed me in a practical way that there is no single measure of ability and that the most effective operations may be built by assembling people with differing skills. It was a lesson that stuck with me in the growing debate about affirmative action.

During the winter and early spring of 1964 I stayed in Washington as my staff fanned out to the places in the Delta and southwestern Mississippi where complaints of violence and voting rights denials were prevalent. The staff reports that came back were staggering. While I had worked in civil rights for almost ten years, I found the accounts hard to believe. There were reports of routine beatings and whippings as a means of retaliation or for no reason at all, crude denials of registration, and instances of police misconduct. They reminded me of a James Baldwin play I had recently seen on Broadway, *Blues for Mr. Charlie*, that dramatized the cruel treatment of blacks in the deep South.

I decided it was time to see for myself. In June, Ned Wolf, a young staff lawyer, and I went to southwest Mississippi. Soon after we reached our destination in Natchez, it became apparent that we were being followed. That night at dinner, our table was surrounded by three young T-shirted white men who simply stared at us as we ate. The next day, Ned and I went to visit the head of an organization called Americans for Preservation of the White Race. Affecting a manner that was affable (if somewhat creepy), the group's leader asked us if this was our first visit to Natchez and advised that we must take in Rosalie and other antebellum plantations in the area, places he assured us that had to be visited at night to appreciate their full grandeur. After we left, Ned asked me earnestly whether we could add this to our agenda and was disappointed when I reminded him of John Doar's rules. Doar had instructed the lawyers in the Civil Rights Division of the Justice Department that they were to conduct business during daylight hours and be off the street by sunset. Ned's reactions to the situation in which we now found ourselves were different from mine. I decided that our differing views might have had something to do with our upbringings. He grew up on the Main Line in Philadelphia with the view that nothing bad could happen to him. I grew up in the streets of New York and (like Yossarian, the bomber pilot in Joseph Heller's *Catch 22*) I knew that there were people out there who wanted to kill us.

Early in our visit we met a Justice Department investigator who, it turned, out shared my view of our circumstances. He had been part of the highly regarded team assembled by Robert Kennedy and Walter Sheridan, a veteran investigator, for the purpose of developing criminal prosecutions of Jimmy Hoffa and the Teamsters Union. But during a lull in their efforts this investigator and others had been assigned to Mississippi to cope with the growing crisis. The trouble was that they had been given no real orientation about what they would face. We briefed the investigator as best we could and agreed that we would meet at the end of each day to share what we had learned. When we completed our work that day, Ned and I went to the investigator's first-floor room at the motel and knocked on his door. We were greeted by a guarded "What?" from inside. We announced ourselves and there followed the sound of furniture being moved away from the door. The investigator's experience had made him apprehensive enough to blockade his room.

I knew how he felt. Earlier in the day Ned and I had visited Father William Morrissey, a Catholic priest who helped Negro residents of Natchez and had contacts with civil rights workers. As we sat in his rectory, we heard a sharp cracking sound outside the window that continued for a couple of minutes. When we inquired, he took us to the window. Across the street at a gas station, a man stood cracking a whip against the sidewalk. "That's the bull whip man," Father Morrissey explained. "Whenever I have visitors who he thinks are connected with civil rights, he sends his message."

These events were unsettling and gave us concern about our own safety (William James's phrase, "the moral equivalent of war," popped into my mind). But far more harrowing were the stories told by black residents of Natchez. Archie Curtis, a funeral-home operator who had encouraged people to register to vote, told us that he had been lured out to a country road at night by a telephone call saying that an ambulance was needed. When he and an associate arrived, they were met by three hooded men who asked for his "NAACP card." He and his associate were blindfolded, forced to strip, and beaten with a pistol and a whip. His medical report stated that he had been struck "with great force by objects of at least three different widths."

At a commission meeting in June, I reported on my trip. In Natchez and Adams County, I said, "a state of fear is prevalent. There had been five or six beatings of Negroes by men with hoods who took them out on the highway at night. There had been shootings and physical intimidation and economic reprisals against merchants who employ Negroes. Natchez has become a city of terror with both white and Negro leadership being intimidated," I concluded, adding that "local law enforcement seems to have completely deteriorated with some possible Klan involvement."

The fact-gathering aspects of the investigation were proceeding well. Black Mississippians were telling us their stories and providing the means for documenting them. And most indicated a willingness to testify publicly, even with the knowledge that the commission could not protect them after the hearing was over. We also knew we could use the subpoena power to obtain the records and testimony of local voting registrars and sheriffs, and we believed their own words and deeds would make a powerful case about the brutality of injustice in Mississippi. Also, the Justice Department appeared to have come to the grudging conclusion that the hearing would go forward. While the department was resisting or delaying our requests for information, particularly about extremist groups, it was not blocking the investigation. And we were developing some of our own sources about extremist activity.

But members of the commission had another objective, which some raised at every opportunity. They wanted the hearing to provide a forum for voices of moderation—people who would speak out for peaceful solutions to the problems that wracked the state. So we worked hard to reach business executives, religious figures, and other opinion leaders to ask that they engage in a dialogue and make such a plea at our hearing.

We got nowhere. Sometimes corporate executives turned us down with the explanation that their businesses could be ruined. Others told us they feared physical harm to themselves or their families. In other cases, our phone calls or letters were not answered or we were flatly refused without explanation.

Then in the summer two life-changing events for Mississippians took place. On July 2, after decisive action by both houses of Congress, Lyndon Johnson signed the Civil Rights Act of 1964. The law barred segregation and discrimination in public schools and other public facilities. It went further to require nondiscrimination by private employers and people who operated hotels and restaurants and other places of public accommodation. For the first time, the nation had something approaching a comprehensive policy of racial justice and both Congress and the president had finally come to the rescue of the Supreme Court.

In signing the bill, President Johnson called on all Americans "to bring justice and hope to our people—and peace to our land. Let us close the springs of racial poison." Those words had to have particular resonance in Mississippi. A week or two later, I met with most of my staff in Jackson after conducting investigations in several parts of the state. For the first time, we were all able to stay together at the Admiral Benbow Inn and to take our meals in the inn's dining room, where the presence of our interracial group evoked looks of consternation from other diners but no incidents occurred. On the last day of our stay, as I was standing in line to pay the bill, I overheard an elderly man say to his wife, "I guess this is something we're just going to have to get used to."

The other cataclysmic event began on June 21 when three young civil rights workers disappeared shortly after being released from a Philadelphia, Mississippi, jail, where they were being held on a speeding charge. Two of the young men were white New Yorkers—Andrew Goodman and Michael Schwerner—and the third was James Cheney, a black Mississippian. The FBI found their bodies on August 4 in a recently built earthen dam a few miles from the jail. Autopsies showed that all had been shot to death.

I was shocked by the tragedy—by its brutality, and by the likely involvement of members of the sheriff's department. That same shock, reverberating throughout the nation in part because two of the victims were white middle-class youngsters from the North, turned a spotlight on Mississippi as never before. It introduced a new element into the calculus of state leaders. For years they had relied on entities like the State Sovereignty Commission to maintain the racial status quo and to keep Klan and other extremists in some check by demonstrating that violence was not necessary to preserve the Mississippi way of life. Now, however, the presence of civil rights workers seeking to help people to register had provoked a binge of violence.

The stability the politicians and business leaders had hoped for was gone. Some of the old fears about the economic consequences of speaking out for moderation were being replaced by new fears—that keeping quiet would lead to disinvestment in the state by outside investors and strong enforcement action by the federal government. By the fall, the commission's efforts to enlist the establishment in speaking out at our public hearing began to elicit a new, more favorable response.

The commission appeared on course for a February 1965 hearing. But one more obstacle loomed. In December, FBI agents arrested nineteen men, including the sheriff and deputy sheriff of Neshoba County, on federal conspiracy charges in connection with the murder of the three young men. On January 15 the nineteen were indicted. Within a few days I received a call from Nicholas Katzenbach, the acting attorney general, requesting that the commission postpone or cancel its February hearing on grounds that it could prejudice the trial. His position differed from that of Burke Marshall, head of the Justice Department's Civil Rights Division, who saw the hearing as a problem only if its timing coincided with that of the criminal trial. I told Katzenbach that, because I could not convene the commissioners on such short notice, I would canvass each of them (these were the days before conference calls), present his arguments, and get back to him.

The commissioners were unanimous in wanting to go forward. On Saturday, January 23, I called Katzenbach back and reported the results of my canvass. He exploded. "You son of a bitch, you cocksucker, you loaded the dice, you couldn't have told them my reasons." I took a deep breath. "If you want a meeting with the commission, I'll arrange one as soon as I can."

The meeting was held on January 28, by coincidence the very day on which President Johnson nominated Katzenbach as attorney general. Katzenbach appeared and was adamant, rejecting commission arguments that the hearing would occur well before the trial and was in a different part of the state. (One commissioner told me afterward that he was surprised and puzzled by how emotionally distraught Katzenbach seemed.) In the end, the commissioners decided unanimously to go forward. In the view of John Hannah, the commission's chairman, the agency's integrity was on the line and a cancellation would be a betrayal of all the Mississippi witnesses who had agreed to testify at great personal risk. Finally, as several said, progress in Mississippi could not come by criminal trials alone but by setting out the facts for all to see, a mission to which the commission could make a contribution.

Appointment in Jackson

So, after our long odyssey, in February we arrived in Jackson for the hearing. Under the commission's governing statute we first had to hear in private testimony that would tend to defame or degrade witnesses and to provide them with an opportunity to respond. Then the commission convened in public session on February 16 at the recreation hall of the Veterans Administration Center in Jackson for five days of testimony concerning the right to vote and the administration of justice. The great bulk of the testimony came from ordinary citizens, black Mississippians who had been denied the right to vote, who had been intimidated, beaten, and/or arrested for seeking to exercise their rights. They spoke mainly in matter-of-fact tones about their experiences, but the impact on me and others listening was overwhelming.

One compelling piece of testimony encapsulated the history of race relations in Mississippi. Jake Cain was a seventy-eight-year-old farmer who lived in Carroll County in the Delta. He told how his uncle had been killed and his father wounded in a mass killing of Negroes at the local courthouse during a trial in 1886. At the time of the hearing, only five Negroes of a voting-age population of about twenty-eight hundred were registered. Cain was one of the five, having been solicited to register by local authorities after several criminal convictions were overturned for failure to have a Negro on the jury (the jurors were drawn from the list of registered voters). But the registrar told Cain that being registered did not mean he could vote and that he had better not try.

By the early '60s, believing that conditions were improving, Cain encouraged his adult daughter (the only one of his seven children remaining in Mississippi) to try to register. Previously, she had gone to the courthouse to try to do so, but fear had prevented her from going in. This last time, Mildred Cain said, she had gone through with it. One of the commissioners asked whether she thought it was better to go with a group or alone. She replied, "Well, I wasn't alone because I had prayed and I believed that somebody was with me. That's why I had the courage I had when I went there." She was refused registration.

In contrast to the black witnesses, most of the local authorities subpoenaed to testify—voting registrars, sheriffs, local prosecutors—seemed resentful, angry that they were being called to account for their actions. They seemed particularly upset by the direct probing questions asked by Frankie Freeman, the commission's one black memeber. (Later, when I showed Charles Black photographs of the white witnesses who appeared at the hearing, he said that the expressions on their faces told the whole story.) The commissioners could not believe how in the face of the evidence, state officials could testify that they applied the law fairly. One registrar repeatedly gave black applicants the most complex and technical parts of the Mississippi constitution to interpret while giving whites the simplest parts. Erwin Griswold, growing increasingly impatient, asked the registrar himself to interpret Section 182, a lengthy passage having to do with the state's taxation powers. After consulting with his lawyer, the registrar refused to answer. Griswold, concerned about the abuses that had taken place during the McCarthy period, had recently written a widely admired book urging respect for the protections of the Fifth Amendment against self-incrimination. Nevertheless, he asked the witness whether he was refusing to answer because his answer might incriminate him. The registrar answered in the affirmative.

Griswold was both a formidable intelligence and a commanding presence at commission meetings and elsewhere. An Ohioan who attended Oberlin College and Harvard Law School, he had been dean of Harvard Law School for more than fifteen years when President Kennedy appointed him to one of the Republican seats on the commission. He had the reputation of intimidating faculty and students at Harvard, as well as other colleagues. But I found him to be a more complex and interesting person.

Once, the commission had an emergency meeting at O'Hare Airport and we had to retain a local court reporter to make a transcript of the meeting. The reporter was young and inexperienced and, two or three minutes into the meeting, his machine jammed. After an awkward pause while commissioners waited to be assured that their words would be transcribed, John Hannah, the chairman, said the meeting should resume and asked one of the staffers to take notes. Griswold intervened, saying he thought we should take a recess and allow the young man "an opportunity to repair his machine away from our prying eyes." Hannah acceded and in a few minutes the young man told us he had been successful. I concluded that Griswold felt that it would be bad for the young man's character to be allowed to confess failure.

Another time, I accompanied Griswold to Capitol Hill where he was to present testimony arguing that literacy tests for voting should be abolished. Senator Sam Ervin, chair of the Constitution Subcommittee, was used to playing the role of judge in these hearings, putting witnesses on the defensive in arguing their case to him. But in these hearings I could see that, for the first time, Ervin, a graduate of Harvard Law School, was nervous. He pleaded his case to Dean Griswold saying there was no basis in the Constitution for legislation eliminating literacy tests. Griswold was agreeable up to a point, but Ervin then read a lengthy quote stating that the Fourteenth Amendment had nothing to do with voting. He looked down at Griswold expectantly and asked, "What do you think of that?" Griswold replied, "I'd give that a C-minus." On the way out Griswold said to me, "Do you think I should have said that?"

On occasion Griswold would voice strong views about draft commission reports. Once when he was critical of a draft I had submitted following my own review, he made it clear that it did not meet his standards. "Aren't you being a bit hard on Taylor?" another commissioner asked. "Don't worry about him," Griswold replied. "He's like a rubber ball: bounce him against the pavement and he bounces right back."

At the Mississippi hearings, the chief of police of Laurel, Mississippi, testified about his conduct after the Civil Rights Act of 1964 officially brought the right of African Americans to equal treatment in places of public accommodation under federal protection. On one occasion, he arrested an integrated group of people who sought service at a local coffee shop, charging them with breach of the peace. On another, when he saw two white men wielding baseball bats at two Negro boys who sat down at a lunch counter at S. H. Kress, the chief arrested only one of the attackers and required him to post an appearance bond of $25. The defendant failed to appear and the matter was dropped. At the hearing, the chief opined that that was his option.

The final groups of witnesses were the opinion leaders who had earlier rebuffed the commission's approach—business executives, clergy, and prominent lawyers. At the beginning of the hearing, Governor Paul Johnson unexpectedly appeared to welcome the commission and to voice the colorful plea that critics "get off our backs and . . . on our side." But he emphasized that Mississippians would accept the civil rights laws they had so strongly resisted and that violence would not be tolerated. The leaders whom Governor Johnson said he had encouraged to testify followed suit. The former dean of the University of Mississippi Law School, Robert Farley, lamented the fact that members of the Bar in the South had spent a good deal of time in unjustly criticizing the Supreme Court. Other Bar leaders cautiously suggested that they would take steps to ensure that black defendants in criminal cases would have lawyers. At that time there were only three black lawyers in the entire state to turn to, and very few white lawyers would take the case of a black person.

Owen Cooper, president-elect of the Mississippi Economic Council, said, "We have recognized that the Civil Rights Act is now the law of the land, that we have lost this battle." He recognized that the breakdown in law and order had been in part the responsibility of business executives, which allowed law enforcement officials to believe it would be tolerated. And he set forth a positive agenda of impartial administration of the voting laws, support for public education and training and employment programs for black citizens.

All of this, along with the testimony of black citizens, voting registrars, and sheriffs, was broadcast throughout the state on public television. It was another radical departure for the "closed society," apparently prompted by the effort of the state's leaders to encourage white citizens to accept a new reality.

So, paradoxically, with all the hurdles posed by the administration and by the postponements, the commission's hearing could not have come at a better time. Forged by revulsion against violence and repression, a national consensus for equal justice was emerging. That consensus, concretely represented by passage of the 1964 act, had created the beginning of a new reality in Mississippi. Political and business leaders in the state realized that in political and economic terms they had no choice but to change. And the commission's hearings became an important catalyst for that change.

The hearings also played a role on the national stage. Two weeks after the February hearings concluded, members of a group of some five hundred people marching for voting rights were attacked, tear-gassed, and brutally beaten by Alabama state troopers and sheriff's deputies at the Edmund Pettus Bridge in Selma. The violence sparked a national outcry and a call for new and effective voting rights protections. On March 15, Lyndon Johnson went before Congress with a strong new voting rights bill and the declaration that "we shall overcome."

For more than half a century, Congress and the courts had sought to guarantee voting rights to black people without disturbing state control over the electoral process, only to find that, as each roadblock to the franchise was struck down, states adopted another. Now the Johnson administration and Congress were ready for a bolder step, striking down literacy tests and authorizing federal registrars to take over the voting process if state resistance continued. These were measures the commission had recommended in 1959 only to have them derided as "radical" by Eisenhower's attorney general, William Rogers.

Now their time had come. On May 18, the commission sent to the president and Congress its report, "Voting in Mississippi," summarizing the finding of its investigations and hearings and restating its legislative proposals. On August 6 President Johnson signed the Voting Rights Act into law.

The impact was immediate. Where every previous voting reform had been thwarted by a new device for disenfranchisement concocted by state and local officials, this time the federal government was poised to take over the voting process if the states continued in their old ways. By the end of September, despite some continuing resistance, more than forty-two thousand new Negro applicants were registered to vote in Mississippi. (Previously the total was just over six thousand.) In Leflore County, nonwhite registration went from 281 to 13,567, and in Madison it went from 218 to 10,567. Similar, if less dramatic, progress took place throughout the old South. The commission, by making the case that concerns about states' rights could no longer be allowed to stymie the national interest and constitutional imperative for black enfranchisement, had made a signal contribution to the success of the civil rights movement.

On November 4, the commission issued its report on law enforcement, the other major subject of the Mississippi hearings. A large part

THE PASSION OF MY TIMES

of our concern was the weakness of the federal criminal civil rights laws, which required proof not only of an intent to commit violence but to violate a specific federal right. Even these laws were rarely enforced because the Justice Department was deterred by the likelihood that Southern white juries would not convict. Just as bad, federal law enforcement officials would not make arrests even when crimes of violence were committed in their presence unless they were there to enforce a federal court order. This policy disillusioned a generation of young civil rights workers who had looked to the federal government as their protector.

The commission's report called on Congress to strengthen the law. It also pointed to the existence of a reservoir of federal power to provide protections against violence that, if used wisely, we believed would not fulfill the administration's fears about creating a "national police force." In a speech to the Southern Political Science Association in Raleigh, North Carolina, in November 1965, I said that supplanting rogue local law enforcement officers with federal enforcement officers "would be a serious decision . . ." one that no one "wants either to make or recommend. But if all of the current efforts to persuade and negotiate fail, the choice will lie between leaving American citizens utterly defenseless in the face of lawlessness or protecting them at the cost of a drastic change in the allocation of responsibilities among governments. Only the exercise of courage and wisdom by the leaders of state governments can save us from such a decision."

Fortunately, the decision of state leaders in Mississippi to stop lawlessness by white citizens and by the state's own police made this decision largely unnecessary. In 1968 Congress also strengthened the criminal civil rights laws in the ways the commission had recommended, and federal civil rights prosecutions at last became viable around the nation. Recently, more than three decades after the horrendous events, Southern juries have shown themselves willing to convict the murderers of the children in Birmingham and Medgar Evers in Jackson.

Eras rarely end neatly. In 1966 I was invited to speak at an NAACP conference in Natchez and was impressed that the police who once had followed my car now were politely ushering people into the parking lot for the meeting. But in the summer of 1965, a local civil rights leader had been severely injured when a bomb exploded in his car and, in 1967, a Natchez NAACP leader was killed by another car bomb. No arrests were made in either case.

Black residents of Mississippi made good use of their enfranchisement and, within a decade, African Americans were elected to local and state offices and to Congress. An African-American man became a judge on the state's highest court and the numbers of black lawyers increased. Yet Mississippi's politics continued to be ultraconservative, with only a change in label from Democratic to Republican, thanks to Richard Nixon's successful Southern strategy after his election in 1968. Trent Lott, the state's leading senator, suffered mightily on the national stage in 2002 for his nostalgic paean to the days of Jim Crow (delivered at Strom Thurmond's farewell party) but it is doubtful that he will suffer any repercussions at home. The state's congressional delegation continues to vote overwhelmingly against measures that would provide opportunity or a safety net for its poorest citizens.

In the years that followed, the closed society was replaced by a more open dialogue, due in no small measure to the successful legal campaign of Rev. Everett Parker and the United Church of Christ to deny renewal of the license of the segregationist leadership of WLBT, the NBC-TV affiliate in Jackson and its replacement with a biracial team headed by Mississippi's NAACP state chairman. Still race overhangs most issues and stifles progress.

One personal incident may illustrate the growing pains of moving to a freer system of communications. A few months after the Mississippi hearings I received a call from the chairman of the political science department at Jackson State College in Mississippi. Jackson State is a black public college and, as was typical in those days, the president was a black educator supervised by a white state board of trustees who ruled with an iron hand.

The department chair's call was to invite me to speak at the college. I accepted on the spot, but my caller wanted to tell me more. This was a significant occasion, he explained, because the department wanted me to talk about civil rights and the college had never before had a speaker on that subject. I told him I was doubly honored.

A few weeks before the date set for the speech, the department chair called again. Would I mind changing the topic from civil rights to something along the lines of human relations? I said I would work it out.

When the day I arrived I found that I was speaking at vesper services on a Friday evening. Some eight hundred people, almost all of them students, attended—the largest audience I had ever addressed. I was introduced by the college's president, Jacob Reddix. My speech got a friendly reception, but no questions were permitted. From there we adjourned to a political science department forum, where I was told I could be more informal. Reddix introduced me again to an audience of about one hundred. This time questions were permitted, but they seemed to me very perfunctory. Still I was feeling good about commanding such a large audience.

When the forum ended with refreshments, Reddix departed. A dozen or so students gathered around me to continue the discussion. And they were markedly more animated than before. A tall young man asked the first question: "You are an expert on the Constitution," he said. "Tell me, do you think that, when a public college compels student attendance at vesper services, it is violating my right to religious freedom under the First Amendment?"

The air went out of my balloon.

Mississippi remains a very poor state and, like the rest of the nation, it is a place of haves and have-nots. Tunica County, an area in the Delta tucked in the northwest corner of the state, was long described by the U.S. Census as the lowest-income county in the nation. Now gambling palaces rise out of the cotton fields and provide employment to some residents, but most remain desperately poor.

In the end, my gauge of the success of the civil rights movement and the contribution the commission made to it in Mississippi is the extent to which it enabled people to empower themselves and throw off shackles that prevented them from realizing their potential. Here is an illustration:

One of the witnesses at the Mississippi hearing was Unita Zelma Blackwell of Mayersville. She gave an account of her repeated efforts, ultimately successful, to register to vote and to encourage others to try to do the same. She spoke of the registrar's requiring her to interpret technical provisions of the state constitution, of the fears of black residents of Issaquena County that registration efforts would result in a cutoff of welfare checks in the winter when farm work was not available, of white men flashing shotguns and making threats. Yet she and others persisted because, "It is very important to have the people represented and I wants somebody to represent me."

As to the threats: "You just get to the place you know it's going to happen, but you've just got to stand up and got to do something."

Twenty-seven years later, in June 1992, the MacArthur Foundation announced the award of one of its thirty-three "genius grants" to Unita Blackwell, who had become the first black woman to be elected mayor in Mississippi. The announcement stated, "She succeeded in having her town [Mayersville] incorporated, making it eligible for federal funds and then raised money to provide for basic services such as water, sewage and housing. She continues to work at the local level to create an economic and social infrastructure, while providing a national leadership example."

There are hundreds of thousands of people in Mississippi and around the nation who, like Unita Blackwell, have succeeded by sheer will and effort in leading rewarding and productive lives once the barriers of racism they faced were removed. That, I believe, is the true legacy of the civil rights movement in Mississippi and elsewhere, and what makes me grateful to have been a part of it.

Triumph and Despair

L ooking back on the period from 1965 to 1968, when I served as staff director of the U. S. Commission on Civil Rights, I am amazed by the pace of events. All of us worked unremittingly to gain an understanding of the rapidly changing scene in race relations and to strive for some measure of influence over policy that might channel change in a positive direction. It was also a period when public attention as never before was focused on civil rights. Going back to my clip files, I find that it was not unusual for the *New York Times* or the *Washington Post* to publish two or three stories in a single day about a commission report or a national conference the agency held on racial isolation in public schools. Never before or since has so much debate been focused on the search for solutions to unequal opportunity.

It also seems clear now that our work at the commission ran along two fairly distinct tracks: as hopes raised by the success of the legal civil rights revolution were beginning to be realized, other hopes were dying in the ashes of the fires burning in American cities.

In personal terms, change began for me in February 1965, when Lyndon Johnson nominated me to be staff director of the commission. This position would require confirmation by a majority vote of the Senate. As was often the case with civil rights nominees, the Judiciary

Committee delayed a hearing for several months. In fact, my nomination had already been delayed when the *Vanguard* affair arose during the FBI investigation that preceded the president's decision.

The six commissioners had recommended me for the job, but the president had to decide whether to nominate me. A decision had been pending for some months when John Macy, head of the Civil Service Commission, asked me to come to his office on a Saturday morning. He told me that some issues had arisen in the security investigation the administration was conducting prior to any nomination. Specifically, people from Brooklyn College were giving interviews recalling the 1950 controversy and saying negative things about me.

I gave Macy a detailed account of the affair and followed up with a list of the current positions of the student journalists who had been my colleagues in 1950. Far from being the scruffy band of radicals the administration described, most had gone on to successful careers in journalism or business. Mike Levitas was carving out a distinguished career as a top editor at the *New York Times*. Myron Kandel was well on his way to establishing himself as a leading expert in finance for newspapers (and later for CNN).

I weathered the storm and was nominated in March 1965.

Twenty years later when I secured my FBI file, I discovered what John Macy had been talking about. Harry Gideonse was true to his threat to try to do damage to my career. In giving me a negative recommendation, he told the investigator that there was a "remarkable similarity between the editorials published in the newspaper and the content of Communist literature then in circulation." Possibly in mitigation he added that "SUBJECT [me] had a rather firm character but was very stubborn . . . Possible that he did not suspect the true political ideologies of his friends." Dean Herbert Stroup, one of Gideonse's deputies, told the agent that I was a member of the student council, which "was at this time espousing liberal causes such as the rights of the negro [sic] in the South." In Stroup's view, this was one of the reasons I should not be given a position of trust in the government.

My favorite in these reports was an unidentified faculty member who said I was a "fake liberal" and "under no circumstances" should I be given a position of trust. The agent appended a note that "the Informant refused to sign a sworn statement or appear at any hearing . . . He felt it allowed him more latitude than would be the case were he under oath. He further refused to let his name be known as he felt this would detract from his effectiveness as a teacher."

In any event, having surmounted these obstacles, my hearing date finally arrived.

At the Senate hearing, I got some indication of the gathering storm in race relations when senators' questions to me were not about the new civil rights laws but about civil disorder in the cities. At the end of the hearings Senator Ervin, chair of the subcommittee considering my nomination, took me aside and told me that he would vote against me but that I should not take it personally since he thought I was "very well qualified to head this unnecessary agency." Senator Ervin was also giving me a message that he would not seek to defeat my nomination, but only to record his own opposition. I was confirmed early in August on the same day that the Senate approved Thurgood Marshall's nomination as solicitor general. My swearing-in took place on August 20, which coincidentally was the third birthday of my son, David. David, who by that time had established himself as the most outgoing member of our family, immediately engaged Vice President Humphrey, who had agreed to administer the oath, in conversation. The next day newspapers around the country ran a wire-service photo of the vice president down on one knee, laughing with David. Both had a way with words and were clearly enjoying each other's company.

The Changing South

On the commission's first track, we had a great sense of urgency about making the most of the recently passed civil rights laws. The Voting Rights Act was signed into law on August 6, and the commission moved quickly to distribute information throughout the South on peoples' rights and responsibilities under the law.

In December we put together a conference in Jackson, Mississippi, with four hundred representatives from fifty-two Mississippi counties to help spur the registration movement. Simultaneously, the commission issued an interim report on enforcement of the law, based on our examination of thirty-two Mississippi counties and information gleaned from others. We concluded that while significant progress had been made (some two hundred thousand Negro citizens had been registered, one quarter of them by federal examiners) there was much more to be done. The commission urged that federal examiners be sent to additional counties, that affirmative steps be taken to encourage registration and voting, and that the Justice Department guard against attempts to prevent newly registered Negroes from voting.

Attorney General Katzenbach fired back a seven-page letter to me complaining about the commission's report and recommendations. Apparently still smarting from the commission's rebuff of his plea to stay out of Mississippi, he argued that our report was not comprehensive (coming only a few months after the act was passed, it couldn't have been complete), rejected an affirmative role for the federal government in encouraging people to register, and said the agency's recommendation for protection at the polls was unnecessary "particularly since I had discussed this matter with you personally."

The Katzenbach letter ensured that the commission's report would receive national attention. The *Washington Post* said there "seems to be ample justification for the Civil Rights Commission demand" for additional voting registrars. Peter Osnos, writing for I. F. Stone's *Weekly*, criticized Katzenbach's "legal stubbornness," his refusal to see the need for "the federal government to be proactive, to understand that Negroes fear that registration would mean the loss of farms and jobs."

We continued our work on voting and, in May 1968, published "Political Participation," a study of the participation by Negroes in the electoral and political processes in ten Southern states since passage of the Voting Rights Act of 1965. We were able to report that 1.28 million

Negro citizens had registered since 1965 and that, in Mississippi, registration had gone from 6.7 percent to 59.85 percent of voting-age Negro citizens. At the same time, through the work of a young commission lawyer, Frank Parker, we were able to document more subtle practices that were being used to dilute the minority vote and to change the rules to the detriment of black people. This established an agenda for future renewals of the act.

The commission also included a new chapter in the report, calling on the Democratic and Republican parties to end discrimination and ensure the opportunity to participate to all party members at all levels, regardless of race. In 1964, the Democratic Party had almost self-destructed over the effort to secure Negro participation in the Mississippi delegation to the national convention in Atlantic City. Lyndon Johnson wanted to respond affirmatively to the demands for black representation but feared a mass defection by white Southerners. His proposed compromise of seating two black delegates was rejected bitterly by both sides. By 1968 the issue had been somewhat defused. Howard Glickstein, the commission's general counsel, and I went to Trenton to visit Governor Richard Hughes of New Jersey, who had been designated to chair the 1968 Democratic Convention. He was already working on plans for greater minority participation and welcomed our recommendations.

Today, almost all the gains in equal justice that have been achieved over the past four decades are traceable to the enfranchisement of people of color and the transformation of the Democratic Party. It is true that President Johnson's embrace of civil rights legislation in the 1960s cost the Democrats dearly in the South, something that Johnson predicted and that made his advocacy even more courageous. But on issues perceived as critical to their well-being, such as the Bork nomination in the 1980s, blacks and their supporters were able to have an impact that would not have been possible before their enfranchisement. The conservative South today is still a product of embedded racial attitudes but it also reflects industrial and postindustrial growth that continues to thrive on cheap labor. And Republicans have gained political ground in part by drawing political districts in ways that have packed black citizens into uniracial election areas, thus ensuring the dominance of white Republicans in other areas. While some civil rights advocates and black politicians supported this practice to ensure the election of black candidates, it has not served the goal of increasing minority influence. In many situations, an apportionment of two areas into two 40 percent black districts will ensure more minority influence than an apportionment that creates one 80 percent black district and one 20 percent black district. Indeed, many civil rights advocates have come to realize that multiracial districts create greater minority influence than packed districts. Over time, as the demographic change brings more diversity to the nation, the South and other areas of the country are likely to grow more progressive in seeking to serve the needs of all citizens.

In addition to voting, another major area in which the commission managed to have a significant impact in the 1960s was on school desegregation in the South. With the passage of Title VI of the 1964 Civil Rights Act and the enactment of federal aid to education legislation a year later, the federal government acquired a powerful new instrument for securing compliance with the *Brown* decision. President Johnson and Secretary John Gardner made the critical decision that school districts would have to submit school desegregation plans to qualify for federal funds. Gardner, a Republican who during his career was a philosopher, educator, and philanthropist as well as a public servant, displayed a quiet resolve to resist political pressure and ensure equality of opportunity.

But this still left open the question of what desegregation remedies would be sufficient to redress the violation of the Constitution. On this issue, the Johnson administration proceeded cautiously, seeking to synthesize what courts had said rather than breaking any new ground. By then, the fallback position in much of the South was to adopt so-called freedom-of-choice plans. These retained the old system of racially segregated assignments but allowed parents to opt out of these schools and not have their kids attend with children of other races.

Experience showed what the designers of this freedom of choice expected—that very little desegregation took place.

In the fall of 1965, the commission set out to investigate the operation of freedom of choice. In an interim report that year and in a more comprehensive study published in 1967, the commission found that poverty and economic dependence on whites deterred many black families throughout the South from applying to have their children attend white schools from which they previously had been barred. It also found that some black families who did exercise their options under freedom-of-choice plans became "targets of violence, threats of violence and economic reprisal and that black children were abused in the schools."

In March 1966, HEW indicated that it would adopt the commission recommendations counseling against the acceptance of freedom of choice plans. At the same time, the department was rejecting the rear guard actions of Attorney General Katzenbach who advised against the use of federal fund cutoffs as a sanction for noncompliance.

The federal courts, having found a new ally in the executive branch, began to reject freedom-of-choice plans that did not accomplish desegregation, stating that judges should rely on the expertise of federal officials. In June 1966, Harold Howe, who was serving as commissioner of Education under Gardner, and I met with educators and citizens, white and black, from sixty-four of Alabama's sixty-seven counties and told them we would stand behind federal guidelines calling for effective desegregation.

Finally, in 1968 the Supreme Court decided to review *Green v. School Board of New Kent County*, the first case since *Brown* to examine the proper scope of a desegregation remedy. The Court specifically cited the commission's findings that the threat of violence and their condition of dependence often deterred black people from choosing desegregated schools. But the Court went further. It recognized as the commission had that a new round of litigation to determine whether intimidation existed in particular cases would only cause more delay in the enforcement of rights declared in 1954. So the Court ruled unanimously that the standard for judging a remedy was effectiveness and that freedom of choice would not be accepted unless it produced substantial desegregation.

That was a mandate for real desegregation throughout the nonurban South. Three years later, with its decision in *Swann v. School Board of Charlotte-Mecklenburg County*, the Court approved busing for desegregation and extended its mandate throughout the South.

The result was a dramatic transformation of public education in the South. In the decade between *Brown* and passage of the 1964 act, fewer than two blacks in one hundred attended schools with whites in the eleven states of the old South. By the end of the '60s, more than 40 percent of black children were in majority white schools, and the numbers continued to grow after the Court's 1971 decision in *Swann*.

Most important, desegregation was accompanied in many places by real educational opportunity. By 1980, the respected National Assessment of Educational Progress was able to report that, from 1970 to 1980, black children made substantial achievement gains in reading and closed the existing gap with whites significantly. The greatest gains reported were for black children in the third grade of public schools in the Southeast. This, of course, was where desegregation had taken place most extensively.

The importance of expanding educational opportunity was reinforced by another set of commission hearings in Alabama in 1968 that demonstrated the intransigence of an economic system that subjugated black workers. One incident may serve to illustrate this:

In the course of our investigation of a sixteen-county rural area, commission investigators came upon a sawmill operation in Bellamy, Alabama. The sawmill was part of a company town run by the American Can Company. It was a wholly segregated town: White workers lived in modest cottages provided by the company; black workers lived in hovels with outdoor privies. Two racially segregated public schools served the workers, and all other public facilities were segregated as well. On Sunday morning, each racial group went to its own church. American Can operated the grocery store and other retail facilities, deducting bills from the workers' paychecks. At the end of the month, some of the black workers literally "owed their souls to the company store." When I went to see for myself, I was amazed. I had thought that such operations had ended thirty years earlier.

What followed was at least equally amazing. Two black workers said they were willing to testify about the conditions in Bellamy. A few days before the hearing, management convened a meeting of all its workers. With a lawyer from the prestigious Washington firm of Covington and Burling standing at his side, the plant manager told the workers that their segregated housing might violate the civil rights laws. Two workers planned to testify at public hearings about this and if they did, the plant manager said, the housing would be closed down and everyone left homeless.

When I learned of this, the commission convened an executive session to determine whether the plant manager or the lawyer should be charged with intimidating witnesses. Both backed down from their threats and the black workers testified as scheduled. The American Can Company pledged to dismantle the practices of segregation and exploitation that governed the sawmill operation in Bellamy, and Bill May, chief executive officer of the company, reported to me periodically, even after I left the commission a few months later, about the progress he was making.

Still, the experience demonstrated to me how ingrained existing practices of discrimination were. For instance, the federal government's farm program was a rigidly segregated system of supports and technical assistance operated by private interests that refused to yield to change, even after the commission persuaded President Johnson to write a letter to Agriculture Secretary Orville Freeman urging him to take strong corrective action. Thirty years later, in the 1990s, Negro farmers received some small measure of relief in a court suit for the harm they had had long suffered. Similarly, economic development programs seemed to make only a small dent in the business system that left black workers struggling at the bottom. And, if American Can's company town had not been discovered and exposed by the commission, it might have gone on for years unimpeded by civil rights laws or by any hint of conscience in a lawyer from one of the nation's most powerful law firms. In this environment, educational opportunity and voting were the tickets out of the morass of discrimination and deprivation in the South.

Darkness Ahead

As the commission poured its meager resources (a budget of about $2 million) into civil rights enforcement in the South, it also became clear that we needed to increase our focus on the problems facing minority citizens in cities of the North and West. Those were the places that the greatest numbers of people of color lived. For the most part, the lives of black city dwellers seemed unaffected by the civil rights laws. And beginning in 1964 and 1965, some of these cities erupted in disorders and riots.

As we began our investigations into urban conditions, one commission member, Erwin Griswold, said he was baffled about why economic conditions for blacks had become worse in the cities while the national economy had expanded. He wondered whether these were matters within the commission's mandate to investigate denials of equal protection or whether the problems were more of poverty than of race. As our work progressed in hearings we held from 1965 through 1968 in Cleveland, San Francisco, Rochester, New York, and Boston, there was plenty of discrimination to investigate. Housing conditions were deplorable: Poor black people lived in rigidly segregated public housing. When local authorities decided to clear land for new housing for the middle class ("urban renewal" was the name of the program but "Negro removal" was the familiar title applied by those affected), they made no provision for relocating residents to decent housing and, in Cleveland, stopped enforcing housing codes in the area entirely.

Blockbusting, real estate speculating, and redlining (disqualifying whole areas of cities from receiving loans based on the race of their occupants) were all prevalent practices in the housing industry, and predatory lending practices were widely employed by financial institutions, unrestrained by public agencies that were supposed to guard against discrimination. A high-ranking federal official of the Federal Housing Administration in San Francisco explained his agency's failure to pursue housing opportunities for black families of modest means by saying that he viewed his agency as serving the needs of the housing industry and was concerned that they might stop using FHA if subjected to nondiscrimination requirements.

Similarly, the United States Employment Service continued to fill racially discriminatory job orders submitted by employers even after the enactment of fair-employment legislation. Union leaders in the construction trades were open and defiant in defending their practices of nepotism and minority exclusion. Training opportunities were scarce and jobs were being relocated to new and expanding suburbs that were inaccessible to minority workers.

Other important services were frustratingly difficult for minorities to access. Police response time to emergency calls from Cleveland's Hough ghetto was much slower than elsewhere in the city. Black people living in the isolated area of Portrero Hill in San Francisco had a very hard time getting an ambulance to come to their homes.

Beyond these objective conditions, the commission discovered the sense of despair and hopelessness that characterized the lives of most slum dwellers. They felt they were powerless, unable to control their own destinies or influence persons in positions of authority. The same phrases kept cropping up in the testimony of witnesses, both young and old. They felt "trapped" or "in a cage." One teenager who had a prison record but helped stop the disorders in San Francisco's Hunters Point said that sometimes they thought they saw light but "we turn around and all we can see is darkness ahead."

For the Cleveland hearing in Hough, we procured the services of a young Harvard psychiatrist, Robert Coles, to use his new technique of having children draw pictures of familiar things. The commissioners were skeptical of the value of this effort but the results were revealing. Dr. Coles described the picture a Negro boy drew of his home:

This house is a shambles. It is a confused, disorderly house. The house is deliberately ramshackle. There is a black sky and what might pass for a black sun or in any event a cloud of black. The ground is brown and not green and there are no flowers. It is a dismal place. There is a cross on the door. The child told me that the property was condemned.

Dr. Coles added that the children he had dealt with in Boston and Cleveland became "confused and, at a very early age, filled with despair and depression. They see with clarity the discrepancy between the ethic of equality 'that is proclaimed' and the actual fact of 'what is.' "

By the time the commission held hearings in San Francisco, there had been riots in many cities and the voices of black nationalism and militancy had grown louder. On the same day that the commission opened in its hearings in the Bay Area, the newspapers reported that "a band of young Negroes," members of the Black Panthers, "armed with loaded rifles, pistols and shotguns" barged into a debate of the California General Assembly. The Panthers had come to protest a bill restricting the carrying of loaded weapons within the city limits of Oakland.

At the commission hearing, the chairman of the Mexican American Political Association presented testimony that included an indictment of the commission for neglecting the problems of Latinos, then said he was leaving the hearing "in contempt, anger, and indignation." Several young African Americans excoriated the commission for failing to produce results in changing ghetto conditions and suggested that action in the streets might be more effective than the issuing of reports.

Some commissioners reacted defensively. Father Theodore Hesburgh, president of Notre Dame University, tried to present a world perspective, noting the freedom that existed in the United States and pointing to the fact that housing slums in this country were not as bad as the favelas in South America. Eugene Patterson, editor of the *Atlanta*

Constitution, cautioned a witness who urged a "by any means necessary" approach against going outside the democratic process, noting that such tactics had not served white segregationists well. These observations simply brought more derision from the protesters.

Haynes Johnson, covering the commission's hearing for the *Washington Star,* observed, "Less than two years ago, the commissioners were evoking ovations from Mississippi Negroes. Over the past few years their investigations have supplied facts and figures which later became incorporated in presidential and congressional action in the broad field of civil rights. Certainly, their contribution to keeping the Negro revolution peaceful has been significant. Yet now when they journey north or west to examine national civil rights problems they often find themselves without the support of Negroes and other minority groups in the big cities."

The irony to me was palpable. It was the commission's status as a blue-ribbon, largely white group of prestigious citizens that gave it credibility within the establishment in urging civil rights policies. Yet it was these very same characteristics that were inspiring distrust of our efforts and initiatives among activists in inner cities.

The commission weathered the criticism heard in the Bay Area and began to respond. We had been slow in addressing the problems facing Latinos so we moved quickly to attract Hispanic-American lawyers and experts in Latino issues to produce useful work in that area. We continued to have the support of national civil rights groups that we had worked with for years. And, with the establishment of field offices in four cities authorized by the Civil Rights Act of 1964, we began to learn some valuable lessons on what is important in producing change at the local level.

One striking illustration of the latter point was our experience with Coronet Village in Harvey, Illinois. Coronet Village was a development of about a hundred attached townhouses and apartments built after World War II and inhabited almost exclusively by low-income blacks. By the 1960s, the development was deteriorating rapidly. It was rat-infested, major appliances were unserviced, windowpanes were broken. And there was so much violence on the property that local police had decided not to respond to calls for help.

Some of the residents formed a tenants' union. They got no response from management until the savings and loan association that held the mortgages became insolvent and was taken over by the Federal Savings and Loan Insurance Corporation, a government agency that regulates private lending institutions. When the tenants' union presented its demands to the FSLIC, essentially the new landlord, it was initially rebuffed and its leaders asked the commission's Chicago office, headed by John McKnight, to serve as an intermediary. Although the agency resisted, we were able to persuade its officials to enter into discussions with the union.

I came out to Chicago with Jerry Worthy, a soft-spoken Alabama banker who headed FSLIC. Worthy participated personally in the negotiations and, after receiving some initial rough treatment, he won the confidence of the tenants. The result was a detailed agreement specifying the responsibilities of both tenants and the landlord, including the provision of key services, and reducing and equalizing rents among tenants. Interestingly, the tenants' union held no brief for irresponsible occupants. They were prepared to see tenants evicted for nonpayment of rent or for drug use or violence if they were not prepared to mend their ways.

When I visited in 1968, six months after the agreement was signed, the changes were striking. Many of the apartments had been renovated and painted, the streets were free of litter, and the rats were under control. Plans for a recreation area for children were being developed, and crime and vandalism had decreased markedly. The leaders and members of the tenants' union felt real pride in their community and were exerting pressures on others who were delinquent in their rents or who damaged property to shape up or ship out. The gains made, the tenants felt, should not be jeopardized by the destructive actions of a few.

More than three decades later, I believe that there are growing efforts in inner cities to develop forms of community organization and structures that will serve the needs of residents as the tenants' union in

Coronet Village did in Illinois. But fundamentally, little has changed. While many social critics continue to lament the disintegration of the black low-income family, hardly anything is done to create the employment opportunities that would encourage family stability. And while most people know what effects recessions and joblessness can have in breaking up middle-class families and causing pathology, they do not connect the dots to the plight of the worst-off people in ghettos.

Indeed, the major difference now is that the wider society has simply learned to ignore people in inner cities. With some sporadic exceptions the ghetto is not erupting today, so we are isolated from it in a way that it has almost no effect on our daily lives. A few images stick with me today. In 1997, Frederick Wiseman, the great documentary filmmaker (and a friend and classmate from Yale Law School) produced a film about life in the Ida B. Wells housing project in Chicago. Wiseman does not provide a narrative for his films; he lets his subjects and images speak for themselves. What came through to me was the extraordinary difficulty that residents of this public housing project encounter in accomplishing the daily tasks that for most people are routine. Lacking a car or efficient transportation, and with a dearth of nearby stores, shopping becomes a burden. Lacking convenient access to health care, addressing one's medical needs is a problem. Despite the availability of telephones (though usually without e-mail access, increasingly a communications necessity) many other needs are not easily met. Dealing with government agencies and forms, people can become worn out. Little thought is given to this environment by many middle-class people who still stereotype ghetto residents as lazy or dissolute.

The other image is stimulated largely by memories of the stories told by my late wife Harriett of the experiences she had when judging drug or other criminal cases at the Superior Court in Washington, D.C. She found that many of the defendants in these cases had abilities that emerged during the course of the trial. Young African Americans charged with running drug operations had acquired skills in organizing a business enterprise and in keeping track of financial affairs that would have served them well in school and in legitimate occupations. Truly, in Jefferson's words, there were a mass of talents that lay buried beneath poverty for want of means of development. Under current policies, they will continue to be buried.

LBJ and Racially Isolated Schools

After enactment of the 1964 act it became clear that segregated public school systems in the South would be dismantled. But it was clear that racially isolated schools were a problem not only in the South, where segregation had been mandated by state law, but in the rest of the nation as well. Increasingly, national attention focused on racial isolation of schools in the urban North and West, on its causes and educational effects.

In November 1965, President Johnson, perceiving that there was no ready political solution to the problem, decided to study it. He wrote to the commission, "even with the progress in ending formal segregation of schools, racial isolation in the schools persists" and "presents serious barriers to quality education." He asked the agency to conduct a thorough study.

We put together a staff team, headed by Tom Pettigrew, a social psychologist and race relations expert at Harvard, who served as chief consultant and helped us recruit David Cohen, a very talented young educator, to direct the project. We established a working advisory committee that included the social scientists Kenneth Clark and Robin Williams, who had contributed valuable evidence in the *Brown* case; the educators John Fischer of Teachers College at Columbia and Judson Shaplen of the Graduate School of Education at Washington University in St. Louis; and school superintendents Benjamin Carmichael of Chattanooga and Neil Sullivan of Berkeley. We also commissioned papers from distinguished educators, including John Goodlad of the University of California and Frank Keppel, who had been commissioner of Education, the highest federal education official.

In addition, we found local educators to examine in detail the policies and practices of fifteen school systems throughout the nation. We reanalyzed the data accumulated for the Coleman report, a huge survey of some six hundred thousand school children mandated by the Civil Rights Act of 1964. And through commission hearings in Cleveland, Rochester, Boston, and the Bay Area, we learned about the history and dynamics of racial isolation in the schools and gained the perceptive insights of parents, teachers, and civil rights and education activists.

When we were done, about fifteen months after we had started, we had produced what I believe to be the first major interdisciplinary report ever prepared by a government agency. We learned a good deal about the causes of racial isolation in the schools of the thirty-three states in the North and West that did not have segregation laws in 1954. Primarily, we learned that segregated conditions did not come about by happenstance but were usually the result of choices made by school boards and school superintendents in locating and organizing schools. Often, the state or the city board had had explicit racial segregation statutes or policies in the past—policies that were similar to those challenged in *Brown*—but, even after those policies were abandoned, school systems continued to make decisions that perpetuated segregation.

More important, we learned a good deal about the dynamics and effects of segregation. The Coleman report, while making clear that family background had a very large impact on overall student achievement, determined that school factors, most prominently the quality of teaching and socioeconomic environment of the classroom, had an important influence on educational results. We found in addition that there was a significant racial dimension—schools and classrooms that were isolated by race as well as socioeconomic status were often stigmatized as inferior, depressing the morale and effectiveness of teachers and the self-esteem of students.

The commission explored the growing metropolitan dimension of racial isolation. It recommended that legislation be considered calling on states to develop desegregation standards, crossing lines between city and suburbs where necessary. And, most controversially, we expressed the view that the problems of inequality could not be addressed adequately by the compensatory measures, such as remedial reading, then in use.

When we had completed a final draft, we sent it to President Johnson with a request for a meeting to discuss our findings. We met at the White House at the end of January and it became clear early on that Johnson had either thoroughly read the report or had been briefed extensively on it. He talked about his own experience teaching poor Mexican-American children in southwest Texas in the early '30s and how he had become convinced that these children could succeed if given the opportunity. Responding to the commission's discussion of how peer influence affects children's aspirations and performance, LBJ said he knew from personal experience what we were talking about, because he could see the difference in the work of his own two daughters after they were enrolled in the National Cathedral School in Washington.

The commission could not have asked for a more attentive response from the president. On the way out, Harry McPherson told me that the meeting, which had run for about an hour, was the longest on a domestic matter that Johnson had held since the Vietnam War had heated up. Johnson clearly had been engaged.

But the rewards of the meeting with LBJ were primarily psychic, and little more. By this time, the wave of national conscience that had produced the Civil Rights Act in 1964 and 1965 and the major planks of the Great Society was largely spent. The country was consumed by Vietnam and there was no Sheriff Bull Connor with vicious dogs to make plain the rights and wrongs of conditions in the ghetto. In fact, the tide was running out.

Taking My Leave

By the beginning of 1968, I had pretty much decided that it was time for me to leave the commission. I had been with the agency and working in government on civil rights issues for the past seven years. I had had the extraordinary good fortune to be able to make a contribution to a great transformation in race relations but I felt the time had come to move on.

I had come to understand that lawyers like me could not create the climate that makes major change possible, we could only use our skills to maximize the benefits of a favorable environment. We had caught an enormous wave in the '60s, but who knew when it might come again. I did not feel tired or spent, but only that I was ready to do something else. In the short run, I thought I might write a book about what we had learned about race and cities. For the longer run, I had no idea about what I would do next.

On the evening of April 4, I was at home helping to celebrate the ninth birthday of my daughter Deborah when the call came from my office that Martin Luther King Jr. had been assassinated in Memphis. I think I went into shock. The next day, I went to a previously scheduled meeting of the commission's D.C. Advisory Committee at the Pitts Motor Hotel in downtown Washington. We were all grieving and none of us knew what to say. As I left the motel and walked to Fourteenth Street, I could see smoke rising all around me.

Over the next few weeks, I felt as if I were living in a newsreel. I flew on Vice President Humphrey's airplane to the funeral at the Ebenezer Baptist Church in Atlanta, and I still have images of the packed church and of the mule-drawn caisson in the street. When I returned I saw sandbags piled on Constitution Avenue and soldiers with bayonets on street corners, ready to deal with civil disorders. We went to work on a new Fair Housing Act spurred by national support growing out of the murder of Dr. King. Then, in June, Robert Kennedy was killed in Los Angeles. He had waged an extraordinary campaign for the presidential nomination, picking up the torch that King had carried on behalf of the poor. The deaths of King and Kennedy left me and so many others numb and traumatized. Any feelings that we had of living in an orderly world and having some control over our destinies was dissipated.

I wasn't sure where I was going but I was glad to get out of Washington.

CHAPTER SIX

New Beginnings

The next stop turned out to be a sojourn in New Haven. The precipitating events began some months earlier when my friend Mike Kandel said he wanted me to meet a friend of his, Richard Kluger, an editor at Simon and Schuster. Kluger, it turned out, was seeking someone to write the story of the five communities that made up the landmark decisions in the school segregation cases—the four communities in *Brown* along with a companion case involving Washington, D.C.

Kluger's idea was inspired by two other books about important Supreme Court cases: *Gideon's Trumpet*, Anthony Lewis's account of how Clarence Gideon won the right to counsel to represent him in a criminal case, and Bernard Taper's *Gomillion v. Lightfoot*, the story of the Tuskegee, Alabama, gerrymander that disenfranchised black people. Kluger's proposal was fascinating but daunting. It involved the racial dynamics of five communities, the history of segregation and of the carefully planned campaign to overturn the Court's approval of the separate-but-equal doctrine, and also an effort to penetrate the secrecy of the Court to understand what led to the historic decisions.

Kluger asked if I would take on the task. After some thought I turned him down. It seemed to me that it was such a formidable undertaking that it would probably take five years to complete. While

I thought of myself as a good writer, this book would benefit from the skills of a novelist, which I did not possess. And I wondered how much of an audience there would be after the book was completed.

Kluger then surprised me by asking what kind of book I *would* be interested in writing. I said that I would like to write about racial isolation and cities, to try to sort out the experience I had gained with the commission over the past few years. In short order, I had a contract with Simon and Schuster. Kluger, by the way, decided to take on the *Brown* assignment himself. He had written novels and had a powerful intellect and a real feel for issues of equality. As I had thought, it took more than five years for him to complete the book, but it turned out to be one of the two or three best books ever written about the contemporary civil rights revolution. The book, *Simple Justice*, tells the story of the people and their struggles in Clarendon County, South Carolina; Topeka, Kansas; Prince Edward County, Virginia; Wilmington, Delaware; and the District of Columbia; it traces the extraordinary work of Charles Houston, Thurgood Marshall, and their colleagues in crafting the legal strategy that ultimately led to the decision; and it gets inside the thinking and deliberations of Supreme Court justices who knew what the right thing to do was, but worried about making the court's perceived legitimacy the subject of attack. I have often told students and colleagues that my great contribution to the book was deciding not to write it.

With my contract in hand, I approached Lou Pollak, then dean of Yale Law School, to ask whether he would be interested in my coming to Yale Law School in the fall of 1968 to write the book. He liked the idea, created for me the title senior fellow; and with a small grant from the Ford Foundation to add to my advance from Simon and Schuster, my family and I moved to New Haven for a year in residence to write what became *Hanging Together: Equality in an Urban Nation*.

In many respects the year in academia provided a welcome respite from the cauldron in Washington. I was an invited kibitzer in law school classes dealing with civil rights and education. I devised and taught a course on poverty and urban issues at Jonathan Edwards College in the undergraduate school.

The law school was in turmoil as were so many other education institutions in 1968, with student protests on a variety of issues. I was privileged to sit in on faculty meetings as professors debated how to respond, but was relieved to have no decision-making responsibilities. The city was roiled by an upcoming murder trial of several Black Panthers. The country was in political turmoil, too, and my friend Al Lowenstein came to town to make speeches on a couple of occasions about the Nixon-Humphrey presidential campaign, verging on opposing Hubert Humphrey's candidacy because he did not find himself able to cut his ties with LBJ on Vietnam. I told Al I thought he was being shortsighted, because Nixon would be no better than Humphrey with regard to the Vietnam War, and his conservative domestic policies would certainly hurt poor people on a day-to-day basis. But I did not persuade him and from my perch at Yale Law School I felt remote from the whole political struggle.

The research for the book gave me time for learning and reflection that I had not had in Washington. I read about the history and economics of cities and was exposed to the ideas of thinkers such as Lewis Mumford. Meanwhile forces like suburbanization, the interstate highway system, and the beginning of the information revolution were changing cities in ways no one could fully predict.

When I turned to what I might do next, I was in a quandary. I interviewed at several law schools and responded to a couple of feelers from law firms. One interview brought its own surprise. Richard Sachs, a good friend, was a member of the board of trustees of the New School in New York and he urged me to become a candidate to head up a new department at the school dealing with urban affairs. I told him I might be interested were it not for the fact that Harry Gideonse, having left Brooklyn College in 1962, was now the provost at the New School. Dick assured me that I would not have to deal with Gideonse in any way and he ultimately persuaded me to schedule an interview with Jack Everett, the school's president. When I arrived, Everett gave me a smiling greeting and then turned toward the door I had come through, where stood Harry Gideonse. Gideonse told me that he remembered me and had followed my career with interest. Since I had not yet obtained my FBI file, I did not fully grasp the meaning of his statement. After a cordial discussion with Everett, I withdrew from consideration.

Some friends had also suggested that I might be successful in seeking elective office, but I found myself concerned about how a political career might destabilize family life. That concern was reinforced when Harriett, who was helping a Yale Law School professor with his book on labor law, came down with a mysterious kidney ailment. By the time it was properly diagnosed, it had become life threatening. As she recovered, I thought about what was important in life and all the things I had taken for granted.

Harriett's illness may have helped me focus on what I might do next that would make a contribution. There was, I thought, one striking need in civil rights work—to mount a real effort for administrative enforcement of civil rights laws. There were organizations—notably the NAACP Legal Defense Fund—that provided representation in the courts for persons who had suffered discrimination. There were also organizations that mounted strong lobbying campaigns for civil rights legislation. With their success in securing the Civil Rights Act of 1964 and the Voting Rights Act of 1965, virtually every agency of the federal government had civil rights responsibilities.

But this new situation of government-wide responsibility to ensure that federal dollars were spent without discrimination created a vacuum. What private groups would ride herd on federal agencies to see that they did their jobs? Years of experience with the commission had convinced me that one could not rely on the FHA or the Labor or Agriculture departments to enforce civil rights laws without private monitoring and pressure. And five years after enactment of the laws, no one had yet grasped this mantle.

I decided to try to establish an institution that would make administrative civil rights enforcement its main mission. We would offer our expertise to other civil rights groups to help them petition for rulemaking, comment on regulations that appeared in the Federal Register, and file administrative complaints on behalf of persons who suffered discrimination at the hands of recipients of federal funds. We would also seek publicity for continuing problems of discrimination and perhaps file lawsuits to get federal agencies to do their jobs. The idea of administrative advocacy of course was not entirely new. Ralph Nader was pursuing it by challenging federal policies on auto safety and in other areas. But there certainly was a comparable need in civil rights.

I drafted a proposal to create this new institution and sent it to the Ford Foundation with a request for $150,000 to get us started. The people at Ford reacted favorably and after further discussion agreed to funding with one major proviso: That the new institution could not be freestanding. It had to be affiliated with an already existing organization. Ford was worried, I think, by the growing attacks from conservatives in Congress about its support for civil rights advocacy rather than for more traditional charity. After some searching for a partner, I was put in touch with Clinton Bamberger, who had recently become dean of the Catholic University Law School. Bamberger had spent several years helping to develop and implement the legal services program, a key element of Johnson's War on Poverty.

Catholic University was a stodgy and conservative law school, but Bamberger was chosen by a progressive university president because he reflected the social justice strain of Catholic thinking and would bring a new dynamism to the institution. From my first meeting with him, I had the feeling that Catholic Law School would be a good home for the center. It would provide an opportunity to establish a pioneering clinical program for law students. All over the country, clinical programs were being created at law schools, giving students the opportunity to represent poor people in landlord-tenant court, on welfare claims, and on other matters. Ours would be different, however. Situated in the nation's capital, it could help students learn how to become advocates before federal agencies, something that no one had done up to that point.

So in the summer of 1970 we established the Center for National Policy Review, setting up shop in the basement of Catholic University Law School in northeast Washington. I hired a research director and a handful of lawyers who were expert in specific areas of civil rights. I developed a civil rights course and we accepted applications from students who would receive half of their credits during the academic year for clinical work. I reestablished contact with the Leadership Conference on Civil Rights. LCCR had created a committee on compliance, largely for the purpose of organizing meetings on civil rights with cabinet officers. I proposed a far more systematic and programmatic approach: the center would help to staff the work of a new group of task forces to take on implementation issues. LCCR agreed. We were in business.

The Center's Advocacy

One of the issues we decided to take on almost immediately was the federal role in home finance. I had learned during my days at the commission how influential federal agencies had been in establishing lending policies that denied black Americans the opportunity to purchase homes and that resulted in patterns of strict policies of residential segregation in metropolitan areas. While overt discrimination was now unlawful, we had reason to believe that it continued in many forms.

A break for us came early when the Federal National Mortgage Association (Fanny Mae) decided to enter into the "secondary market" for the purchase of conventional mortgages. This meant that the association would purchase from banks and from savings and loan associations mortgage loans they had made to customers to buy houses that were not government-subsidized (i.e., conventional). The creation of the secondary market would free up lending institutions to make more loans and the impact on the economy was going to be substantial, about $1 billion in the first year.

Fannie Mae had to decide, however, what its standards would be for the purchase of loans. It issued proposed rules. When we saw them, we were thunderstruck. The agency had decided to adopt the most regressive policies that existed in the home mortgage business, policies that would hurt hundreds of thousands of homeseekers.

For example, the proposed rules said that when a two-income family applied for a mortgage loan, only the husband's income could be considered fully in deciding whether to approve the mortgage. The wife's income would be fully or partly discounted because she was not likely to be a permanent member of the workforce. Also, when a person in a low-income area applied for a mortgage, the lender would be required to consider not only the age and condition of the house being sought but of all the other houses in the area. This was a clear invitation to redline.

The list went on. Another rule said that if the age of the mortgage purchaser and the term of the mortgage added up to more than eighty years, the mortgage should not be approved. Yet another said that bonus and overtime income, even when regularly received by an employee, should not be counted in his application. And still another said that *any* past history of credit problems should be deemed as disqualifying the applicant.

The center had already been doing research on several of these policies and had found that there was very little data to back them up as means to prevent defaults. When Fannie Mae came forward with its rules, we were ready. We organized a group of thirty organizations to file a petition to challenge the proposed rules.

But it also struck me that this was a situation where a press conference could have a major impact. So we organized a public event. Ralph Nader challenged the "any past history" provision. Aileen Hernandez, chair of the National Organization for Women (NOW), said the provisions for discounting a wife's income were sexist. A high official of the AFL-CIO took on Fannie Mae's refusal to consider bonus and overtime income. A leading organization representing older people denounced the eighty-year rule. And the NAACP skewered Fannie Mae's endorsement of redlining.

The agency beat a hasty retreat, saying right after the press conference was held on October 3, 1971, that it would take another look at its proposed rules. On December 16, Fannie Mae announced revisions in its guidelines. As the *Wall Street Journal*, the *New York Times,* and the

Washington Star reported, "many of the revised guidelines incorporated proposals made by . . . [our civil rights] coalition." We had scored a clean victory in this round of the battle by organizing a group representing many interests.

The center continued the home-finance battle on other fronts. On the same day that Fannie Mae announced its revised guidelines, the center, with another legal group, filed a law suit against the Federal Home Loan Bank Board. We challenged the board's exclusion of low-income people from a program established under the Emergency Home Finance Act of 1970, which directed the board to use $250 million to provide housing for those in need of help. Our lawsuit alleged that the board had arbitrarily excluded families with low incomes from being eligible for subsidized loans. The board's defense was that savings and loan associations were friendly neighborhood institutions that had good relations with black groups in low-income areas. At one point the judge, William Bryant, who had a distinguished career in civil rights before his appointment to the bench, tartly observed that, when he was young, the message from savings and loan associations to the black community was that they were unwelcome and that blacks would never even think of entering a savings and loan. The case was settled with an agreement by the board to make more loans to people who were truly low-income.

The main thrust of our effort was to persuade the four agencies that regulated most of the banks and savings and loan associations in the nation to acknowledge a responsibility to ensure that these institutions pursued fair lending practices. We began in 1971 with a petition filed with the four agencies on behalf of thirteen civil rights and public interest groups asking each of them—the Federal Home Loan Bank Board, the Federal Deposit Insurance Corporation, the Federal Reserve, and the Comptroller of the Currency—to adopt civil rights regulations. Progress was slow, sometimes glacial. In 1971, the Bank Board agreed to begin collecting racial data on mortgage loans so that it could detect patterns in the lending patterns of individual institutions. The board agreed also to adopt credit guidelines and to use an "effect standard" in judging the validity of a practice. This meant that banks and savings and loan associations could not escape responsibility for practices that hurt minority applicants simply by claiming they were not intended to discriminate.

Still, little change was taking place. We then went to the Senate Banking and Currency Committee to ask that oversight hearings be scheduled to examine the activities of the four agencies on fair lending. Senator William Proxmire, who chaired the committee, had a keen interest in opening housing opportunities to all people and in ensuring strong implementation of the civil rights laws and the recently passed Equal Credit Opportunity Act. The hearings became a vehicle not simply for calling top agency officials on the carpet to get them to account for their lassitude and pledge to do better, but to gather data about the nature and extent of the problem.

Armed with a great deal more information about lending practices, we decided to go to court. In 1976 we joined with the National Committee against Discrimination in Housing to file suit on behalf of the National Urban League and other groups against the four agencies. The judge was Gerhard Gesell, who, as a private lawyer, had headed a commission that President Kennedy created to examine discrimination in the armed forces. Judge Gesell was a no-nonsense jurist who informed all the parties early on that the case would be settled without a trial and that he was prepared to lock us all in a room until we came out with an agreement.

So motivated, all of the parties worked hard and in 1977 we achieved a settlement. The agencies agreed to collect and analyze racial data on loan applications, to train bank examiners to identify possible discrimination in their regular review of bank records, to appoint civil rights specialists, and to use the same sanctions against lending institutions for civil rights violations as were used in other areas of bank misconduct.

We viewed the settlement agreement as a victory for our side. The establishment of systems for racial data collection and analysis was a key element. In the days before the enactment of the 1964 act, many civil rights advocates regarded the collection of racial data as a wrong, believing that the possession of such information could be used as an instrument of discrimination. Slowly, however, they came to recognize that discrimination was accomplished without the aid of data systems and that indeed data collection was needed to identify and correct discriminatory practices. These days, civil rights opponents like Ward Connerly are urging the elimination of racial data collection, arguing that we now live in a "color-blind" society. Despite his success with anti–affirmative action referenda in California, Connerly lost his proposed referendum to eliminate racial data collection in 2002, suggesting that voters understand that problems cannot be cured by hiding their existence.

After our settlement, Roger Kuhn, my codirector at the center, established regular contact with representatives of the four banking agencies to work with them in creating effective operations. He helped them internalize their new responsibilities and the institutional change persisted even after the expiration date for our agreement. Today, while it is hard for me to assess with precision the impact of our efforts, I do think that significant change has taken place. Our legal efforts ran parallel to the growth of community organizations like the National People's Action, headed in Chicago by the late Gail Cincotta, which exerted pressures on banks to adopt policies for reinvesting in the community. Certainly, all of this has resulted in easier access to credit for middle-class people of color and in the revival of some neighborhoods. At the same time, fewer banks and savings and loan associations are engaged in extensive home mortgage lending and, in some places, predatory lending practices pursued by disreputable businesses have continued to victimize poor people and have not been effectively controlled by state or federal laws.

The Value of Coalition

As the center's work was becoming a central part of the program of the Leadership Conference during the 1970s, the conference was growing and changing. Through the end of the '60s the Leadership Conference was a coalition of African-American organizations, mainly the NAACP, supported by labor unions and religious groups dedicated to legislation to eliminate racial segregation and the residual effects of slavery. But with the success of the black civil rights movement, other organizations were established to attack gender discrimination, to deal with biased practices based on nationality and ethnicity, and to assert the rights of people with disabilities to fair and unequal treatment. These new groups sought to become members of the Leadership Conference in order to work for the kinds of legislative protections contained in the Civil Rights Act of 1964.

In retrospect, the question of adding these groups to the roster of Leadership Conference organizations seems like an easy one, but to many it was not a self-evident proposition at the beginning. For some black groups and their supporters, racial discrimination, with its roots in slavery and segregation, was different from other forms of discrimination—more pernicious and deeply embedded in American society. This led some to the conclusion that broadening the mission of the Leadership Conference to other forms of bias would dilute the focus and weaken the drive against race bias. In addition, members of the LCCR were susceptible to some of the same stereotypical thinking as were other Americans. Some still wanted to preserve elements of the traditional role of women in society; some thought of people with disabilities as having less to contribute to society than others. And in a few areas, the possibility of conflicts of interest existed. Immigrants from Mexico and elsewhere, for example, might be employed to keep the wages of black workers low.

While recognizing that some of these views were deeply held, it seemed to me that the arguments for expanding the coalition were far stronger than any reflexive opposition to doing so. For one thing, racial, religious, gender, and ethnic bias seemed to me to be all strains of the same virus—a refusal to understand and value people as individuals and a willingness to make harmful judgments based on stereotypes. Just as important for organizational purposes, the practical value of working in coalition struck me as inestimable. The experience of pulling all of these organizations together to blast Fannie Mae's biased lending guidelines in 1971 was a graphic demonstration of what we could all gain by working together.

This was the view that prevailed in the Leadership Conference, and it has grown since the '70s from a membership of fewer than one hundred groups to the 180-member roster of organizations today. The process of working together and trusting one another has not always been easy. In 1975, during the Ford administration, David Matthews, the secretary of Health, Education, and Welfare, decided it was too burdensome to investigate all civil rights complaints that his department received. So his Office for Civil Rights let it be known that they proposed to pick and choose among complaints, and suggested that racial and ethnic groups would benefit from the new discretionary policy because women's organizations were more articulate and better organized in getting complaints filed.

We decided in LCCR to present a united front in urging the department to investigate all complaints, and we scheduled a press conference to discuss our position. The conference got off to a rocky start. Ron Brown, representing the Urban League, said something that the president of NOW interpreted as sexist. When she rose to speak, she criticized Ron, but then went on to say that HEW "could not be so blind" as to ignore the rights of women. That remark offended the representative of disability groups. As moderator of the press conference, I could see my friend Judy Lichtman, of the Women's Legal Defense Fund, in the back of the room, drawing her hand across her throat to signal me to end our predicament. I responded by saying, "We are all just getting to know one another." And so we were. Despite our awkwardness, Secretary Matthews got the point and withdrew his ill-advised proposal. Through succeeding years, our groups worked together on various kinds of civil rights legislation, sometimes on bills that affected the rights of one group, and other times on bills that have affected the rights of all groups. On the latter type of legislation there were often issues of strategy or tactics on which there were disagreements in the coalition. It was not uncommon for groups

Here I am (*left*) entering the Supreme Court for the historic Little Rock School case argument on September 11, 1958, with Jack Greenberg, William Coleman, and Thurgood Marshall (*right*).

(**BELOW**) This picture was taken on Governor's Island in 1957 after I had won on the quiz show "Tic Tac Dough."

(All photos are part of the author's collection unless otherwise noted.)

(ABOVE) The U.S. Commission on Civil Rights meeting with President Kennedy on February 12, 1963, to celebrate the centennial of the Emancipation Proclamation. Front row, *left to right*: Commissioner Robert Rankin, Staff Director Berl Bernhard, Commissioner Robert Storey, President Kennedy, and Commissioners Spottswood Robinson, Erwin Griswold, and Theodore Hesburgh. I am in the back row, far left, next to M. Carl Holman and Clyde Ferguson.

(LEFT) In this photograph, I am shaking hands with Vice President Humphrey.

My children, Lauren, David, and Deborah, with Vice President Humphrey at my swearing in as Staff Director of the U.S. Commission on Civil Rights on August 20, 1965. It was also David's third birthday.

(**LEFT**) My wife Harriett and I with Roy Wilkins, Executive Secretary of the NAACP.

Civil rights commissioners Frankie Freeman and Theodore Hesburgh with me at a hearing in the 1960s.

I am shaking hands with President Johnson. Clyde Ferguson, former General Counsel of the Commission, is in the middle.

(**ABOVE**) Members and staff of the U.S. Commission on Civil Rights meeting in the Cabinet Room of the White House to discuss their report on Racial Isolation of the Public Schools of the North and the West with President Lyndon Johnson in January 1967. Clockwise from far left: Carl Holman, Deputy Director of the Commission; Erwin N. Griswold, Dean of Harvard Law School; Robert Rankin, Professor of Political Science, Duke University; Frankie M. Freeman, attorney; John Hannah, President of Michigan State University and Chairman of the Commission; Eugene Patterson, Editor of the *Atlanta Constitution*; Rev. Theodore Hesburgh, President of Notre Dame University; Me; Clifford Alexander, Deputy Counsel to the President; Harry McPherson, Counsel to the President; President Johnson; Howard Glickstein (back to camera), General Counsel of the Commission.

(**ABOVE**) President Johnson's Commission on Human Rights. Among those pictured are Supreme Court Justice Tom Clark, Averill Harriman, A. Philip Randolph, Governor Robert Meyner of New Jersey, presidential aide Clifford Alexander, and Warren Christopher. I am standing behind LBJ.

(**ABOVE LEFT**) Here I am standing with Baynard Rustin in the 1970s. Rustin was the chief strategist for the March on Washington in 1963 and later served as Chair of the Executive Committee of the Leadership Conference on Civil Rights.

(**LEFT**) My late wife, Judge Harriett R. Taylor. Senator Orrin Hatch sought to remove her from the bench.

(RIGHT) I am standing at the podium next to Arthur S. Flemming, co-founder of the Citizens' Commission on Civil Rights

(BELOW) Ossie Davis and Dorothy Height (*front*). Julian Bond and me (*back*).

At the White House in 1998, I spoke to President Clinton. The occasion was the 35th anniversary of the Lawyers Committee on Civil Rights, talks led by President Kennedy to provide legal assistance for black people in Mississippi. I was one of two people at the Clinton celebration who had been at the Kennedy meeting in 1963.

Back at Brooklyn College in 2001, I am standing with my son David and granddaughter Simone in front of the portrait of Harry D. Gideonse, the president who in 1950 had threatened to ruin my career. (Nicole Bengiveno/*The New York Times*)

representing one set of interests to be unwilling to compromise on their issues even if an inflexible stand might defeat the bill. But somehow we worked our way through all of the difficulties. We learned to trust each other and to deal pragmatically with the legislative process.

We also expanded our techniques of advocacy in the '70s. One example came with the advent of the Nixon administration, when the federal government moved to convert programs in which federal grants to the states were targeted to specific purposes (categoricals) to block grant programs (in which states had broad discretion to use federal money as they chose).

The largest of these new programs was general revenue sharing, a $30 billion grant to the states with virtually no strings attached. This new approach was worrisome to civil rights groups and their allies. While the nondiscrimination provisions of the civil rights laws applied to these grants, states were free to structure them and to describe the uses of the money in any way they chose. After all, the money was fungible and, if the states or localities wished to impress the public that the funds were being used for some popular purpose, they could state that this was the use while shifting local money from one account to another. Similarly, if jurisdictions were worried about the vulnerability of a particular area, say law enforcement, to a civil rights challenge, they could avoid stating that they were using the money for that purpose in order to create a defense against a legal action.

To cope with this challenge, the center joined with the League of Women Voters, the Center for Community Change, and the National Urban Coalition to mount a monitoring project on the operation of general revenue sharing. With a sizeable grant from the Edna McConnell Clark Foundation, we set out to ensure that funds broadly available to states and local jurisdictions were not used for discriminatory purposes. We also worked to determine the impact of revenue sharing on equity for poor people and to help develop the capacity of citizen groups to analyze budgets and to influence spending decisions at the local level.

The revenue-sharing project represented a comprehensive partnership between Washington-based groups working on issues of national policy, and local organizations seeking to influence decision making in their own communities. The center's partners in the project helped publish guidebooks to assist their local affiliates in analyzing budgets and riding herd on decisions by mayors and city councils. At the same time, the local groups were able to gather data that helped in dealing with national issues. And we jointly established a clearinghouse to disseminate information about revenue sharing around the nation. While these are commonly recognized as important techniques for influencing national policy today, in the '70s they were still new.

The center's primary role in the project was to provide legal expertise and advocacy on civil rights issues. In 1972 we were retained by Renault Robinson, president of the Afro-American Patrolmen's Association in Chicago, and by other organizations, to persuade the Department of the Treasury to stop giving revenue-sharing money to the City of Chicago until the City eliminated job discrimination in the police department. When Treasury failed to take action we helped prepare a lawsuit asking a federal court to direct the department to withhold funds from Chicago until the City took corrective action on job discrimination. Judge John Lewis Smith ruled that Treasury had the authority to defer revenue-sharing payments and ordered the agency to begin the enforcement process.

Still the Office of Revenue Sharing was reluctant to take action and, in 1975, Judge Smith transferred our case against Treasury to a federal district judge in Chicago who was struggling to get the mayor to carry out his obligation to remedy practices of discrimination in the employment and promotion of members of the police department. The mayor was the same Richard J. Daley whose clout in the 1960s led President Johnson to direct his administration to back down from proceeding with a complaint challenging school desegregation in Chicago. It was also this Richard Daley who had resisted a federal court order to find sites in white neighborhoods to locate public housing units, which until then had been built by the city only in black areas. Daley's recalcitrance had led a federal judge to compare him to George Wallace:

> There have been occasions in the past in parts of the country when chief executives have stood at the school house and the state doors with their wattles flapping and have defied the federal government to enforce its laws and decrees.

It was an anomaly, Judge Richard Austin wrote, for the "law and order" chief executive of the city to "challenge and defy federal law." Still Daley resisted.

But in the revenue-sharing case the stakes were raised. Judge Marshall ordered the revenue sharing payments to be deferred and, by January 1976, $95 million had been withheld from the City of Chicago, with more at stake in the future. This time Daley folded his cards and complied with the court orders. Judge Prentice Marshall was impelled to observe that "the most effective remedy to cure [Daley's] constitutional malaise is the economic sanction of withholding revenue-sharing funds" until the defendants comply.

Also in 1976, our groups persuaded Congress to strengthen the civil rights provisions of the revenue sharing law and Treasury began to take more interest in enforcing the law, particularly to provide job opportunities for minorities in police and fire departments. Indeed, by the end of 1977, the *Washington Post* was able to report some striking civil rights successes in the revenue sharing program. In a December 22 front page article, staff writer Susanna McBee set forth the following among several cases:

"Item: Jacksonville, Fla. Mayor Hans Tanzler said on March 17 that the idea of having a lot of women on police and fire forces was 'so idiotic, so ridiculous, so unrealistic . . . it's not going to happen, there's no way it can happen.'

"Five days later the city council passed one of the toughest affirmative action ordinances in the country and the city is aggressively recruiting women and blacks for jobs.

"Why? Because the federal Office of Revenue Sharing threatened to cut off $2.3 million in quarterly revenue sharing payments unless the city complied with federal anti-discrimination laws.

"Item: In Claremont, N.C., Russell Shuford has been battling local officials for seven years, ever since his father was killed when his house was burned down and the family didn't have enough water to fight." Things got worse three years ago when Claremont started taxing the Shufords for services, and Shuford indignantly refused to pay because he wasn't getting any services—such as a road, a water line and a streetlight.

"Shuford complained to the Office of Revenue Sharing here that the town of 90 was discriminating against him because he is black and suddenly in July wheels started turning.

"Faced with a cutoff of $25,000 in revenue sharing money, the townspeople raised $4,700 and Shuford now has a road, a water line and a streetlight . . ."

The article credited the strengthened law, the Chicago case and the willingness of ORS to cut off funds for the results.

By 1980, however, support for the general revenue-sharing program had weakened and Congress did not extend it. The fundamental problem with the program, I believe, was that it violated a key principle of good government—that the people who raise the money through taxes should be the people who are held accountable for how it is spent. Here the federal government raised the revenues and then "left the money on the stump" for states to use as they pleased.

Nevertheless I think our work on general revenue sharing did some lasting good. Along with strong regulations we secured under the Law Enforcement Assistance Act, another block grant program that was ultimately repealed, we helped gain acceptance for the notion that federal funds spent anywhere in state and local government should give rise to a broad obligation by the recipients to provide equality of opportunity. This principle was applied decisively by Congress in the Civil Rights Restoration Act of 1988, which reversed a narrow ruling of the Supreme Court. Through our efforts, we also increased the capability and interest of local groups in ensuring fair treatment of minorities and the poor in local budget processes.

Back to School

Needless to say, working on behalf of school desegregation and equality of educational opportunity remained a central preoccupation of mine at the center. To be effective advocates, my colleagues and I proceeded along two paths.

Starting in 1970, our first endeavor was to persuade the Department of Health, Education, and Welfare to carry out its obligations to enforce Title VI of the 1964 act by redressing unlawful segregation. After the Johnson administration's extraordinary performance in implementing desegregation, Richard Nixon came to office in 1968 determined to pursue a "Southern strategy" designed to induce bigoted white Southerners to become Republicans.

When Nixon ordered HEW to stop enforcing the civil rights laws on school segregation, the NAACP Legal Defense Fund responded with a lawsuit against the agency, requesting an order that HEW carry out its responsibilities. While the center was not formally a part of the litigation, we assisted the fund and Joe Rauh, the principal lawyer, in gathering information for the suit.

But I was also interested in the desegregation of public schools in the northern and western areas of the nation. In 1973, the Supreme Court spoke for the first time on the obligation of these districts, declaring in the *Keyes* case that deliberately segregative practices, even if not encoded in a statute or policy, could give rise to remedies similar to those in the South. HEW, after recovering from the Chicago fiasco, had begun to conduct smaller-scale investigations in northern school districts, but it had not engaged in any real enforcement.

I knew from my experience at the Legal Defense Fund and the commission that segregation in most northern and western public schools was not accidental, but had come about through deliberate decisions by public officials. We decided to conduct a study and, with the help of Roger Mills, a student intern in our program, published a report in September 1974, *Justice Delayed and Denied*, documenting HEW's failure to mount an enforcement program against discrimination in the North. We gathered much of our information through a lawsuit under the Freedom of Information Act, which had been enacted in 1968, and our suit also impelled Congress to amend the law to make information more readily accessible to the public.

In July 1975, the center, joined by the NAACP and the NAACP Legal Defense Fund, brought an action against HEW officials, seeking an order requiring them to take enforcement action against school districts that were illegally segregating their schools. We represented black parents from eight districts where HEW was delaying action.

With a court order looming, HEW bestirred itself to begin enforcement action. Finally, in 1977, with the Carter administration in office, we were able to negotiate a comprehensive settlement of our case, by then known as *Brown v. Califano*, and two other similar suits. (In lawsuits brought on behalf of several plaintiffs, lawyers can choose who should be the "named plaintiff." We chose a child whose last name was Brown, as an emblem that the case was a legacy of *Brown v. Board of Education.*) HEW was required to investigate and act on school discrimination complaints within specified time frames and to clean up its backlog by September 1979. It also agreed to begin investigations of systemic discrimination in big city systems and to hire nine hundred additional staffers to do the job.

The result was some modest progress in the North and West, mainly in small and medium-sized districts. HEW secured desegregation agreements from school districts such as Bakersfield and Fresno, California; Joliet and Cahokia, Illinois; Springfield, Ohio; and Fort Wayne, Indiana, and began enforcement proceedings against others. (Later, in the 1980s, when the Fort Wayne agreement failed to desegregate elementary schools, I was hired to bring a private suit that resulted in a successful desegregation plan.) Our work called for continued monitoring. Shortly after the settlement, we found the need to seek a contempt citation against HEW for failing to initiate proceedings to terminate federal funds to New York City for discriminating in several areas including its treatment of children with disabilities. New York soon agreed to take action to end the discrimination.

The success we attained in doing battle with HEW, however, did not address the huge problems of segregation and educational deprivation that continued to prevail in America's largest cities. In a growing number of these cities, the problem was not simply one of racially segregated schools *within* a district. With the continued migration of black people from the South to central cities of the North and the South, and with the growing suburbanization of whites and the exclusion of blacks from housing in the suburbs, whole school districts became one race. The typical pattern became a central city school district that was 80 percent or more African American in its enrollment, surrounded by suburban districts that were 90 percent or more white.

Having explored the issues at the commission in our 1967 "Racial Isolation" report, I decided that the center should serve as a forum to discuss strategies for attacking racially isolated schools on a metropolitan basis. When I convened a meeting of lawyers, educators and representatives of advocacy groups soon after the center's establishment, I discovered that many people had the same thoughts and some were contemplating litigation.

The most promising case was long-running litigation to desegregate the Richmond, Virginia, school district. By the time the suit finally came to a head at the end of the 1960s, the district was more than two-thirds African American in its enrollment. At the same time, the surrounding suburban school systems in Chesterfield and Henrico counties were more than 90 percent white. The judge, Robert R. Merhige Jr., a Johnson appointee, clearly felt that the remedy for decades of segregation should produce substantial desegregation and he let it be known that he would be receptive to hearing evidence to support a metropolitan-wide remedy.

Our basic argument for an interdistrict approach was based on the original *Brown* decision. Education was a state responsibility and, as the decision said, when a state undertakes to offer public education, it must do so on equal terms. While local districting was to be respected it could not override the demands of the Constitution. A state could not, for example, retain local political districts without change when population had so shifted that current lines would violate the principle of one man, one vote.

These arguments, we thought, had particular salience in Virginia, which was a bastion of segregation and the intellectual cradle of massive resistance to the *Brown* decision. While our opponents inveighed against busing, we were able to point out that during the heyday of school segregation, Negro children living in areas where the black population was sparse were transported hundreds of miles to black schools, boarding there during the week and being transported home on weekends. That kind of busing to maintain segregation had been deemed acceptable by the authorities.

The case was being prosecuted by the NAACP Legal Defense Fund, which had retained Lou Lucas, an able trial lawyer who was a member of the first integrated law firm in the South. Lou asked me to join the legal team as a participant in the case rather than just as an adviser. In establishing our center I had told our sponsors at the Ford Foundation that the center would not litigate because there were enough litigating organizations. But when I broached the subject with my program officers after the Lucas request, they approved my participation in what was clearly going to be a high-profile case. They may have had different thoughts a few months later when anti-desegregation groups organized a boycott of Ford automobiles because of the center's participation in the case.

We laid out our case in a trial that took several weeks in 1971, showing how Virginia's policy dictated segregation both in public schools and housing. The atmosphere was charged. Judge Merhige was receiving death threats. Floodlights were installed at his house, and his wife and son were accompanied by federal marshals when they went out into the community. Despite all this, the judge seemed relaxed, maintaining friendly banter with the lawyers on and off the bench.

On January 11, 1972, Judge Merhige issued a 325-page decision finding that a metropolitan remedy was called for and directing the defendants to come up with a plan for merging the three districts. The decision was a big news story around the nation. In a commentary on CBS, Walter Cronkite said:

> So far as school desegregation is concerned, if Judge Merhige's ruling is upheld, there'll be no place to hide. Lily-white suburbs, even northern ones, are not isolated islands but parts of larger metropolitan communities and must share the responsibilities. Sometime in the not so distant future, the message to white suburbanites will be clear: when the school bell tolls for integration, it tolls for thee.

The key words, of course, were "if upheld." The case was appealed to the conservative court of appeals for the fourth circuit. There, a three-member panel of the court came up with the convoluted notion that metropolitan relief would be justified only if we were able to prove that the three districts conspired with each other to keep the metropolitan area segregated. Since the districts had been busy trying to maintain segregation within their individual borders, the idea of an interdistrict conspiracy seemed both farfetched and irrelevant. Then we asked the Supreme Court to review the case and the Court agreed.

The state of Virginia retained Philip Kurland, a conservative constitutional scholar from the University of Chicago, to argue the case and the Legal Defense Fund asked Bill Coleman, by then known as one of the ablest lawyers in the country, to present our case. With only a short time to prepare, Coleman mastered the extensive record and presented a fine argument. But one member of the Court, Lewis Powell, recused himself from participating, presumably because he had once served as chair of the Virginia Board of Education. This resulted in a 4–4 deadlock, which had the effect of upholding the court of appeals decision and nullifying the metropolitan remedy. The Court's custom in such a situation is to issue no opinion and to treat the case as setting no precedent. So everything would depend on the next metropolitan case to reach the Court.

I had hoped it might be a case that was proceeding in a lower court in Wilmington, Delaware. Wilmington was one of the four communities originally involved in *Brown v. Board of Education*. Although it had desegregated its schools fairly promptly, by 1970 80 percent of the school district's students were black, surrounded by suburban schools (some of them quite affluent) that were 90 percent or more white. Early in 1970, Lou Redding, the lawyer who had represented black plaintiffs in the Delaware part of the *Brown* case, wrote to me saying that there were a couple of lawyers from the American Civil Liberties Union who were considering a metropolitan suit but needed expert assistance, and asked that I advise them. In examining the facts, I discovered that Delaware, a few years earlier, had temporarily changed its school district reorganization law to make it easier for districts to consolidate, but had barred Wilmington from eligibility to participate. Wilmington then had 40 percent of all the African-American students in the state, and it was difficult to believe that race had nothing to do with the differential treatment.

Given those facts and the possibility that the Court would be troubled by resegregation in one of its seminal cases, Wilmington seemed like a good candidate for considering metropolitan remedies. But we were winning in the lower court and the case was not ready for review. (Ultimately we did prevail in the Supreme Court and a good plan was implemented.)

So, as it happened, the next case to reach the Supreme Court came from Detroit, Michigan. This was unfortunate for a variety of reasons. First, while Richmond and Wilmington were relatively small districts in small metropolitan areas, Detroit was one of the largest districts in the nation and was surrounded by a very large aggregation of suburban districts. Although there were sound logistical ways to desegregate the metropolitan area, they were not self-evident to many citizens. Secondly, when the case reached the Court in 1974, it was less than a year after the Court had spoken for first time on the obligations of school systems in the North and West. Just when Northern communities were examining for the first time changes they might have to make, they were faced with the possibility of undertaking a huge, unsettling task.

Third, in the 1972 Democratic primaries in the presidential race, George Wallace had made a very strong showing in Michigan, demonstrating that racial fears and prejudices had a firm hold in the North as well as the South.

The Detroit metropolitan school case came about in a strange way. It began as an effort to desegregate only the city schools, supported by extensive evidence that, historically, school officials had worked to keep black children (and at one point even Jewish children) in separate schools. In the late '60s, however, a movement arose to establish subdistricts of big city school systems to allow for "community control." In Michigan, an alliance developed between conservative Republicans in the state legislature interested in breaking up large school districts and a handful of African-American legislators interested in increasing black political influence. They moved successfully a bill requiring Detroit to prepare a plan for four or five subdistricts in the city.

Soon thereafter I received a call from Abe Zwerdling, a lawyer who was president of the Detroit school board and a friend from my Americans for Democratic Action days. If Detroit was compelled to establish subdistricts, he said, he wanted to do so in a way that would give voting power to black parents. But to do so, since black registration was lower than white registration and far lower than the black school population, he would have to draw lines that would result in racially isolated schools. What was my advice, he asked. My only thought was that school assignments did not have to conform to the boundaries set for the subdistricts. While this might be cumbersome, resulting in some parents living and voting in one subdistrict while their children attended school in another, at least it would not enshrine racially isolated schools.

Zwerdling agreed and his plan for subdistricts also included a plan for desegregating schools. The state legislature responded negatively by rescinding the desegregation plan. With this action, the state was made a party to the litigation and an interdistrict remedy became an issue. For being so politically imprudent as to follow my advice,

Zwerdling was recalled by Detroit voters in a referendum and soon moved to Washington, D.C., to practice law.

The Detroit case was well prepared in the lower courts. The judge, Stephen Roth, an immigrant from Hungary, initially seemed inclined to the view that the black experience in this country was very similar to the immigrant experience and that blacks could succeed without the intervention of the courts. But as he listened to the testimony of witnesses, particularly a black "realtist" (the name that black real estate agents were compelled to use by state law) who was the judge's own age and who had been rigidly isolated in seeking to develop opportunities for black home-seekers, Judge Roth came to realize how much larger the racial barriers were, compared to those faced by many immigrants.

The record was replete with instances of racial discrimination that crossed district lines. Michigan had established a suburban elementary school district—the George Washington Carver district—to serve black children. But when children reached high school age, school authorities determined there were too few of them to establish a high school. So they bused them past white suburban districts to black high schools in the Detroit school district. Moreover, there was overwhelming evidence that the State of Michigan along with federal government had supported and implemented policies from restrictive covenants to FHA loans to race bias in the location of subsidized housing. These practices kept black people contained in central cities, and therefore eligible to enroll their children only in substandard neighborhood schools.

Judge Roth found that the school and housing practices constituted a violation of the Constitution that justified a metropolitan remedy. The Court of Appeals sustained his decision, but decided not to consider the housing violation because it believed that the discriminatory school practices were sufficient.

On July 25, 1974, by a vote of 5–4, the Supreme Court declared that there was no obligation to pursue a metropolitan desegregation remedy in Detroit. The justices in the majority in several ways played fast and loose with judicial principles. Instead of addressing the fundamental tenet of state responsibility for public education, they spoke of "local control." Four of the justices said they would not deal with the issue of racial residential exclusion because the court of appeals had not ruled on the issue in the belief that the school violation was sufficient to justify a metropolitan remedy. But proper procedure would have been to return the case to the court of appeals for findings on housing. The Supreme Court had performed a magic act to make housing disappear as an issue.

But one justice in the majority—Potter Stewart—apparently did consider the housing evidence and found it wanting. In the key passage of his opinion, Stewart, who often was the swing vote in closely contested cases, said:

> It is this essential fact of a predominantly Negro school population in Detroit—caused by unknown and perhaps unknowable factors such as in-migration, birth rates, economic changes, or cumulative acts of private racial fears—that accounts for the "growing core of Negro schools," a "core" that has grown to include virtually the entire city.

He added that unless the State had contributed to this situation, there was no constitutional remedy in the courts. In his elliptical language, Justice Stewart was presumably referring to high black birth rates in the city, to white movement to the suburbs in pursuit of new jobs, and to white flight ("cumulative acts of private racial fears"). But this analysis fails to explain why black families were not found in the suburbs. While Justice Stewart said that he did not find the evidence of housing discrimination persuasive, he did not discuss it nor did he offer any plausible rationale for the fact that, while twenty thousand black workers were employed in the auto plants of the industrial suburb of Warren, Michigan, only seven black families lived there.

In dissent, Justice Thurgood Marshall got to the heart of the matter:

Today's holding, I fear, is more a reflection of a perceived mood that we have gone far enough in enforcing the Constitution's guarantee of equal justice than it is the product of neutral principles of law.

Three months later, I attended my twentieth reunion at Yale Law School. At the event, one Yale Law School alumnus on the Supreme Court, Byron White, presented an award to the other Yale alumnus on the Court, Potter Stewart. In his presentation, Justice White described Justice Stewart as the "flywheel" of the Court, explaining that the flywheel operated to slow down the speed of a machine when it threatened to get out of kilter by going too fast. I could not help but think that Justice White, who was a dissenter in the Detroit case, was explaining Justice Stewart's vote with the majority. No doubt Justice Stewart, and perhaps Justice Blackmun as well, feared the consequence of a popular attack on the Court that would surely have followed the upholding of a metropolitan remedy. No doubt both hoped that the Court's decisions and the Civil Rights Acts passed by Congress would ultimately work to the benefit of poor citizens living in ghettos as well as other minorities. Unfortunately, they turned out to be wrong.

The Court's majority in Detroit had described situations, such as cases where states had manipulated boundaries, where interdistrict remedies would be appropriate. In the years that followed, we won our case in Wilmington, Delaware, and Tom Atkins and I represented the Indianapolis school board in a successful effort to convert a single district remedy into a metropolitan remedy in that city. My longtime friend, Galen Martin, who headed the Kentucky Civil Rights Commission, helped preserve a metropolitan desegregation victory in Louisville by inducing the city school board to dissolve and become part of suburban Jefferson County.

I also negotiated a desegregation settlement for the NAACP within the Cincinnati school district, the judge having ruled out a metropolitan remedy. In Cincinnati as in several other districts, the settlement made extensive use of magnet schools which gave families the option of choosing schools that specialized in particular curricula offerings or particular teaching methodologies. Some time later, I realized that our efforts had been responsible for the establishment of public Montessori schools, which had proved very popular. Magnets in general helped blow some fresh breezes through the public school system, by giving dynamic principals the opportunity to choose their own teachers and fashion their own programs.

Coincidentally, my work in Cincinnati brought *Vanguard* back once again. Having been asked by the NAACP to negotiate a settlement with a trial date looming, I felt a need for intensive briefings on the situation, briefings to be conducted during breaks in a 14-to-15-hours-a-day negotiating schedule. So I asked a young colleague to identify and arrange a meeting with a local educator who knew the specific needs of minority students in the public schools. He reported back that he had just the person I needed—the dean of the School of Education at the University of Cincinnati, and that he had arranged a breakfast for us the following morning. The name, I asked? "Hendrik Gideonse," my colleague replied.

When Dr. Gideonse arrived the next morning, any doubt was dispelled. The silver hair, the dark bushy eyebrows, along with other features, were all too familiar. In fact, it seemed to me that his appearance was almost a dead ringer's for his father's some thirty years earlier. At breakfast he gave me helpful answers to my question about the schools. After we were done, I told him I had a different kind of question for him. "I'm a graduate of Brooklyn College," I began. "Oh, no," he replied, "I get this all the time." "There's more to it than that," I said. "I was the last editor of *Vanguard*."

He remembered it all very well. He told me that his father was a very difficult man and that for many years, beginning in about 1950, he and his brother Martin (who became a teacher at Harvard) had barely any relationship with their father. In fact, he said that they had reconciled only recently on the occasion of Harry's eightieth birthday and the dedication of the Brooklyn College library in his name. Hendrik and I continued to work together on the litigation and he became a friend.

In 1980, the NAACP had asked me if I would help seek metropolitan relief in a long-running school desegregation case in St. Louis. I found some irony in the request. In 1955, after I joined the Legal Defense Fund, it appeared that St. Louis had responded very affirmatively to the *Brown* decision, so affirmatively that June Shagaloff, the fund's education expert Howard Wood, editor of the *St. Louis Argus*, and I discussed the possibility of writing a script for television on the success of desegregation in St. Louis. But things are not always what they seem. Missouri was the state of the *Dred Scott* decision, the state that sent black students to other states to go to college (the *Gaines* case), the state of racially restrictive covenants (*Shelley v. Kraemer*), the state that did not repeal its segregation laws after *Brown*, and the state of widespread housing discrimination (*Jones v. Mayer*).

Minnie Liddell, a local community activist, filed suit in the 1970s when her children were sent to rundown black schools in St. Louis. The NAACP joined in the suit to seek a remedy on behalf of a wider class of children. The City Board of Education decided to join in the quest for a metropolitan remedy and hired the Washington law firm of Hogan and Hartson to represent it. This was good news because Hogan's education department was headed by David Tatel, a very good friend with fine credentials as a civil rights lawyer. The resources that the firm could bring to the case meant that we could do a thorough job of documenting the history of discrimination in the St. Louis metropolitan area.

Some of the history was similar to that in other cases. In the 1930s, there were small settlements of black people outside the city in St. Louis County. Since no high schools were provided for black children in the county, and it was then unthinkable to send them to schools with whites, the state authorized contracts between the suburban districts and the city to send the students to racially segregated high schools in the city. Ultimately, the black settlements, unsupported by schools or other community institutions, disappeared. These and other government acts to contain the black population had long shaped the demography of the area and its schools.

The presiding judge in our case was William L. Hungate, who had served in Congress for several terms and had been a member of the Judiciary Committee that recommended the impeachment of Richard Nixon. Judge Hungate did not much care for lawyers, particularly those from out of town; he had an unconventional approach to his judicial duties but seemed disposed to give fair consideration to our metropolitan claim.

Meanwhile, the case promised to be a tough one. White citizens' groups organized to oppose us and the more extreme hinted at violence. The state's attorney general, John Ashcroft, and the county executive, Gene McNary, whipped up racial sentiment with expressions of defiance even to voluntary desegregation efforts.

When we began negotiations at the urging of Judge Hungate, lawyers for the twenty-two opposing districts told us that their clients would not stand for desegregation. While these may have been good negotiating tactics, what struck me even more were the expressions of raw prejudice that came from the mouths of some of the lawyers. In these meetings, David Tatel played the friendly cop while I tried to play the tough cop. Even so, we didn't seem to be getting anywhere.

Then Judge Hungate did an odd thing. He appointed a group of three experts to examine potential remedies should the plaintiffs prevail. The procedure was particularly odd since the Supreme Court had previously said that the scope of any remedy should be tailored to fit the scope of the violation—which of course had not yet been determined in St. Louis. After the experts reported, Judge Hungate announced that, if he found a violation, he would likely merge all the twenty-three districts in the area into a single consolidated district.

His pronouncement sent shock waves through those involved in the case. David Tatel and I were afraid that the decision would result in a reversal of any judgment favorable to us, because the judge had improperly decided what the remedy would be before determining how extensive the violation was, and we supported our opponents in their appeal. But the court of appeals was more relaxed about the whole matter, indicating it would decide on the question of remedy at the appropriate time. (In this appeal and throughout the litigation, the Court of Appeals was guided by Judge Gerald W. Heaney, who later said that in his many years on the court, the St. Louis desegregation plan was "the best thing I have done.")

Then it occurred to me that Judge Hungate's statement might provide us with the opportunity for a breakthrough. I called David and asked if he would join me in telling defendants that if they would agree to a good interdistrict desegregation plan, we would not insist on consolidation. When David agreed, I called Bruce LaPierre, a law professor appointed by the judge to serve as a mediator, and gave him our proposal. When our negotiations were reconvened, it was clear that the atmosphere had changed. Several of the lawyers let it be known indirectly that their client school board members and administrators cared a lot more about the political rewards of continuing to run their principalities than about desegregation. If there was even a chance that they might lose power through consolidation, they did not wish to risk it.

There was a lot more negotiating to do. The defendants appointed a subcommittee of their more skilled and reasonable lawyers to replace the previously unwieldy group. We worked hard to ensure that transferring students would be treated fairly and equitably in their new schools, that they would not be relegated to classes for slow students, that a group would be established to engage in affirmative outreach to parents and students and to ensure a friendly ear as problems arose. We also wanted to ensure educational improvements in central city schools and the establishment of more high-quality magnet schools in the city. The suburban districts wanted assurances from the state that they would receive ample payment for their agreement to accept students. We agreed ultimately that each district (some of which had only token numbers of African-American students) would accept transfers until its enrollment reached 25 percent African American, a proportion that it would then maintain.

Judge Hungate, after holding the required hearing to ensure that the agreement was fair to the class we represented, entered the settlement as a court order. John Ashcroft sought to take the case to the Supreme Court, but later lost. Although Judge Hungate has kept in touch with me in the years since his retirement, I have never had the nerve to ask him whether his opinion on consolidation was deliberately intended to evoke the response it did. When journalists asked me what I thought, I said that perhaps it was an illustration of Samuel Johnson's aphorism that "nothing concentrates the mind so wonderfully well as knowing one is to be hanged in a fortnight."

Although our negotiations in St. Louis were usually intense, there were moments of comic relief. One such moment came when we were on the verge of settlement late one winter evening, I called Tom Atkins, then general counsel of the NAACP, at his home in Brooklyn, to obtain approval of the agreement. I said to him, "Tom, there are three key points to consider and I'll give them to you briefly." I went through the first point. Tom said nothing, which I thought was a bit strange since he is ordinarily a very voluble person. But I went on to the second point and again was greeted with silence. I had started my third key point when the sound of soft snoring came through my receiver.

There was nothing to do. I hung up and called back the next morning. Tom told me he had awakened with the telephone still in his hand.

With more legal struggles that I will detail in chapter 10, the St. Louis agreement has now been in effect for two decades and more than one hundred thousand children (twenty thousand–plus of them being African Americans) have had the benefits of a desegregated education that they would not otherwise have had. The results have been very positive, with black children, the great majority poor, finishing high school and going on to college at rates that are two and three times as great as those who remain in racially and socioeconomically isolated central city schools. St. Louis is still a troubled city in many respects, but I sometimes think that, were it not for the narrow defeat in the Supreme Court, we might have been able to replicate the school achievements in other places in ways that would have made this a better country.

The Center for National Policy Review stayed in business until the end of 1986. After three years, the Ford Foundation commissioned an evaluation by Hugh Price, a consultant who went on to become a vice president at the Rockefeller Foundation and then president of the National Urban League. Hugh's analysis was accurate and prophetic. He said that the work of administrative enforcement was so "immensely important" that it should be an area for fruitful activity by all civil rights organizations. By 1986, the center's work had been institutionalized in many of the groups in the Leadership Conference on Civil Rights and I felt there was less need for a separate organization.

Hugh's report also raised the question of whether the center should become increasingly involved in broader problems of social and economic justice in employment, housing, and education. I think we did that to some extent with our attacks on institutional discrimination in lending practices and in several other areas. But the fact was that we had our hands full with civil rights issues. We had to confront the Southern strategy of the Nixon administration, and in the '80s we had to fight off the regressive tactics of the Reagan administration. In 1981, Reagan fired Arthur Flemming as chairman of the U.S. Commission on Civil Rights, and Flemming and I decided to form the Citizens' Commission on Civil Rights, a bipartisan group designed to monitor federal civil rights policies. Between that enterprise (which continues to this day) and fighting new civil rights battles in Congress, along with our struggles in the courts, we have had a pretty full schedule.

But the battle for social and economic justice remains a central element of the unfinished agenda. While the civil rights groups I have worked with have had a good record in preserving the antidiscrimination protections of the laws of the 1960s and 1970s against attack, the gap between haves and have-nots in this country has grown. Poor people, almost exclusively African Americans and Latinos, increasingly have been confined in ghetto areas of central cities where they have been cut off from employment and educational opportunities. So the battle for social and economic justice remains a central element of the unfinished agenda.

Fighting Back in the '80s

The Voting Rights Act

In the spring of 1980, the Supreme Court handed down a decision in the case of *City of Mobile v. Bolden* that seriously weakened the quest for voting rights. A majority of the justices ruled that, even though the practice of holding at-large elections for state offices impaired the possibility of African Americans electing candidates of their choice, it did not violate the voting guarantees of the Fourteenth and Fifteenth Amendments. The reasoning was that at-large elections had been adopted in Alabama almost a century earlier when black people were disenfranchised and that, therefore, race could not have been the motivating factor. A majority of the justices was unwilling to go beyond the question of motivation to examine the harmful consequences to black people of at-large elections.

The *Mobile* decision was the opening salvo in a decade-long assault on the gains launched in the 1960s in the courts and the executive branch. I still marvel that our coalition was able to repel each assault, with three landmark pieces of civil rights legislation and the defeat of Robert Bork's nomination to the Supreme Court.

If *Mobile* was a defeat, the election of Ronald Reagan was a blow to the solar plexus for liberals and civil rights advocates. Reagan's views on race were best exemplified by his campaign trip to Neshoba County, Mississippi—site of the murders of Schwerner, Goodman, and Chaney in 1964—where in a stunning exhibition of insensitivity the candidate exalted the doctrine of "state's rights."

Late in the fall, the Ford Foundation convened a meeting of voting-rights litigators to discuss a response to the *Mobile* decision. I was not involved in the *Mobile* litigation and therefore was not invited to the meeting, but when I learned of it I was puzzled by the assumption that dealing with *Mobile* was solely a litigation matter. Since the Supreme Court had just decided the case—albeit by a 5–4 vote—there was little likelihood that it would change its mind or that any help could be found in the courts. If there was any remedy, it would have to come from legislation; fortuitously, Congress was scheduled soon to address the renewal of key provisions of the Voting Rights Act of 1965.

I persuaded the conveners at Ford to add legislation to the agenda and solicited an invitation to attend the meeting. I went to the session to argue that the response should be legislative and that the Leadership Conference on Civil Rights, the coalition that had led all previous campaigns for civil rights, was the group to take on this new battle.

This, I realized, was a considerable act of chutzpah on my part. First, the Leadership Conference had not yet discussed a legislative response to *Mobile*. Second, the conference was not in the best of shape. Its part-time director had resigned and the organization, while seeking a full-time successor, had not yet found a suitable candidate. Also, there were some wounds within the coalition that had not completely healed from the last voting rights renewal in 1975. That year, Latino groups had urged the creation of a new category of voters—non-English-speaking minority voters or those with limited English skills. The new category would be eligible for protection under provisions of the act that required voting changes to be approved by the Justice Department before going into effect. Also, under the proposal, language assistance would be provided at the polls. The 1975 proposal had resulted in a rift in the Leadership Conference with opposition led by Clarence Mitchell, its legislative chairman, who feared that such a broadening of coverage might bring down the whole Act. While the provision had passed after Joe Rauh and other leaders supported it, the battle had not been forgotten. Vilma Martinez Singer, president of the Mexican American Legal Defense Fund, was at the Ford meeting and pointedly asked how she could be assured that her group's interests would be protected. Again I went out on a limb to express my complete confidence that we would not have a repeat of the 1975 rift.

Early in 1981, the Leadership Conference convened a meeting on the subject and, to my relief, we achieved a consensus that reversing the *Mobile* decision would be a priority in our efforts to renew the Voting Rights Act. Then, in March, after a couple of turndowns from top-flight African-American lawyers who had served in the Carter administration, we found our new director, Ralph Neas. To outward appearances, Ralph seemed an unlikely choice for the Leadership Conference. He was a white male Catholic Republican who had gone to Notre Dame, where he devoted himself to becoming an officer in the ROTC.

But I supported Ralph for the job because of other qualities. We had met in the early '70s, when he was an aide to Edward Brooke of Massachusetts, the only African American in the Senate. Brooke had taken on the task of resisting the growing number of amendments being offered to cut back on the remedies for school segregation. Ralph and I collaborated in organizing meetings to build support for strong desegregation remedies. I admired his energy, his passion, and his strategic sense of how to approach issues, based on a thorough knowledge of Senate procedures. Early in 1979 just after he had gone to work for Dave Durenberger, another moderate Republican senator, Ralph was stricken with Guillain-Barre syndrome, a form of polio that left him completely paralyzed and at death's door for months. His battle back from the disease to good health impressed me and other friends with his extraordinary will and determination.

The campaign to renew the Voting Rights Act presented daunting challenges. The provisions scheduled to expire included Section 5, which allowed for the appointment of federal registrars and required a federal review of any proposed voting change to ensure that it did not harm minority interests. Many legislators regarded Section 5 as an emergency provision when it was adopted in 1965 because it so intruded on functions long regarded as belonging to the states, and they believed that the provisions should be terminated once the emergency was over. Since African Americans were now registered to vote in large numbers, we faced a real challenge to persuade legislators that the provision should be renewed. Moreover, we had little more than a year to accomplish our goal since the special provisions were scheduled to expire in 1982.

It was interesting to watch how Ralph worked. Presiding over a large and often unruly coalition, he created what he called a "steering committee," which consisted of every interested organization and met every week to consider all pending issues. The meetings often had twenty or more people and were an unwieldy apparatus for decision making, but the steering committee gave everyone a feeling of inclusion in the process. Meanwhile, much of the important work in drafting and planning strategy was taking place at least initially in smaller groups.

The biggest potential cleavage in our group was between the "lobbyists" and the "litigators." Recognizing the importance of the impending battle, several major civil rights groups had sent their voting rights lawyers to Washington to participate in the legislative effort. The litigators, steeped in the legal arcana of voting rights and aware that unsympathetic judges could interpret a law in ways that would deprive people of an intended remedy, sought to fashion legislative language so specific that it would deprive judges of any wiggle room. The lobbyists understood the concerns of the litigators, but believed that the only way to get the needed consensus in a large and diverse Congress was to be more flexible in drafting language. Too great a degree of specificity would risk alienating many people in the middle, who wanted to be known as supporting voting rights but would be susceptible to attacks on the legislation for "going too far."

While I had a foot in both camps, having worked in the courts as well as Congress, my sense of political practicality led me to support the approach of the lobbyists. Unlike the United Kingdom, where laws are often drafted in extraordinarily detailed terms, the diversity of the population and of interests in the United States often leads to broadly drafted compromises in the legislative process. We leave it to the regulatory process and the courts to give full content to the legislative words. I could not see how we would win if we tried to dictate in the statute itself the outcome of every controversy.

These days, the dilemma I have described would be even more thorny. The courts have become far more conservative than they were in 1981, making it riskier to leave any ambiguity in the legislation. Yet it is even harder than it was then to pass strong and specific legislation.

One of my major tasks was to draft language for the new bill to propose to Representatives Don Edwards and Peter Rodino, who would be the chief sponsors in the House. One problem we had to deal with was that the words "discriminatory effect" had become a weapon in the hands of conservatives. Only a year earlier, I had tangled with Senator Orrin Hatch, when he launched an attack on amendments to the Fair Housing Act that used an "effects test" to determine violations of the law. Hatch claimed this was a disguised quota and was unyielding at the negotiating table when, at Senator Kennedy's request, I represented him in an effort to reach a compromise. We lost when Hatch led a successful filibuster against the bill.

This time I proposed language for the voting bill that spoke of practices that "resulted" in discrimination. My idea was to increase our chances of reversing the *Mobile* decision by using new terminology. The litigators accepted this formulation and, although I thought it was fairly transparent, it seemed to help in defusing the conservative attack.

Our first major challenge in the House was to demonstrate that discrimination against black citizens continued in many areas even if it was sometimes less blatant than when the law was enacted. For this, public hearings were essential and Edwards's committee scheduled several days to hear from witnesses in May and June. Here the litigators played an invaluable role identifying black people throughout the South who had experienced discrimination.

The House committee hearings were designed to persuade the entire committee that, while great progress had occurred, there were still major barriers to full enfranchisement. At the last hearing, held on June 12 in Montgomery, Alabama, it became clear that we had achieved our purpose. Henry Hyde, a key conservative on the committee who later went on to greater fame as chairman of the Clinton impeachment committee, made it dramatically clear that his eyes had been opened. Hyde said he was distressed by testimony about how difficult some officials had made the registration process. He noted that, in some areas, registration could take place only between nine a.m. and four p.m., a practice designed to keep working people from registering; that registration and polling places were often located in areas that were inaccessible to black applicants; that there were few black election officials; and that sometimes the right to cast a secret ballot was being compromised.

He viewed all of this as "outrageous" and told Steve Roberts of the *New York Times*, "you're being dishonest if you don't change your mind after hearing the facts." Hyde then announced that he would support both the requirement that state voting changes be approved in advance by the Department of Justice and that practices be judged by their effect, not the more rigorous standard of intent.

We were elated. This was a great breakthrough, opening the way to strong bipartisan support for a strong voting rights bill. But there were still obstacles to overcome. One was that Hyde wanted to put his own imprint on the bill. For example, Section 5 contained a "bailout" provision that allowed voting districts to escape supervision after a number of years of nondiscriminatory performance. Hyde wanted to fashion what he deemed a reasonable requirement for bailing out while the voting litigators wanted to put the heaviest burden of proof on applicants for bailout, allowing only "angelic" districts to escape.

Ralph Neas and I, as well as others experienced in the legislative process, thought these differences could and should be negotiated.

Some of the litigators railed against "premature" compromise, arguing that we could probably achieve a win in the House without compromise. But Ralph argued forcefully that what was needed was a timely compromise, one that would come soon enough to enable us to win a big enough victory in the House to provide the momentum needed to overcome the onslaught we would face in a Republican-controlled Senate.

While we threaded our way through these difficulties, we also had to contend with likely opposition from the Reagan administration. A few of us paid a visit to Ken Starr, then a young assistant to Attorney General William French Smith. Starr greeted us affably, listened to our plea for support and then announced that the administration would not take a position until it had completed its own study of voting rights, which might be weeks or months away. He seemed bland and nonconfrontational, a far cry from the Starr who emerged in the '90s as Clinton's inquisitor. Some in our group thought that the administration's delay was a setback, but I viewed it as a tactical victory enabling us to continue to build momentum without having to contend with an opposing position from the administration.

On July 29, 1981, everything hit the fan. Ralph's steering committee had put constraints on our ability to negotiate directly with Henry Hyde and the task fell to staff of the House Judiciary Committee under the leadership of Alan Parker, a veteran congressional staffer who did not have much use for the Leadership Conference. Parker called us together on July 29 to announce that he had fashioned the best compromise possible and that he had cleared the language with Representatives Edwards and Rodino and other key Democrats.

My quick review of the document made it plain to me that the compromise would be unacceptable not just to the litigators but to me and other "moderates." We sought and gained an emergency meeting with Edwards, who listened to the staff and to us and then said that his support of the compromise had been contingent on acceptance by the Leadership Conference and that, lacking such acceptance, he would not support it. I had known and worked with Don Edwards for almost twenty years and admired greatly his quiet but firm commitment to justice and equality. So I was ready when he turned to me and said, "Bill, you now have to stay here and put this thing back together again." Meanwhile, Parker's staff had made available copies of their compromise, and several of the members of our coalition, thinking we had sold them out, were furious. Working primarily with Althea Simmons, who had succeeded Clarence Mitchell as the NAACP's Washington representative, I drafted a counter offer for Edwards's consideration. What was now the dissident faction in the coalition, consisting of some but not all of the litigators and a few young representatives of organizations who had experience neither in litigation or legislation, stormed over to Edwards's office, demanding to see our new draft. When I showed it to them, they were partially mollified, agreeing that I wasn't giving away the store.

There followed a new round of negotiations with Hyde, with me drafting offers and counter offers to Hyde's proposals and Edwards's engaging in shuttle diplomacy. By evening, we had narrowed the differences substantially and felt we had a compromise that would be acceptable to most of the Leadership Conference. We met with Edwards and Rodino, and Ralph assured them that most of the coalition including the largest and most active groups—the NAACP, the AFL-CIO, the League of Women Voters, the Catholic Conference, among others—would fully support the compromise now at hand. Each of the groups spoke up to ratify Ralph's position while a few unhappy dissenters remained silent.

The next day, as the Judiciary Committee assembled to consider the bill, an unsigned two-page press release was circulated, purportedly drafted by civil rights advocates, blasting the compromise as a sellout. The dissenters, having tried unsuccessfully to get support from members of the Congressional Black Caucus and other leaders the night before, resorted to the tactic of an anonymous pamphlet. All that became irrelevant almost immediately when, as the session got underway, Henry Hyde backed away from his own compromise. He insisted on including in the bill a bailout provision allowing some state legislatures to opt out of the preclearance process even when the state contained cities or counties that were not eligible for exemption.

Hyde's reversal threw the committee into confusion and it now adjourned without voting. Edwards decided that the only course was to seek a new Republican partner and to come forward the next day with a strong bill. Time was of the essence because Congress was about to take its August recess. Edwards found two new partners. The principal one was Hamilton Fish, a member of a New York state family whose record of public service dated back to the American Revolution. Fish had a conservative record, but he was strongly committed to the cause of civil rights. The second was James Sensenbrenner of Wisconsin, who had shown no previous interest in civil rights issues, but seemed to be propelled by a strong dislike for Henry Hyde.

Our remaining challenge was to craft a new bill that would secure all our major objectives while attracting the widest possible support in the committee. The committee staff washed its hands of our efforts. They told our advocates' group as the evening began that we were destined for failure and that, while we were free to use their offices, they were going home. Several of us, both litigators and lawyers, set to work on a bill we could present to our legislative leaders. We determined that we would include Hyde's language whenever it did no harm to the principles we were seeking to protect, but that we would make sure that on critical issues, such as the results test and the bailout provisions, we would not be ambiguous. One of my attorney collaborators in the group was Armand Derfner, based in Charleston, South Carolina, who had wide experience in voting-rights litigation. While fully committed to the cause, he had the ability to see both sides of a question and thus gained the respect of almost all of the coalition. The one drawback to his approach was that he appeared at times to be indecisive. He confessed to me one day that he was worried that this trait was carrying over to his family. The previous evening, he said, he had asked his two small redhaired sons, "Do you want hamburgers or hot dogs for dinner?" One replied, "I don't know, can we see them both first?"

In our circumstances that evening, however, Armand was a very helpful bridge builder. Our group worked harmoniously until almost three a.m., when we completed what we all agreed was a good substitute bill. I then went home for a few hours' sleep with the knowledge that I had to return at nine thirty in the morning to brief our new Republican chief sponsor Hamilton Fish on his bill so that he could help lead the discussion. Groggily, I appeared in Fish's office, concerned that the subject was so technical that he might have a hard time mastering it so quickly. I need not have worried. Fish had that fine legislators' talent of being able to grasp the essential elements of legislation upon presentation. He asked me a few penetrating questions and pronounced himself satisfied. When the committee session began, in the formal chamber that the House Judiciary Committee used both to hear witnesses and later to "mark up" (agree upon) legislation, he joined Edwards in making a persuasive case for the bill.

Ralph was expecting a fairly narrow victory in committee. But Edwards cleverly began by giving great credit to Hyde, saying, "We've taken ninety-five percent of your bill and we thank you for it." Hyde was very angry that a new substitute had been sprung on him, but he had been outmaneuvered. While predicting the ultimate demise of the bill, Hyde voted for it and helped to produce a 25–1 victory for a bill that almost all of us felt was much stronger than anything we had expected in the preceding weeks. On October 5, 1981, the House passed the bill by the overwhelming vote of 389–24.

With that great endorsement by the House, the coalition was able to persuade sixty-one Senators to cosponsor the House-passed bill. But we knew we were not secure yet, because cosponsors often can be persuaded to water down a bill. The bill was referred to the Senate Judiciary Committee, where Orrin Hatch mounted a full-scale attack on the results test we had devised, arguing that it was a covert device for requiring "proportional representation," which he characterized as a kind of quota system for electing representatives that had earlier been pushed by left-wingers in New York City in the '40s. Only proof that a voting practice was racially motivated, Hatch said, would justify calling it a violation of law. Moreover, Strom Thurmond chaired the committee and controlled the timetable, a not inconsiderable problem as the August deadline for reenactment approached.

As we pondered our latest problems, I got a phone call from Ralph. Would I come to the Hill to meet with him and an aide to Senate Republican leader Robert Dole? I met with Ralph and Sheila Bair, a legislative assistant to Dole. It turned out that Dole, who had not declared himself publicly on the voting rights extension, wanted to play a leadership role in enacting the bill. He was not unhappy with the House-passed bill but needed some language of his own that he could offer as a compromise.

I went to work on new language. Drawing from the wording of a 1973 Supreme Court decision, my draft said that black persons can successfully challenge a law as discriminatory when they can show that, as a result of the operation of that law in their community, they have less opportunity than whites to nominate or elect representatives of their choice. Several factors would be weighed in determining whether black people were harmed by such a law. I also added a disclaimer to respond to Hatch. Nothing in the bill was to establish a right based solely on the absence of proportional representation (a bugaboo that Hatch portrayed as establishing racial quotas rather than assuring some representation for minority interests). In sum, I had found a way to codify the effects test in a way that opponents could not easily dispute.

I found Bob Dole very easy to work with. He was pragmatic and had a stinging sense of humor that he sometimes directed against his colleagues. Dole asked me to come in on a Saturday afternoon to meet with Strom Thurmond's chief legislative aide. "You don't have to make any concessions," he said, "just make sure he comes away feeling we have paid some attention to Senator Thurmond's concerns." We had a meeting that lasted a couple of hours during which I offered linguistic variations on our theme, none of which changed any substantive point. Later, Armand Derfner helped reinforce my effort. He learned that Senator Thurmond was going to a meeting in South Carolina with black mayors of his state and that Thurmond presumed they shared his opposition to proportional representation. Armand called two or three mayors he knew well and briefed them on what Thurmond was seeking. Thurmond came back to Washington with the clear understanding that he would not be able to peel off members of the black community.

Most knowledgeable people recognized what we had done. One day in the Senate cafeteria, Art Briskman, an aide to Senator Howell Heflin of Alabama, came to the table where Ralph and I were seated and said, "I know what you guys have done. You have drawn a picture of a horse and put a label on it reading 'cow.'" And my colleagues were pleased as well. Lani Guinier, one of the litigators with demanding standards, whose own theories on proportional representation later became controversial when President Clinton sought to nominate her to the top civil rights slot at Justice, wrote later, "What began as a compromise, however, proved to be one of the great treasures of the Voting Rights Act."

On June 18, the Senate passed the bill by a vote of 85–5 with Strom Thurmond joining the majority. On June 29, I attended the White House signing ceremony and heard President Reagan say that "this legislation proves our unbending commitment to voting rights." While I know a great many people in the civil rights community, I recognized only a handful of people at the White House ceremony. Most of those attending, black and white, were the president's political supporters who had nothing to do with extending the Voting Rights Act. Somehow, I found, it did not matter.

In the years that followed, some of the fears of the litigators were partially realized as the Supreme Court invalidated as racially motivated the oddly shaped political districts that were designed to help elect black candidates to office. On the other hand, I found myself distressed by the advocacy of some of my colleagues who insisted on including enough black citizens in a district to ensure the election of a black candidate. My concern was that, just as distributing people of color in small numbers in several districts diminished their political influence, packing them all into one or two districts limited their influence to those districts and no others. The aim of the law was not to ensure the election of greatest number of candidates of color but to maximize the influence of black voters. The two outcomes are not always synonymous. In this effort, the voting rights advocates were often joined by Republicans who saw and continue to see packing minorities into a few districts as a way to ensure the election of more Republicans in others. Thankfully, this view of the aims of the Voting Rights Act seems to be waning, although packing continues to be a problem.

One of the last issues we confronted in the legislative battle was how long the extension of Section 5 would be. Our objective was a permanent renewal, but in the end we had to settle for twenty-five years. Most of our group thought that was a reasonable compromise, but Frank Parker, who had worked with me at the Civil Rights Commission and then relocated to Mississippi to devote his considerable legal talents to advocating for voting rights, was unhappy. When I asked him if he didn't think things would be considerably better in twenty-five years, he replied, "I doubt it."

I think of that conversation as we approach the year 2007, when the act will be up for renewal. In the late '80s, I persuaded the Leadership Conference to take on as a legislative issue an effort to make voter registration easier. The bill we drafted at that time permitted voter registration by mail and also enabled people to register when they obtained their driver's licenses or went to other government offices for services. The bill also required that better access to registration sites be provided to people with disabilities. After a long struggle, Congress finally passed the National Voter Registration Act and President Clinton signed it into law in 1993. Yet, as the 2000 presidential election in Florida vividly illustrates, minority voters are still shortchanged by inferior voting equipment and ill-staffed polling places. These problems will not be solved until states are required to equalize conditions throughout their jurisdictions and ensure that the critical right to vote is not subject to local control. And, of course, real enfranchisement for people of color will not be fully realized until their economic conditions and educational opportunities improve. Clearly, there will be a need for some form of extension of the Voting Rights Act in 2007. We will fight for its renewal because, as so many events have demonstrated, from the defeat of Supreme Court nominee Robert Bork, to the election of civil rights hero John Lewis to a leadership position in the House of Representatives, to the resignation of segregationist Trent Lott from his leadership position in the Senate, the act has been a huge success.

In personal terms, the campaign for renewal of the Voting Rights Act in 1981 and 1982 brought great rewards to me. One result was the beginning of a personal and professional relationship with Congressman Hamilton Fish, one that lasted until his death in 1996. Fish was a fascinating person in many ways. As noted earlier, his family line went back to colonial times, the first Hamilton Fish having been named for Alexander Hamilton. Ham's father was an ardent opponent of FDR and a red-baiter. President Roosevelt helped the elder Fish gain fame by bracketing him with two other obstructionist legislators with a scornful reference to "Martin, Barton, and Fish." Ham himself was anything but flamboyant—he was a soft spoken chain-smoker with a wry sense of humor. Once I wrote an article for *The Nation* about Reagan's attack on the U.S. Civil Rights Commission, in which I described Fish as a "veteran legislator." He told me he didn't like the adjective. I asked what he would have preferred. "Respected" would have been nice, he said.

He was conservative on most issues but had a passion for advancing the civil rights of minority citizens. We worked together into the 1980s and '90s on the Civil Rights Restoration Act, the Civil Rights Act of 1991, and other matters. But our collaboration occurred in odd circumstances. Fish was the ranking Republican on the Judiciary Committee and the Republican committee staff reported to him. But as the Republicans on the committee, led by Hyde and Sensenbrenner, became more conservative, Fish found himself increasingly isolated in his own pro–civil rights views. To make matters worse, the committee staff was not loyal to him but to the other committee members. So Ralph and I found ourselves visiting Ham to make proposals and plan strategy in secret, without the usual complement of committee staff, and perhaps only one personal aide of Fish's in attendance. Despite the cloak-and-dagger aspects of the relationship it worked out well and, with Ham's leadership, we were able to count on the relative handful of moderate Republicans to provide the support we needed in the House.

After Ham's death, his son Hamilton, the first Democrat in the family and publisher of *The Nation*, asked me to come to Garrison, New York, on the Hudson River to deliver a eulogy at the 1997 annual dinner at the Fish-Donaldson library attended by many of the late Congressman's friends and constituents.

At the dinner, the *Vanguard* episode came back one more time. An award was to be given to Pete Seeger, the great folk singer, and his wife Yoshi, for their environmental efforts to save the Hudson River. When I arrived, Seeger was regaling a group at the reception with tales of the political attacks on him and his folk group, the Weavers, during the 1940s and '50s. I introduced myself to him and said that I had a story of my own about my experience at Brooklyn College. "Ah, Harry Gideonse," he replied. "That's very good," I said. "I have a reason for remembering," he replied. "I was not permitted to sing on the Brooklyn College campus until Gideonse left in 1962."

When I was writing the eulogy I thought that his passing also marked the passing of the era of the moderate, pro–civil rights Republican. Through the '80s and early '90s, there was a cadre of strong civil rights advocates in the Republican party—Senators Jacob Javits of New York, Hugh Scott of Pennsylvania, Lowell Weicker of Connecticut, Charles Mathias of Maryland, and Governor Nelson Rockefeller among the elected officials; and great jurists like John Minor Wisdom in the South. These were politicians who were motivated by a passionate concern for equality, feelings of paternalism, family ties to the party of Lincoln when it truly deserved that appellation, and some combination of all these forces. I never actually asked Ham about what motivated his passion for equality, but when I learned that his right-wing father had commanded an all-black regiment known as the

Harlem HellFighters in World War I, I realized that, unlikely as it might have seemed, there may have been some family influences on him that I hadn't known about.

The new Republican party—the one that capitalized on the defection of Southern Dixiecrats, and devised election strategies based on racial resentments—could not be more different. Now one can count on the fingers of one (or at most both) hands the number of Republicans who can be relied on to support civil rights legislation. That will change eventually, as the changing demography of the country causes Republicans to consider their strategy. But the absence of the moral force of a Hamilton Fish in the party makes racial reconciliation all the more difficult.

The major dividend of the Voting Rights campaign for me was the beginning of a personal friendship and professional relationship with Ralph Neas that is now in its third decade, with Ralph serving as president of People for the American Way. We have worked on many campaigns since, most of them victories mixed in with a few defeats. Although we come from different backgrounds we share a passion for justice.

Ralph's great strategic sense about legislation and his organizational abilities have helped put me in situations where I could use my own skills to the greatest advantage. When President Reagan signed the bill, I obtained an official copy and later asked Don Edwards and Hamilton Fish to sign it. Don wrote, "To the real author of the Voting Rights Act." I was very touched by the sentiment, but I realized of course that victory has a thousand parents while defeat is an orphan. And it was working as a team with Ralph and so many others that enabled me to receive Don Edwards's accolade.

Fighting Back in the '80s: Part II

The Battle of Bork

L ooking back on the successful campaign to defeat the nomination of Robert Bork to the Supreme Court, I am surprised to realize that it spanned less than four months. Ronald Reagan announced his intention to nominate Bork to the Court on July 1, 1987. The Senate rejected Bork's nomination on October 23, 1987, by a vote of 58–42, the largest majority ever to defeat a candidate for the Court. Those intervening days were extraordinarily eventful.

The Reagan years leading up to the Bork nomination were a time when progressives and civil rights advocates felt constantly beleaguered. Early on, Senators Helms and Thurmond, along with other conservative legislators, aimed what could have been a mortal blow at the Constitution with their "court-stripping" amendments. While they conceded that the Court was empowered by the Constitution to say what rights the Constitution guaranteed, their theory was that Congress could decide what if any the remedy for a violation would be. With their attempts to pass court-stripping amendments, they proposed to deprive the federal courts, including the Supreme Court, of the authority to prescribe an effective remedy for state practices that mandated segregation, or prohibited abortions, or breached the barriers between church and state. Helms and Thurmond received support from the Reagan administration in this effort. Indeed, Attorney General William French Smith warned the courts to heed the "groundswell of conservatism evidenced by the 1980 election." The Helms amendment severely limiting desegregation remedies actually passed the Senate but was stopped in the House after a spirited campaign. Although the amendment would still have required ratification by thirty-eight states if passed by the House, it posed a grave threat to our constitutional system.

The campaign against court-stripping legislation was the first venture for a new organization, the Citizens' Commission on Civil Rights, which I had helped Arthur Flemming to form. Flemming, an extraordinary public servant who was President Eisenhower's secretary of Health, Education, and Welfare, was fired by Ronald Reagan as chair of the U.S. Commission on Civil Rights as part of the administration's campaign to rid itself of an agency that was deemed too independent in its work. In response, Arthur and I decided to establish a private commission, bipartisan in its composition, that would undertake with a much smaller budget the civil rights monitoring that the federal commission had done. Our first report was on the court-stripping efforts. With Republicans like Erwin Griswold, former solicitor general and dean of Harvard Law School, and Elliot Richardson, a former attorney general who had resigned in the infamous Saturday night massacre when ordered by President Nixon to fire special prosecutor Archibald Cox (Robert Bork finally performed the task), our report had great credibility.

On another front, the Administration sought to nullify civil rights remedies by placing the major enforcement agency—the Civil Rights Division of the Department of Justice—in the hands of William Bradford Reynolds, a hardline opponent of the laws he was entrusted with enforcing. Reynolds announced from the beginning that he would not even follow principles established by several Supreme Court cases. He browbeat the professionals in the division who objected to this, leading several of them to leave. The department became an easy mark for the exercise of political influence, the most notorious instance being the Bob Jones University case. At the instigation of a then-obscure congressman from Mississippi, Trent Lott, the Reagan administration reversed the position of its predecessor. It decided a university that practiced racial discrimination could nonetheless be entitled to a federal tax exemption. The Supreme Court appointed a special counsel to argue the position the Reagan administration had abandoned and the Court decided 8–1 against Bob Jones. Meanwhile, a report that I supervised for the Leadership Conference entitled "Without Justice," along with other studies, documented the Justice Department's misdeeds and attracted the attention of members of Congress who began to scrutinize with care the activities of the Civil Rights Division. Later, the Judiciary Committee rejected the Reagan administration's effort to promote Reynolds to a higher position.

Beyond court-stripping and administrative nullification, the primary strategy of the Reagan administration for rolling back the civil rights and economic justice gains of past decades was to populate the courts with ultraconservative judges. The administration had a long agenda of decisions from the Warren era that it sought to reverse— including broad remedies for racial and other forms of discrimination, expansive readings of the First Amendment to permit free speech, ensuring the separation of church and state, protecting the procedural rights of criminal defendants, and upholding Congressional use of the Commerce Clause to promote health and safety and to safeguard the environment.

The administration had another strategy, as well: Appoint young people who could be expected to serve on the courts for many years. Appoint academics whose conservative writings would provide an accurate forecast of how they would be expected to rule as judges.

In the early years the administration enjoyed a fair degree of success, securing the confirmation of strongly conservative judges like Alex Kozinski, Richard Posner, J. Harvey Wilkinson, and Frank Easterbrook to federal courts of appeals around the nation. All of these were capable lawyers who could have been challenged only on their judicial philosophies. A few were ciphers, like Daniel Manion, who had handled almost no cases of significance and whose legal briefs were ungrammatical and incoherent, but who won confirmation by a single vote as a result of a sordid vote-trading scheme in which Senator Slade Gorton of Washington changed his vote on Manion at the last minute when promised a favor by the Reagan administration. In a few instances—like the nomination of Jefferson Sessions—we won, or the nomination was never sent forward, usually because of blatantly racial speech or conduct by the prospective nominee. Sessions, for example, a U.S. Attorney in Alabama, prosecuted black civil rights activists for voting fraud, action which an appellate court found to be racially and politically motivated, called the NAACP "un-American" and said a white lawyer who handled civil rights cases was "a disgrace to his race." Sessions was later elected senator in Alabama, where he could begin voting to confirm judges.

When Reagan was reelected in 1984, it was apparent that the judicial threat was very real. Nan Aron, a dynamic lawyer with a great ability to network, had become director of the Alliance for Justice, a coalition of public interest lawyers from various fields, whose mission was to promote public policies to assist the underrepresented. I had become the first chairman of the alliance. Together with Herman Schwartz, a passionate constitutional scholar at American University Law School, we hatched a plan to establish a new entity within the alliance to focus on judicial nominations. Herman and I went to see Larry Gold—then general counsel of the AFL-CIO, which had been increasingly adversely affected by the decisions of Reagan judges—to ask for support. He secured a small grant for us and the new Judicial Selection Project was on its way. Along with the Leadership Conference it began to lay plans for combating the expected judicial onslaught. In addition, People for the American Way, a relatively new organization established by Norman Lear in 1980, joined the Leadership Conference and, with strong investigative and research skills, became an increasingly effective advocate on judicial nominations.

In 1986, the Reagan administration achieved the breakthrough it had been seeking since 1980. Warren Burger retired as chief justice and the president named associate justice William Rehnquist to take his place. For the vacancy, Reagan then named Antonin Scalia, a federal judge on the Court of Appeals for the District of Columbia circuit. Rehnquist had been nominated to the Court by Nixon, and managed to be confirmed, despite a clear record of hostility to civil rights. As a law clerk in the '50s to Supreme Court Justice Robert Jackson, Rehnquist had advised the justice that separate but equal was a correct doctrine and that the challenge to it should be rejected in the *Brown* case. Later, as a Republican lawyer in Arizona, he appeared at the polls to challenge the voting rights of black people. After his appointment by Richard Nixon in 1971, he was for a long time a lonely voice in dissent on civil rights and other issues. But by the mid-1980s his influence was growing.

Scalia was a smart lawyer with a sarcastic wit, who purported to be a devotee of "original intent"—a doctrine used to curb the vindication of claims for civil rights or civil liberties protections.

I was pleased but not surprised when Ted Kennedy told me that he was ready to lead the opposition to Rehnquist's nomination. In an aside he noted that, when Rehnquist paid him a courtesy visit, he found that shaking his hand was like holding a cold and clammy fish. The confirmation debate garnered thirty-three votes in opposition to Rehnquist, more than any other ballot on a chief justice, but it was obvious that, despite new revelations about Rehnquist's pre-Court anti–civil rights activities, it was nigh impossible to deny confirmation to a sitting justice. With attention directed toward Rehnquist, Scalia's nomination skated by, although the nominee had exhibited an unwillingness to answer questions about his legal philosophy, including such fundamental matters as his views on the Court's power of judicial review.

I have often wondered how one discovers the true biases of a nominee through the confirmation process, where the bias is not already a matter of record. Scalia has since said some horrifying things from the bench. In 1990, in a case about affirmative action in broadcasting, he said during the oral argument that he did not see how having "Negro blood" affected one's political views. Justice Thurgood Marshall responded by questioning Scalia's choice of terminology. In 2003, in the argument in the landmark Michigan University affirmative action case, Scalia referred to people who were "obviously unqualified," meaning students of color, without explaining how their qualifications could be determined from their appearance. But these utterances all came after Scalia became a Supreme Court justice.

Then, on June 26, 1987, Justice Lewis Powell submitted his resignation and a few days later, on July 1, President Reagan announced his intention to name Judge Robert Bork as his replacement. With Bork added to Rehnquist and Scalia, the Court would have a solid cadre of justices vehemently opposed to the protection of individual rights and liberties. With the help of Sandra Day O'Connor, the first woman on the Court and a conservative pro–states' rights jurist, the conservatives might well achieve a majority to reverse decisions made by the Warren Court. During the week of the Bork nomination, I read everything I could that he had written, most notably a wide-ranging article published in 1971 in the *Indiana Law Review*. From this article I learned that he rejected the Supreme Court's decision in a 1948 case holding that courts could not enforce racially restrictive covenants, and that he thought courts were powerless to deal with poll taxes even though they were used to disenfranchise Negro citizens. Later Bork wrote that he believed Congress had no power to bar discrimination in restaurants, hotels, and other places of public accommodation as it had done in 1964. I learned that Bork spurned the idea that a right to privacy was implicit in the Ninth Amendment to the Constitution. That meant that states were free to ban married couples from using contraception in the privacy of their bedrooms, that states could decide that interracial couples could not marry, that states could compel the sterilization of people deemed mentally or morally defective and, of course, that women had no recourse against state laws prohibiting abortion.

The list went on. Essentially, Bork believed that in almost any case where individual rights were pitted against the majority will as expressed in legislation, the latter prevailed, except in those rare cases where a right was specifically enumerated in the Constitution. At the same time, when an exercise of legislative authority conflicted with executive power, Bork almost always sided with the executive—even where the issue was one of life and death, like the bombing of Cambodia.

What struck me in reading his work was how extreme and intemperate Bork was in the expression of his views. He belittled the plight of the poor and racial minorities, and ridiculed justices, such as Earl Warren, with whose views he disagreed. Later it would be said by Bork supporters that his writings were academic speculations and musings and were not to be taken literally as expressions of his belief. But that conclusion could not survive an examination of his work. Bork was an angry man and was ready to put his anger into decisions if he ascended to the Supreme Court.

Later I told Mike Pertschuk and Wendy Schaetzel, who wrote a book about the Bork confirmation fight, that I believed after reading all Bork's writings and speeches that "if you gave that body of material to the United States Senate and said, 'please sit down and read this, and then, based on this alone come to a conclusion,' a clear majority of the Senate" would have voted no. I told them that I thought the same conclusion would be reached by the great majority of modestly informed American citizens. I also said then, and still believe, that what the anti-confirmation campaign was all about was getting the information to people and seeing that they did not get deflected from the main issues.

But my aim of getting senators to reject Bork by focusing on his extremist judicial views faced formidable obstacles. He had been named to the federal court of appeals in 1982, rated as "exceptionally well qualified" by the American Bar Association and confirmed by the Senate without a dissenting vote. While on the bench he almost always favored business interests over the claims of consumers and environmentalists, and seemed to apply different standards in reviewing government action, depending on which group was adversely affected. But these were hardly blockbuster cases. A further difficulty was that there was almost no contemporary history of opposing judicial candidates on philosophical grounds. One had to go back to the nominations of Brandeis and Parker, much earlier in the century, to find such arguments, and the opposition to Brandeis in 1916 had been tainted by anti-Semitism.

Added to all that was Bork's standing with the Washington establishment. While the phrase is amorphous, there is in the nation's capital a seemingly permanent cadre of people whose dedication is not to policy goals but to preserving their own social status and access to power. They adapt their political views and their invitation lists to whichever party is in power. Bob Bork had many friends in the establishment, among them newspaper editors and influential lawyers, and they would be personal allies in his effort to be confirmed.

But our prospects seemed somewhat brighter when the Leadership Conference convened a meeting on July 2, less than twenty-four hours after the announcement of Bork's nomination. The leaders of forty organizations, including some like Ralph Nader's that were not even members of the Leadership Conference, appeared and jammed the conference room. There was no dissent. Everyone felt that a full-scale effort had to be made to oppose the nomination. Ralph Neas, who had been thinking about strategy for the weeks that the nomination had been in the offing, was at his best. He organized the groups into task forces to work on research, communications, grassroots support, and lobbying. One of his more inspired choices was to ask Althea Simmons, Washington representative of the NAACP, and Kate Michelman, recently installed as head of the National Abortion Rights Action League, to serve as cochairs of the grassroots task force. The two had not worked closely together before and were temperamentally different, but each represented an interest—civil rights and a woman's right to choose—that was directly threatened by the Bork nomination and each was able to communicate directly with many thousands of members. Later I told Pertschuk that Ralph was the engine that got the campaign off the ground. "He was both Wright brothers," I said. Once the campaign was launched, there were other people who helped keep it airborne.

It soon became clear to me what roles I could usefully play in the Bork effort. One was to take the mountain of research material compiled by People for the American Way and other organizations, and distill it into a series of simple but accurate points that would reach the concerns of interested citizens and legislators. So, for that first meeting on July 2, I wrote an eight-page "talking points" memo that spelled out the central themes I hoped we would follow. I began with the statement, "The primary reason for opposing nominee Bork is that he has aligned himself against many of the landmark decisions protecting civil rights and individual liberties that the Supreme Court has rendered over the past four decades." I followed that with separate sections dealing with race discrimination, other forms of discrimination, restrictions on the right to privacy, and restrictions on free speech.

The Pertschuk-Schaetzel book notes that these themes were later refined through focus group tests and polling that the participating groups commissioned, but that the memo contained the "bedrock of issues on which the ensuing campaign was to be constructed."

A second role that was chosen for me was to help mobilize law school professors to oppose Bork. About a week after the nomination, Melanne Verveer, by then vice president of People for the American Way, suggested that she and I have lunch with Carolyn Osolinik, who was to be Ted Kennedy's chief aide in the nomination fight. At the lunch, they suggested that I should put together and contact a list of legal scholars who might be inclined or persuaded to oppose Bork. I had done some work with academics on Nixon's unsuccessful nominations of Clement Haynesworth and Harold Carswell in the '70s and on the more recent Manion nomination. I said I would think about it. Not more than a half hour after I returned to my office, I received a call from Senator Kennedy, telling me how grateful he would be if I would undertake this task. I told him I would. Then I tried to reach Carolyn Osolinik, who was not at her desk. I left a message saying "I didn't see the light. I felt the heat," which she kept posted on her door for months.

In beginning the task, it struck me that if two or three of the most prominent constitutional scholars who held divergent views about many other issues could be persuaded to sign a letter appealing to their colleagues to oppose the nomination, we might win a strong mandate in the academic community. Finding a liberal constitutional scholar was easy. Larry Tribe of Harvard Law School was an obvious candidate. Finding a conservative one was more challenging. I had learned that Phil Kurland, a noted conservative scholar at the University of Chicago, was advising Senator Joe Biden, chairman of the Judiciary Committee, on the Bork nomination. I decided to try him. Kurland's conservative credentials were impeccable. Indeed, as I have noted, in the 1970s when our Richmond metropolitan school case reached the Supreme Court, Bill Coleman, who argued for our side, was opposed by Phil Kurland representing the State of Virginia.

My draft of the letter for Tribe and Kurland began:

As teachers of law and as citizens concerned with the preservation and enforcement of constitutional rights, we ask that the Senate withhold its Consent to the nomination of Robert H. Bork to be an Associate Justice of the Supreme Court of the United States.

None of us has reached this decision easily. Judge Bork is a highly skilled lawyer. He has also been a colleague in the teaching of law where his skills and experience are widely respected.

We have decided to oppose his nomination because of a substantive concern that we believe to be so important as to override matters of credentials or personal considerations. Judge Bork has developed and repeatedly expressed a comprehensive and fixed view of the Constitution that is at odds with most of the pivotal decisions protecting civil rights and civil liberties that the Supreme Court has rendered over the past four decades.

The letter went on to make the case and to express concerns about judicial regression that would threaten the fairness and justness of our society and the health and welfare of the nation. It concluded:

> Finally, we note that the issue before the Senate is not properly a partisan matter or one that may be summed up by labels such as "liberal" or "conservative."
>
> Rather, the responsibility of all Senators is to assure that a member of the life tenured judiciary does not disdain the Bill of Rights or the Fourteenth Amendment's command for equal protection of the laws and due process.

I was somewhat amazed and definitely pleased that my draft was accepted with very little change by Professors Tribe and Kurland. It told me that there would likely be wide recognition of the fundamental constitutional and societal issues at stake in the Bork confirmation struggle and that these might override the usual political and partisan skirmishing. When I began contacting law school deans and constitutional scholars, one who had helped on the Manion nomination told me not to expect much success because the fight about Manion, he felt, had been an effort to protect the standards of the profession against incompetency. In the case of Bork, he said there was no question of competency.

But this judgment was incorrect. By the time of the hearings in September, thirty-three deans and seventy-one constitutional scholars had signed two similar letters opposing Bork that were essentially my initial draft for Tribe and Kurland. Moreover, the letter had given rise to a desire by many other law professors to express themselves. John Haber, a field representative at People for the American Way, and I organized an effort in which we identified one or two faculty members at each law school to collect signatures. In the end, 2,000 law teachers at 153 law schools, more than 40 percent of all the academics at accredited law schools, had signed on to our letters opposing the nomination. In contrast, the White House countereffort to enlist academics who favored Bork produced only one hundred signatures.

After Bork was defeated, some of his allies complained bitterly about the academic opposition, suggesting that the liberal establishment in the university community was more concerned about Bork's apostasy than about public issues—and that, as is said of some academic conflicts, the fight was so bitter because the stakes were so small. This was a total misreading of what motivated the academic response to Bork. At the law schools, a great many teachers were people whose lives had been touched by the work of the Supreme Court and who had invested large portions of their professional lives thinking and writing about the great issues the Court had taken on in the last half of the twentieth century. Nor were these teachers appeased by the notion that Bork's writings were merely scholarly musings. While they understood that there was a place for such speculative writings, Bork's work clearly did not fit into that category and many teachers resented the suggestion that powerful academic work had no influence on the direction of the judiciary.

Finally, Bork's candidacy aroused a reaction among students. For several years, law students with progressive views had been largely quiescent while wealthy donors helped organize associations such as the Federalist Society, dedicated to the propagation of conservative legal views by law teachers and students. Bork had furthered his candidacy for the Court with conservatives by making speeches to the Federalist Society; liberal students understood the high stakes and acted on the issues in the confirmation fight.

As a group, liberal students did not again become mobilized until the University of Michigan affirmative action case arose in the new century, when they rallied in support of policies favoring diversity.

After the vote denied Bork confirmation, I told Ted Kennedy with a smile that little did I think I would enter the autumn of my career by mounting an effort to empower law professors. But actually I was quite proud of the role I played in encouraging people to articulate their highest ideals.

Yet another role I played in the confirmation battle was to try to ensure that it was a fair fight. Along with others I was aware that struggles over appointments to office, unlike most battles over legislation, are inevitably personal and can inflict pain on the individual. This problem is only partly mitigated by the fact that the individual in the spotlight has usually achieved a degree of successes and influence that will ensure a soft landing if he does not achieve his office. In any case, it was very important to me and to my colleagues that we were fair and accurate in what we said about Robert Bork and his record.

I am convinced that we largely achieved that objective. Immediately after the nomination, Ted Kennedy took to the Senate floor to warn of the danger of "a land in which women would be forced into back-alley abortions, blacks would sit at segregated lunch counters. . . ." While the speech was tough, it accurately described the plausible consequences of positions that Bork had taken if they had prevailed. Kennedy believed that it was important to portray the issues in stark terms before some of his colleagues slipped into their usual position of accommodating the administration. Later, however, an official of NOW said that her group and others would "bork" the nominee, introducing a new, disrespectful word into the lexicon. At the hearings, Senator Howell Heflin of Alabama capitalized on Bork's socialist student days and bristling red beard to say that he was a man with "proclivities." Heflin, an astute former judge who was deeply concerned about Bork's judicial philosophy, was apparently searching for a way to justify a negative vote to his constituents. That was not fair.

But these were isolated incidents in a debate that was waged on the merits. People for the American Way was in the spotlight because the organization was prepared to use media advertising to bring information and its views to the American people. I was asked to review ad copy for accuracy. I worked closely with David Kusnet, a gifted writer, who went on to be a chief speechwriter for Bill Clinton and Hillary Clinton. The objective was to describe Bork's positions clearly and directly without either clouding them with legal obfuscations or stating them so simplistically as to distort his views. So, for example, the ads said that Bork "defended" poll taxes and literacy tests, not that he personally favored them, but that he did not believe the federal government was empowered to eliminate them. The most widely broadcast ad was narrated by Gregory Peck. Peck agreed to do an ad because he was greatly concerned that the elevation of Bork to the Supreme Court would damage the rights of poor and minority citizens.

But he wanted to give the most careful scrutiny possible to any words that were used in his name. So after the ad was drafted I was dispatched to New York City along with People for the American Way vice president Melanne Verveer to meet with Peck. He went over the draft line by line until he was satisfied that there was factual support for every statement and that the ad treated the nominee fairly. Only then was he prepared to go forward.

In the years following the Bork confirmation hearings, right-wing politicians have used the purported unfairness of the battle to justify below-the-belt tactics with respect to their Senate opponents or other nominees. So then-Senator John Ashcroft, at the end of President Clinton's second term, launched a sneak attack on the nomination to a federal district court judgeship of African-American Judge Ronnie White, then a state court appellate judge. According to Ashcroft, Judge White was "soft on crime," a charge that did not withstand even a moment's comparison of the records of White and his judicial colleagues, several of them Republicans. More recently Senators Orrin Hatch and Jefferson Sessions have outrageously accused Senate colleagues of being "anti-Catholic" when they question Bush judicial nominees about their views on privacy and abortion. But these modern-day mudslingers, while arguing that the Democrats started it all in the Bork campaign, cannot point to any instance in which civil rights advocates or senators distorted Bork's record or twisted the facts about a nomination in the way Republicans now do routinely.

What is harder to figure out in the current atmosphere is how to establish a degree of cooperation in the judicial selection process that has been absent for more than a decade. Any sensible solution would begin with the president consulting about appellate court nominees with members of the opposition party. Such consultation would respect the Senate's constitutional role to "advise and consent" in nominations. But George W. Bush has resolutely refused to enter into such discussions, appeasing his base by sending ideological extremists, many of them in the Bork mold, to a Senate narrowly controlled by Republicans. Bill Clinton, on the other hand, named people widely regarded as moderates and then in several instances abandoned them if they became controversial. In time, and with a thoughtful president, it is likely that a degree of bipartisan cooperation will be restored, but meanwhile the courts are being harmed.

One other role I helped play with others on the Bork nomination was in suggesting to the committee the witnesses I believed would best present the concerns of the civil rights community. We wound up with an all-star list.

Bill Coleman was Thurgood Marshall's former adviser and the then-dean of civil rights lawyers. He had been secretary of Transportation in the Ford administration and had been selected by the Supreme Court to argue the Bob Jones case when the Reagan administration refused to defend the position taken by its predecessor. Bill was a Republican, conservative in most matters except civil rights. Barbara Jordan had burst on the political scene in the '70s when as a junior member of the House Judiciary Committee she articulated the constitutional imperative of impeaching Richard Nixon in a way that was extraordinarily compelling. Andy Young had been Martin Luther King Jr.'s trusted aide, Jimmy Carter's ambassador to the United Nations, and the second black mayor of Atlanta. Although little noted at the time, it was a commentary on progress that these three leading witnesses on the Bork nomination were all African American and that hardly anyone would regard them as special pleaders, but rather as persuasive voices for American values.

We engaged in one other effort to add to this lineup. Melanne Verveer and her husband Phil had made friends with Bill Clinton years earlier when all were undergraduates at Georgetown University, and now Clinton was the progressive governor of Arkansas. When Clinton came to Washington, Melanne arranged a dinner for a few of us to talk about the Bork nomination. We met at the Yenching Palace, a venerable and modest Chinese restaurant on Connecticut Avenue. Once we had broached the subject, Clinton began by telling us that Bork had taught him constitutional law at Yale Law School in the early '70s. He respected Bork's intellect, Clinton said, and he liked him personally. But, having thought about the nomination, Clinton told us, he had concluded that Bork's ascendancy to the Supreme Court could reopen racial wounds in the South, wounds that were finally healing. As a boy, Clinton had grown up in Arkansas and well remembered Governor Orval Faubus's obstructionism tactics in Little Rock. Since Clinton was dedicated to racial reconciliation, he said he would testify against Bork if we thought it would be helpful. We were overjoyed; in many ways Clinton's approach as a modern Southern governor cut to the heart of the matter. He prepared testimony, but when Bork stayed on the witness stand for several days longer than originally expected, Clinton had to honor a trade mission to Europe and so missed his Senate date. His statement is part of the hearing record, however, and still stands as an important part of the case against Bork. And I found, as so many have, that my first meeting with Clinton at the Yenching Palace drew me powerfully to his later candidacy for the presidency.

When the Senate hearings opened on September 15, we felt we had done everything we could to present a strong case and that people throughout the nation were informed in a way that rarely occurred with a judicial nomination. But we had little reason to be confident of the outcome. Much would depend on Bork's testimony. In anticipation, we had arranged to gain access to Room 115 of the Russell Senate office building, where we set up shop with all our Bork records and reports, television monitors, and telephones. The idea was to position ourselves to be able to inform committee staff almost immediately if the nominee misrepresented the facts or his views. The room also provided a quiet place where we could assess what the main story of the day was in speaking to the media. On that score, we found ourselves having some spirited discussions. Much of the substantive work was entrusted to me and to Eric Schnapper, a very gifted lawyer who had worked for years for the NAACP Legal Defense and Education Fund. It turned out that Eric and I often saw things quite differently. He fixed his attention on how Bork was softening some of his positions, noting that Bork appeared quite ready to contradict his previous positions to win Senate support. Believing that senators would react negatively to such inconsistency, Eric wanted to emphasize what he called "confirmation day conversions." In contrast I thought it important to show that, on the central issues, Bork remained rigidly conservative. At times Eric and I expressed our differences strongly. Some weeks later, Rickie Seidman, who was managing our "war room" (or "boiler room" as I preferred) confessed that she had been afraid we might come to blows, but later decided that this was "just the way two New York lawyers had a conversation with each other." In any event, we were able to work out statements that encompassed both themes.

On the other mission, making sure that senators and their staff were completely informed, there was less to do than we had anticipated. Most senators who were critical or skeptical of the nomination had prepared for the hearings as if they were boning up for a critical examination in constitutional law. In addition, unlike students, they brought to the hearings years of practical experience in the workings of government. While some pundits later portrayed the hearings as a cynical political struggle, I found them an uplifting experience. Lawmakers were engaged in a high-level dialogue about the meaning of the Constitution, the roles of the coordinate branches of government, and the unique place of the Supreme Court in our system. Rarely in our history have such discussions taken place in a public forum.

Bork was on the stand for five days and certainly demonstrated his command of constitutional theory. But his theoretical approach was often at odds with practical reality and the problems that often land people in court. One example is a discussion that Bork had before the Senate hearing not with the Senate but with Jack MacKenzie and other members of the *New York Times* editorial board. MacKenzie asked whether Bork's belief that there was no right of privacy to be found in the Constitution would lead him to the conclusion that courts would have to approve a Chinese-type policy of mandating abortions. Bork, after protesting the unlikelihood of such a policy in this country, agreed that there would be no constitutional protection against state-mandated abortions. Similarly, at the hearings, Bork, who only reluctantly acknowledged a constitutional basis for the Supreme Court's 1954 ruling in the *Brown* case, could find no basis for outlawing segregation in the companion case in the District of Columbia, which was under federal jurisdiction and governed by the Fifth, not the Fourteenth, Amendment. Bork's approach to these matters stood in stark contrast to Lewis Powell, the man he wished to succeed. Powell, while a conservative, had been a skilled trial lawyer prior to his judicial nomination. For him, facts were very important.

In the end, Bork harmed his own chances seriously during his testimony. On his last day as a witness, he was thrown a softball question by Senator Alan Simpson, one of his main supporters. Why did he want to become a justice of the Supreme Court? Bork said his first answer was that "I think it would be an intellectual feast." When we heard that in the War Room, Eric and I exchanged glances. We were stunned and then elated. Bork had confirmed the growing belief that he had little interest in the impact of the Court's work on the lives of real people.

The subsequent testimony of Bill Coleman, Barbara Jordan, Andy Young, Larry Tribe, John Hope Franklin, and others painted an eloquent portrait of constitutional ideals and contemporary hopes for American society. At the end of Coleman's testimony, in an exchange that was not transcribed, Coleman replied to complimentary words from Committee Chair Joe Biden. "Thank you, Senator," Coleman said, "but look at the people here with me [a young African-American lawyer and a young Asian-American lawyer who were his aides]— these are the people who are the future." To me, his words summarized all our hopes—we would not go back to where Bork would take us; the future would be a very different kind of America.

As the hearings ended, the outcome seemed clear. The debate had reached millions of Americans (extraordinary for a judicial nomination) and they had responded. The Committee chair asked that civil rights groups forego their opportunity to testify and—over the vigorous objection of two of our number—Ralph Nader and Molly Yard, head of NOW—we agreed. There was no point to arguing your case after you have won.

On October 23, after three days of floor debate, the Bork nomination was defeated 58–42. The next day, by happenstance I was scheduled to address a conference of voting rights advocates in San Antonio. In preparation, I compared the Bork vote to the 1964 vote on the historic Civil Rights Act. In 1964, twenty-one Senators voted against the new statute, all of them Southerners and all from the eleven states of the old Confederacy. The lone supporter was Ralph Yarborough of Texas. Of the twenty-two senators who held these same seats in 1987, sixteen of them voted against the nomination of Robert Bork. Several of the votes in opposition were by staunch conservatives like John Stennis of Mississippi. Again, it was the power of the Voting Rights Act that made the difference. While the South would remain the most conservative region of the nation, its representatives would not defy a clear mandate from women and people of color that their rights and opportunities be protected.

Along with the Voting Rights Act extension and the defeat of the Bork nomination, two other successful legislative struggles that we waged in the '80s helped ensure that the Reagan revolution would not include significant regression in civil rights.

Both were efforts in Congress to reverse Supreme Court decisions that curbed the remedies available in civil rights cases. The first was our campaign to nullify the effects of a 1984 Supreme Court decision in the case of *Grove City v. Bell*. The Court's 6–3 decision held that the words "program or activity" in Title IX of the Education Amendments of 1972 were to be so narrowly construed that, if federal aid for loans to students was received by the financial office of a university, the only sex discrimination prohibited would be that which occurred in the financial office. Differential treatment of men and women students in athletics would not be affected nor would biased practices against women faculty members. Similar constrictions would apply to other statutes barring discrimination by recipients of federal funds on the basis of race or handicap or age.

The *Grove City* decision ran counter to lower court decisions and to the general understanding of the reach of these laws. In the Leadership Conference, we decided that we had to act quickly to induce Congress to set aside the decision, not just for Title IX, but for all the antibias funding statutes.

In the beginning, it seemed to me that a legislative solution could be fairly straightforward. The words in the law that no person shall be subjected to discrimination "under any program or activity receiving federal financial assistance" should be defined as applying to the operations of the entire institution—the entire university or school district—not some office or subdivision of the entity. But there were complications. Title IX was subject to numerous exceptions and qualifications, including a provision that religious organizations which controlled educational institutions could opt out of coverage for practices that might offend the religious tenets of the group. I urged my colleagues to try to cut through the morass quickly because I could see more problems coming down the road. But in 1984, although we were able to secure House passage of a good bill, it never reached the Senate floor.

In 1985, the crisis hit. Abortion, barely mentioned in legislation discussions the first time around, became a major obstacle to passage of our bill to restore the rights negated by the *Grove City* decision. The problem was that the regulations adopted by the Department of Health, Education, and Welfare in 1975, after enactment of Title IX, said that college hospitals or health facilities had to treat pregnancy or the termination of pregnancy in the same way as they treated other temporary disabilities. The Catholic Conference feared that restoration of Title IX would force Catholic institutions with health facilities to offer abortion services, while women's groups feared that such services would not be available in the absence of a clear mandate. I thought the issue was a red herring since no complaint involving the provision or denial of services had arisen since the passage of Title IX. But the controversy, real or hypothetical, was enough keep the bill from moving forward.

One of the obstacles was that opponents of the legislation demanded that, if we were seeking to restore the law, we should be able to state in great detail what the law was prior to the *Grove City* decision. That, of course, entailed articulating a body of case law developed through administrative regulation or through the lower courts that was not always clear. One aide to Senator Kennedy said to me in frustration one day, "Can't we just write a provision that says 'whatever the law was on the day before *Grove City* was decided is what it is today'?" In dealing with these tactics of obstruction, our principal obstacle was Senator Orrin Hatch.

I had first dealt with Senator Hatch in 1980 when, in seeking improved remedies under the Fair Housing Act of 1968—the weakest of the federal civil rights laws—we encountered strong opposition from the Utah senator. Ted Kennedy asked if I would try my hand at negotiating directly with Hatch, whom I found had an odd negotiating technique. Whenever I would indicate that I was prepared to recommend to my colleagues that we make a concession, Hatch would toughen his position. It became clear that he did not want a settlement and, in the fall of 1980, he mounted a successful filibuster to stop a majority of fifty-five Senators from passing the bill.

I found Hatch to be a kind of peculiar amalgam of two Dickens characters—Uriah Heep and Ebenezer Scrooge. Like Heep, he wanted to be liked. So after his filibuster, as our Leadership Conference group stood in the lobby of the Capitol, he shook the hands of all the men and kissed all of the women (few of whom he actually knew) and promised to work with us on a new bill next year. The Fair Housing Amendments finally passed over Hatch's continuing objections in 1988. But in addition to his obsequious ways, Hatch, like Scrooge, has consistently demonstrated a mean streak. He would not articulate a principled position on civil rights legislation. Rather, he found a label—"quotas" is one of his favorites—that served as his mantra in fighting all proposals.

On the Civil Rights Restoration Act, Hatch kept intervening to sabotage progress. One evening when Brad Reynolds of the Reagan administration had come to discuss the bill with Senator Kennedy, we seemed to be making some progress. Senator Hatch burst into the room and conducted his own filibuster. Later, Reynolds asked if he and I could talk privately to try to reach an accommodation. While I replied affirmatively, I knew that Hatch and Reynolds' right-wing colleagues at the Department of Justice would stymie further negotiations. As the session ended Senators Dole and Kennedy called a meeting to make a last-ditch effort at reaching agreement. It was a senators-only meeting with two exceptions: Reynolds was asked to serve as staff for the conservative senators and I played the same role for the liberal senators. Hatch objected to this arrangement from the beginning. He said he needed his staff with him. Both Dole and Kennedy replied that this would not be helpful, Kennedy adding that the large growth in staff over recent years sometimes impeded the Senate in legislating. Hatch continued to object, adopting a whining tone. During a short break he said to me, "You can see what they are doing to me, Bill; it's not fair. I'll make sure you have a hearing next year." I found it hard to believe that he thought I would be a receptive audience to his plaint. Finally, Senator Thurmond entered the room late, giving Hatch the opportunity to go into the corridor and return with a staff member. The meeting broke up without an agreement.

The bill was delayed again by the Bork nomination in 1987. It then was vetoed by President Reagan in 1988, but the Congress overrode the veto. A provision was included professing that the bill was agnostic on the question of abortion, neither adding to or subtracting from whatever authority previously existed. The important thing was the all-important principle that, when one dips one's hand into the federal treasury, a little democracy must cling to what is withdrawn, was kept intact and our hard-won gains were preserved.

As the Restoration Act moved toward final passage, new challenges to civil rights protections were arising. The Supreme Court issued a series of decisions in 1988 and 1989 interpreting fair-employment laws that threatened job opportunities for minorities and women.

Of the six major decisions that came down during this period, two are vivid in my memory even today. One case, *Patterson v. McLean Credit Union*, involved an interpretation of a law first adopted in 1866 during Reconstruction that said, "All persons shall have the same right as a white person to make and enforce contracts." This law, and another Reconstruction statute intended to secure for black people the right to acquire property without discrimination, had been nullified by the post-Reconstruction Supreme Court under the guise that the Constitution did not permit government to prohibit private acts of discrimination. There comes a time, Justice Bradley declared in 1883, when a black man "ceases to be the special favorite of the laws." Eight decades later, however, the Warren Court and later the Burger Court rescued these laws from the dustbin of history and gave them the content originally intended. But in the conservative backlash on the Supreme Court in the 1980s, some justices were prepared to revisit the key decision that black people had the same right as whites to make and enforce contracts.

In 1988, a majority of the Supreme Court took the unusual step of setting the *Patterson* case for reargument on matters not raised by the parties in the initial argument. A group of 66 Senators and 118 members of the House decided to file a friend of the Court brief asking the Court to uphold the Reconstruction law. The lawyers they retained included Larry Tribe, Ed Levi, former attorney general in the Ford administration, John Pickering, John Payton, and their colleagues at the firm of Wilmer, Cutler and Pickering, and myself. Again, as in the Bork battle I felt uplifted by the distinguished bipartisan company I was privileged to keep.

The Court decided in 1989 not to undo these prior decisions. But it provided no help to Mrs. Patterson. She had alleged that she was verbally abused at her job as a bank teller because of her race. Justice Kennedy, for five members of the Court, said that by its plain terms the statute covered only the making and enforcement of contracts and not their terms and conditions.

In dissent, Justice Brennan pointed out that, in legislating in 1866, Congress was aware that slavery had been replaced by coercive systems of employment in which the "use of the whip" to coerce Negroes to work harder was not unusual. He concluded that, if an employer offers a white and a black applicant the same written contract, but then tells the black employee that her working conditions will be much worse than those of the white employees because there is a lot of harassment going on in the workplace, and that she will simply have to endure it, no one could conclude that there was an equal right to make such a contract. He thought there was no relevant distinction where these contractual expectations were unspoken. It was clear, said Justice Brennan, that Congress needed to act to provide a remedy for such outrageous situations.

The second major case—*Wards Cove v. Atonio*—was an explicit effort by the Court to overturn *Griggs*, a 1971 decision that had become the bedrock of fair-employment law. Although the Court had become more conservative in the intervening period, its later decision to revisit was surprising because *Griggs* had been a unanimous opinion written by Justice Burger and because Congress had reviewed the fair employment law in 1972 and made no change in the interpretation of the law.

The *Griggs* decision took a pragmatic approach to employment discrimination. If there were significant disparities in the employment of whites and minorities on the job, the Court examined the practice that produced the disparities, for example a paper-and-pencil hiring test, to determine whether it was necessary to the maintenance of an efficient work force. If its conclusion was negative, the Court required the employer to find another means of screening applicants that would not have a discriminatory impact. In *Wards Cove*, the majority switched gears entirely. Minorities—Filipinos and Native Alaskans—held low-skilled, low-paying jobs in a cannery, while whites had better-paying jobs. Hiring was done through separate hiring channels and was influenced by nepotism, and the workers were housed in segregated facilities. Despite all these facts, the Court said the burden was on the complaining employees to show discrimination, and the employer could escape liability by showing merely that his practices were convenient, not necessary.

In 1973, the Court had said of its *Griggs* decision that "it was rightly concerned that . . . deficiencies in the background of minority citizens resulting from forces beyond their control not be allowed to work a cumulative and invidious burden on such citizens for the remainder of their lives." Now the majority seemed to be saying that minority citizens would face such lifetime burdens unless they could overcome large legal barriers currently being erected.

The effort to restore the principles of *Griggs* became a complex struggle. Republican leaders had learned in the Reagan administration that there was political paydirt in practicing the politics of racial division. So they continued to do so in the Bush administration, labeling legislation that was designed to reinstitute the decision of a conservative Republican chief justice a "quota bill." In some ways, the negative feelings may have been genuinely felt by some. I remember attending a meeting about the bill with C. Boyden Gray, the White House counsel to President Bush. He told us, in all seriousness, that he knew what it was like to be the object of discrimination because he was treated badly when in college when he was the only WASP on the staff of the Harvard *Crimson*.

Bush vetoed the act in 1990 amid Republican charges that it was "quota" legislation. But he lacked crucial allies. Many of the largest corporations in the nation had come to understand that diversity in their work forces was good for business, and they joined with civil rights groups in seeking a strong and sensible bill. The Bush veto survived by a single vote in the Senate in 1990. When the bill was resubmitted in 1991, it passed with virtually the same key provisions, reversing *Patterson* and restoring *Griggs* and other important fair-employment principles. This time President Bush only grumbled, then signed the bill.

People sometimes ask me whether I think the Bork battle was worth fighting, since the seat was ultimately filled by Anthony Kennedy, also a strong conservative. There is not a question in my mind that the Bork battle and all the others of the '80s were worth fighting. What we were witnessing during that decade was a strong counteroffensive to the civil rights revolution that in some ways resembled the successful effort to end Reconstruction in the previous century. I am convinced the forces behind the counteroffensive were actuated consciously or unconsciously by fears about the loss of white privilege. The outcome was not foreordained. In the 1980s, conservative Republicans gained control of the presidency and one house of the Congress. If Bork had joined Scalia and Rehnquist on the Court, they would have formed the core of a movement to roll the clock back. But this time, there were forces at work that prevented major regression. The voting rights laws had enfranchised blacks, who had also made great strides educationally and economically. There were new powerful allies in the struggle for equality—other people of color, women, and people with disabilities.

Still, in the new century, we continue to face some of the old battles, particularly in the effort of the current administration to populate the courts with judges who believe that almost every piece of social legislation enacted since Franklin Roosevelt took office is unconstitutional. But I believe that the battles of the '80s established a baseline beyond which retreat will not occur. White conservatives who continue to oppose civil rights have considerable wealth and power, and in many areas they are using it effectively. But they are essentially engaged in a defensive effort to retain unearned white privilege. While the struggle against injustice in its many forms is likely to continue for many years, I believe that the apostles of white privilege will never reclaim the control they once had.

CHAPTER NINE

The Thomas Nomination

I f the debate over the Bork nomination brought a moment of moral clarity to American public life, the struggle over the nomination of Clarence Thomas to the Supreme Court four years later demonstrated how much issues of race still clouded our thinking.

With the retirement of Justice Thurgood Marshall from the Court in 1991, it was widely expected that his successor would be an African-American lawyer or jurist. But the nomination of Clarence Thomas by President Bush was a cynical act. Thomas was a lawyer who had made his mark by serving in two civil rights positions in the federal government in the Reagan and Bush administrations, where he had opposed the use of key remedies for violations of anti-discrimination laws. Bush had nominated him to the Court of Appeals for the District of Columbia Circuit in October 1989, a post in which he put in a little more than a year of undistinguished service before being nominated to the Supreme Court. Thomas had written very little and none of his articles or speeches gave any hint that he was a student of the Constitution.

Bush put forward the Thomas nomination on July 1, 1991, just a year after he had vetoed a civil rights bill containing affirmative remedies and labeled it "quota" legislation. If the ordinary meaning of quota is hiring someone unqualified or barely qualified for a position in order to accomplish a racial purpose, that is exactly what George Bush was doing in nominating Thomas to the Court. Yet Bush insisted with a straight face that Thomas was the "most qualified" person for the job, a statement that caused puzzlement even among some Bush supporters.

If Bush was being hypocritical, however, his action was politically astute. The NAACP's national convention was scheduled just a few days after the nomination was announced. While Thomas opposed almost every civil rights policy the NAACP favored, people at the convention were divided about his nomination and some insisted he would change once he got on the Court. The result was a delay of one month while the NAACP pondered its position.

Wade Henderson, then the Washington representative of the NAACP and now director of the Leadership Conference on Civil Rights, called me as soon as the convention was over. He said that it would be important to induce respected African-American leaders whose civil rights credentials were impeccable to declare publicly their opposition to Thomas in order to ensure that the full NAACP would ultimately enlist in the campaign to deny him confirmation. I offered to call John Hope Franklin, the great American historian who had provided such eloquent testimony in the Bork hearings and who had been a friend of mine for many years.

Dr. Franklin was irritated by my request. "These people [NAACP leaders and members] know what they should do," he said. "I am a life member, but they shouldn't need me to tell them." Nevertheless, he said he would consider writing something. By the end of July, Dr. Franklin had written an essay for the NAACP, tracing the history of the self-help doctrine that Clarence Thomas espoused from Booker T. Washington to the present day. "Self-help," he said, "is admirable so long as it encourages initiative and achievement in a society that gives all its members an opportunity to develop in a manner best suited to their talents. . . . Judge Thomas, in failing in his utterances and policies to subscribe to this basic principle, has placed himself in the unseemly position of denying to others the very opportunities and the kind of assistance from public and private quarters that have placed him where he is today."

The NAACP publicly declared its opposition to Thomas on July 31 and the *New York Times* printed Franklin's essay as an op-ed the next day. Two weeks later, Dr. Franklin sent me a letter saying, "I called you all sorts of names for pushing me into the fray. In the end I am glad that you pushed, ever so slightly." He ended his letter with, "I am reminded of the time when a white historian friend of mine had African-Americans in his class for the first time. In an encounter with me he expressed great distress that one of them was performing very poorly and he wondered what he should do. I asked him what he would do if the student were white. He replied promptly that he would flunk him. I said that he had no problem: merely apply his usual standards! We must see to it that the Senators stand up."

That of course was precisely the point. But the four-week delay in the NAACP's decision would prove costly. In the Bork nomination battle, we had gained the initiative by acting immediately. With Thomas, our delay enabled our opponents to gain an edge. They portrayed Thomas as a poor boy from Pin Point, Georgia, whose success was a kind of Horatio Alger story and whose ascension to the Supreme Court would bring a diverse point of view to that privileged bench. Never mind that Thomas shared the antigovernment assistance biases of conservatives already on the Court and had even talked contemptuously in public and private about his own sister, who had accepted welfare payments to support her family.

In the third week of July, I went on a D.C. public affairs television program to discuss the nomination. My opponent was Allan Keyes, a conservative polemicist who later ran for president on a platform to the right of Pat Buchanan. Since Thomas's record was otherwise so sparse, one issue was his stewardship as chairman of the Equal Employment Opportunity Commission (EEOC). Keyes spoke of Thomas's tenure in glowing terms. I pointed out that Thomas had allowed hundreds of complaints filed by older people claiming age discrimination to lapse and that Congress had criticized Thomas and had to come to the rescue of these petitioners by extending the time period for EEOC action. "You are a liar," responded Keyes, startling both me and the moderator, Maureen Bunyan, who called me the next day to apologize, saying she had no idea that Keyes would engage in such behavior.

When the program was over I told Keyes that I thought he should be more careful in his choice of language. He shook a finger at me and said, "You and your friends aren't going to lynch me and you are not going to lynch Clarence Thomas." While this was an incendiary remark, I thought nothing more of it until a few months later, on the day in October when Thomas, faced with charges that he had harassed Anita Hill, described the Senate hearings as "a high-tech lynching for an uppity black who in any way deigns to think for himself." Thomas insisted that he prepared his statement without any assistance or consultation. But thinking back to my encounter with Allan Keyes, I concluded that the "lynching" card was one Thomas and his allies planned to use from the outset if needed.

The hearings themselves were frustrating. Thomas backed away from his previous ultraconservative pronouncements and refused to be drawn out on any important issues. As a group, senators seemed reluctant to press him for answers. He had an enthusiastic sponsor in Senator John Danforth, for whom Thomas had worked in Missouri when Danforth served as state attorney general. Danforth's harsh criticism of Thomas opponents may have persuaded some senators that this was a fight they didn't need.

John Hope Franklin decided not to testify. He explained, "I saw that they [senators] were going to let him back off anything he had ever said. I decided that if they weren't going to do their part I couldn't run with the ball for them. I didn't think those white men had the nerve to speak out courageously against a black man . . . I gave up on it."

One morning during the hearings, three African-American constitutional law authorities testified against Thomas. Drew Days taught at Yale Law School and was later to become solicitor general of the United States, Charles Lawrence taught at Stanford, and Christopher Edley at

Harvard. Their testimony was a tutorial on constitutional theory and analysis and on the critical issues of the day. After they were done, I found myself in a discussion in the corridor with Ralph Neas, then director of the Leadership Conference, and Melanne Verveer of People for the American Way, when Senator Arlen Specter of Pennsylvania approached us. "I know that trouble is brewing whenever I see the three of you together," he said.

"No, Senator," I replied, "we were just commenting on what an extraordinary session on constitutional law that was, and that Clarence Thomas does not even have the ability to talk the same language."

"Well, what would you have the president do?" he asked. "Those panelists are all liberal Democrats."

"There certainly are qualified Republicans," I said, mentioning Bill Coleman, who, while a civil rights advocate, was a conservative Republican and a hugely respected lawyer.

"But the president doesn't know him personally," Specter said. "He does know Clarence Thomas."

His comments left me speechless, particularly when he added, presumably to prove his own civil rights credentials, "Drew Days is wonderful; he should be a senator." A few minutes later, Drew Days came down the hall and said, "The strangest thing just happened; I ran into Senator Specter and he told me I should be a senator."

Specter's brand of muddled thinking seemed to prevail. Although the Judiciary Committee deadlocked 7–7, it seemed clear that Thomas would have a small but adequate margin on the Senate floor. Then the allegations by Anita Hill broke into public view. The Judiciary Committee, in my judgment, then mishandled the whole affair. Senate rules require that any testimony which might "defame or degrade" a witness be heard in private session, at least initially. Fairness both to Anita Hill and Clarence Thomas would have dictated that this rule be followed, but committee chairman Joe Biden decided to treat all of it as a public matter, leading several senators, including Senator Specter, to embarrass themselves with their misogynistic attitudes. In the end, Thomas was approved by a slightly narrower margin than anticipated, 52–48.

In the years since Thomas was confirmed, some have tried to rewrite history. Juan Williams, who while still a journalist at the *Washington Post* engaged in a vituperative campaign to secure Thomas's confirmation, has tried to persuade people that, although Thurgood Marshall disagreed with Thomas, he respected him. As Justice Marshall's public pronouncements and the incident at my last lunch with him (see chapter 2) make clear, nothing could be further from the truth.

Those who were in for the rudest shock were the people who had convinced themselves that, once Thomas was on the Court, he would be a more temperate and humane person than he had been before. That notion was dispelled within six months. Thomas had told senators that, when he saw outside his window at the Court of Appeals prisoners being transported to their cells, he thought, "There but for the grace of God go I." In one of his earliest decisions, however, Thomas wrote a solitary dissenting opinion that a shackled prisoner who had been severely beaten by two guards had suffered no loss of constitutional rights. On cases ranging from disability rights to environmental law to federal authority to regulate commerce or prevent discrimination, Thomas has usually teamed with Scalia to advocate the most extreme position. When, as often, Rehnquist, Kennedy, and O'Connor agree with the result, the five justices become the dominant majority, with Thomas and Scalia typically desiring to go even further in restricting rights than do the others.

Collectively, in civil rights, the five justices have essentially called a halt to desegregation of public schools, effectively reversing the landmark decisions of the 1970s without ever acknowledging that this is what they were doing. Once the Court declared that districts are entitled to reassert "local control," some states have gone back to segregated "neighborhood schools," reinstating the condition that the Court's decision in the *Brown* case sought to redress.

Back to Schools

Saving Desegregation in St. Louis

Fortunately, the Rehnquist-Thomas doctrine has not adversely affected my own major school cases. In St. Louis (and also in Fort Wayne) I was able to negotiate settlements that either did not provide for an end date or specified that, even after districts were freed from the detailed provisions of a plan, they were still obligated to keep their schools desegregated.

In St. Louis, much of the bitterness that surrounded our battles with Attorney General Ashcroft and some of the suburban districts subsided after we reached a settlement in 1983. The agreement provided for the establishment of a community center to engage in recruitment and outreach for students to participate in the interdistrict plan. The center, part of the Voluntary Interdistrict Coordinating Committee, was ably led by Susan Uchitelle who, along with a number of school officials, provided effective counseling and assistance to students who were having problems. By the fifth year, the number of black children enrolled in suburban schools exceeded eleven thousand (it eventually reached thirteen thousand), making St. Louis the largest voluntary interdistrict choice plan in the nation. Six of the sixteen suburban districts had reached their goal of having an African-American enrollment of 25 percent or more and three more were on the verge of reaching the goal.

This level of participation by African-American parents and their children (it has since grown) is even more remarkable than the raw numbers may suggest. Often parents have to get up before sunrise to put their children on buses for long rides to suburban schools. In some cases, children in the same family attend different schools with different schedules. Participation requires that families make sacrifices. Why, in light of these circumstances, do so many families participate? The reasons vary. In some cases, the dominant factors have to do with the negative environment of inner-city schools, including the physical dangers as well as drugs and negative peer influences. But, more than anything, parents and youngsters are influenced by the belief that they will receive a better education in these suburban schools. Over the years, I have learned that lawyers and social scientists may debate concepts like desegregation, but parents tend to think in more concrete and practical terms. They will embrace programs that seem attainable and that offer educational benefits that promise to lead to greater opportunities for youngsters. That is what has happened in St. Louis, as documented by Amy Stuart Wells and Robert Crain in their 1997 book, *Stepping over the Color Line.*

The faith that parents placed in the suburban transfer program has been justified to a very high degree. The transfer students performed somewhat better on assessments of achievement. But, more important, by the time we had to go back into court in 1996, several studies showed that students in the interdistrict program graduated high school and went on to college at two to three times the rate of students in inner city schools in St. Louis and elsewhere. Although some assumed that the transfer students were predominantly middle class, this was not the case. Three out of four were eligible for free or reduced-price meals, which meant that they were marginally or actually poor. The transfer program provided them real opportunity and mobility that they would not have otherwise gained.

During the years following the settlement, other changes also took place in central city schools. New magnet schools were created in St. Louis, a few of which are very good. One, Metro, is outstanding. Capital improvements helped rebuild schools that were in disrepair. Libraries were added to schools that had not had them. Class sizes in the elementary grades were reduced to enable teachers to give more individualized attention to students. But the school improvement program in the inner city did not result in significant achievement gains. I came to the conclusion that the critical failing had to do with the qualifications and preparation of teachers.

Until the 1970s, the teaching profession in public schools had long attracted a remarkable array of talented people. But they were a captive audience: women had been excluded from almost every other profession except nursing, and people of color had also faced discrimination in business and the professions. Once the civil rights laws became effective, the situation changed dramatically. Women and racial minorities went into law, medicine, business, and other occupations from which they had been excluded. And almost everywhere, the monetary rewards and status were greater in those fields than in teaching. Soon, public schools began to suffer a major brain drain.

Certainly, talented people remain. But there are simply not enough of them. As the quality of education in public schools declined, many of the lower-tier graduates went on to teachers' colleges and were recycled back into public schools, continuing the downward spiral. I met several older teachers in St. Louis during this period who were able, committed, dedicated to their children and frustrated by the overall decline in teaching quality.

For about eight years, the interdistrict program continued to grow and prosper, and the school improvement remedies were implemented despite continual bickering between officials of the state of Missouri and local officials over financing issues. When we reviewed the minutes of meetings by the committees charged with implementing the settlement, arguments about money dominated the proceedings and the interests of children were rarely discussed. Occasionally, we felt we had to take issues back to court. By this time our judge was Steven

Limbaugh, Rush's uncle. When we sought data comparing the achievement of students transferring to the suburbs with that of resident students in the suburban districts, Judge Limbaugh denied our request, saying that this would be like "comparing apples and oranges." We found that reference offensive because the whole point was to provide opportunities for inner-city students to perform at the same level as successful suburban students. Despite this unfortunate statement, however, I found Judge Limbaugh to be generally fair.

Beginning in 1991, we faced a new attack. By this time, Missouri's attorney general was Jeremiah "Jay" Nixon, unlike Ashcroft a Democrat. To our disappointment, Nixon turned out to be cut from the same cloth as Ashcroft in his belief that practicing the politics of racial division would take him to higher office. Nixon began by filing a series of motions in federal court. These were designed to end the state's multi-million-dollar annual obligations to fund remedies for the educational damage the state was largely responsible for creating. Nixon was not totally lacking in legal support for his position. In 1991, the Supreme Court issued the first of three decisions suggesting that states and school districts could be declared to have achieved "unitary status," i.e., fulfilled their legal obligations, if they had complied with court orders for desegregation for a period of time. But it seemed absurd to conclude that after a century of segregation and decades of defying the mandate of *Brown*, the State of Missouri could be given a pass after only a few years of offering opportunity to African-American students.

We managed to deflect the State's motions for several years. But the Court scheduled a hearing for March 1996 to decide whether the State had met its obligations. Our prospects did not seem very rosy. In 1995, the Supreme Court had relieved the State of Missouri of many of its legal obligations in Kansas City, an extremely costly case that had achieved very little desegregation. In doing so, the Rehnquist majority had gratuitously reinterpreted *Gautreaux*, a 1976 Supreme Court decision that obligated the federal government to remedy racial segregation in public housing in Chicago by providing affordable housing in the suburbs. A metropolitan housing remedy was available in Chicago, the

Court said in *Gautreaux*, because local officials were not involved in approving federal housing assistance. So, too, in our school case in St. Louis, the Court of Appeals had said there was no issue of local control since the suburban districts had voluntary agreed to the metropolitan remedy.

Now the Supreme Court seemed to be suggesting that more was required for a metropolitan remedy—an actual finding of an interdistrict violation.

If applied to St. Louis, this argument could invalidate the favorable ruling requiring the state to fund the metropolitan remedy. Since we had settled with the suburbs, there never was a decision on our claim of an interdistrict violation. When the State raised this argument, I responded that the least we would be entitled to was a trial on the question of whether there had been such a violation and if the State wanted such a trial we would be glad to oblige. The State then dropped its claim and stayed with the position that it had completed all its obligations.

The two-week trial in March was a kind of docudrama about the state of race relations and education in St. Louis. We sought to demonstrate that the interdistrict program was going well and should be continued. At the same time, the improvement program in city schools was going badly, and needed to be revamped, not ended. In response, the State's private lawyers produced a stable of experts, several of whom made their living by testifying for pay that their State clients were faultless. One, David Armor, argued that the gap in achievement between black and white students was due almost entirely to differences in socioeconomic status of black and white students, not to any deficiencies in the education black children were receiving. Armor based his conclusions on neighborhood poverty and made a huge error in his calculation, overstating the numbers of students surrounded by poverty by about 30 to 40 percent. On the witness stand under my cross-examination, he had to concede the invalidity of his testimony. Another witness for the State was economist Eric Hanushek, whose thesis was that money makes no difference in the educational process. Our judge by this time was George Gunn, a conservative Republican who had previously served on state courts. Judge Gunn was a practical person, and he asked witness Hanushek whether it would make any difference to the education of children whether there were fifteen or forty students in a classroom. Hanushek said there would be no difference. Judge Gunn was so stunned by this response that he asked every expert who took the stand later the same question. All of course said the forty-student classroom would not provide a good educational environment.

At one point, having introduced evidence that fewer than 30 percent of students entering high school in St. Louis graduate in four years, I asked an expert witness what happens to ill-educated students who drop out of school. Before the witness could answer, Judge Gunn interjected. "I know what happens to them," he said. "I see them in my courtroom every day for sentencing."

I concluded then that our judge got it. I was further encouraged when, after the trial, he acceded to a request I had made before the trial—the appointment of a settlement coordinator. The person he named was William H. Danforth, recently retired as chancellor of Washington University in St. Louis, a medical doctor and a very widely respected figure in the community. He was also the older brother of Senator John Danforth. Although not an expert on elementary and secondary education, he had been asked several years earlier to conduct a study of education for a business group and had grasped the issues very quickly.

Dr. Danforth and most of the parties decided that the challenge was to persuade the State legislature to find a way to replace the $150 million-plus annual contribution that Missouri was making under federal court order, so that the programs would continue after the case was closed. But the State, under Jay Nixon's leadership, was not seeing it this way. He produced a plan that offered $304 million, barely enough to keep the program going without new applications for two years, after which schools in St. Louis would be resegregated and without resources. Nixon also decided to seek to close down the interdistrict program immediately and, when he had no success in the district court and court of appeals, he asked for review in the Supreme Court. It was summer of 1996 and the Court was not sitting; so the petition for a stay went to the individual justice designated to accept filings for the Eighth Circuit— Clarence Thomas. That concerned me until I read the petition, filed by a prominent Washington firm that specializes in practice before the Supreme Court. In a long passage in the document, the State laced into Dr. Danforth, calling him biased and referring to him in demeaning terms. I could not believe my eyes. Senator John Danforth had been Thomas's chief guru and protector during the confirmation battle. Whatever temptation Justice Thomas might have had to wade into the desegregation controversy, he had to be put off by what would be regarded as an assault on the Danforth family. It was surprising that the fancy Washington law firm did not know enough politics to avoid this major gaffe. It was at least equally surprising that Nixon and his state lawyers who had to know the politics allowed the brief to go forward in that form. Sure enough, Thomas turned down the motion for a stay.

Nixon kept up his attack. When school opened in 1997, Nixon held a press conference on the steps of Vashon High School, a symbol of black pride that was in deteriorated condition. He announced that he would continue his campaign to end the transfer program and would obtain $100 million in order to build new schools in the city to house the African-American students who would be returning from the suburbs. The *St. Louis Post-Dispatch* carried my reply to Nixon the next day on page one. I compared his statements to those of Southern segregationist state leaders in the 1950s. Those leaders, too, pledged to fix up old schools and also promised to build new ones for black children. But Nixon was even worse, I noted, because, unlike the South of the '50s, the schools in St. Louis were desegregated and Nixon was proposing to resegregate them. By that time Nixon had announced his campaign for the U.S. Senate in 1998 and it was clear that he hoped to follow the same segregationist path that had worked for John Ashcroft fourteen years earlier.

On September 24, 1997, President Bill Clinton went home to Little Rock to join in a commemoration of the fortieth anniversary of the entry of nine Negro students into Central High School after President Eisenhower had ordered federal troops to protect them against a mob stirred up by Governor Orval Faubus. President Clinton was at his best at the ceremony. He affirmed his continuing support of school desegregation, saying that "the alternative to integration is disintegration."

The following day, in the same edition of the *St. Louis Post-Dispatch* that reported the Clinton speech in Little Rock, there was a brief announcement that the president would appear in St. Louis in November to support the candidacy of Jay Nixon. It took me a moment to recover from this news. I then picked up the phone and called Representative Bill Clay, the senior congressman from Missouri and ranking member of the Committee on Education and Labor. Bill and I had known each other for many years and I had consulted him in preparing the St. Louis case. "Have you seen the newspaper?" I asked. "What should we do about this?"

"You write the strongest letter you can for my signature, telling the president he should not go to St. Louis to support Jay Nixon," he said, "and I'll sign it."

That was just the response I had hoped for. Bill Clay is a person who has always spoken his mind, occasionally using incendiary words when dealing with injustice. I knew I had a mandate from him. The letter ultimately sent to the president summarized Nixon's demagogic actions and statements. It concluded, "I am sure that if Orval Faubus in the past had sought your support for a Senate campaign you would not give it. You should not give it to Jay Nixon today. Mr. Nixon should be told directly and forthrightly that unless and until he abandons his opposition to desegregation and other equal opportunity measures for St. Louis school children, you will not come to St. Louis on his behalf or support him in any other way."

Congressman Clay's letter was rapidly followed by letters and calls from other black elected officials in Missouri and an editorial in the *St. Louis American*, the local black newspaper, all urging President Clinton not to come to St. Louis on behalf of Nixon. Very soon thereafter, I received a call from Craig Smith, the political director at the White

House. He informed me that he knew that I was "behind this whole effort" and that I was "destroying the best opportunity the Democrats had to capture a Republican senate seat." He also told me that he knew Jay Nixon personally and that he was not a bad guy. I responded that I would rather see the seat retained by the Republicans than have it turned over to a hard-line segregationist Democrat. In the days that followed, I received several calls from Smith, but I did not budge, urging him to use his friendship with Nixon to bring about a constructive result.

Our campaign had its desired impact. Jay Nixon was informed by the White House that the president's visit would be postponed and he was encouraged to work things out in the desegregation case. Still Nixon dragged his heels, even after a meeting that Clay arranged with a powerful St. Louis labor leader who urged him to come to terms. Eventually, Nixon moderated his opposition and in time he even became a supporter of efforts to secure legislative action that would settle the case. But all of this came too late to rescue his political campaign. In the November 1998 election, Senator Christopher Bond, the incumbent, won easily, bolstered by 33 percent of the black vote, about three times the proportion he had received in the past. Looking back, I still find the whole episode fascinating in its entanglement of race, law, and politics. It was proof again that the enfranchisement of black voters had changed the electoral equation in important ways.

In seeking to settle the case, our major task was to persuade the State legislature to guarantee sufficient funds to pay for the interdistrict program, school improvements in the inner city, and magnet schools for at least ten years. It was a very heavy lift because St. Louis and Kansas City—the two major urban areas of the state—were not regarded with great affection by many rural and suburban representatives and desegregation was not exactly a popular cause. Moreover, when I went to the State Capitol in Jefferson City to press my cause, I was generally viewed as an interloper, if not an outside agitator, and was variously accused of seeking to cash in with a big attorneys' fee or to prolong the litigation for my own benefit. (In this, as in other civil rights litigation, our compensation depended on the trial judge's ruling on plaintiff's request for fees once the case was over.)

But there were a number of things working in our favor. One was that Dr. Danforth, committed to a constructive solution, had secured the services of a former state budget director to help work out the finances. Another was that the Missouri legislature was a far more accessible and informal place than the United States Congress. With the help of Dr. Danforth's aide I was able to obtain a hearing before the appropriate committees with a minimum of notice.

It was also very helpful that among the hundreds of legislators there were a few who cared deeply about education issues. Steve Stoll, a representative and former teacher, and Ted House, a state senator— both from outside the St. Louis area—decided to hold regional hearings on school desegregation and school finance. The witnesses were public officials and community leaders, and the tenor of the testimony was surprisingly positive. In October 1997, a hearing was held at a high school in St. Louis. So many people signed up to testify that the hearing stretched past midnight. While resistance to the interdistrict program persisted in some quarters, there had been a palpable change of attitude from prior years. Transfer students, black and white, who had graduated high school and were now in college, came back to say how useful the program had been in preparing them for higher education and for adult life. While in the '80s, almost all the vocal response from suburbia had been negative, now there was a cadre of white parents who were strong supporters of desegregation.

As I sat through the evening waiting to testify as one of the concluding witnesses, I found myself chatting with Senator Jack Danforth. In his passionate campaign for the confirmation of Clarence Thomas, Senator Danforth had used harsh, even McCarthyite, language in assailing the civil rights groups that opposed his candidate. His stance had angered me at the time. Yet here we were espousing the same cause and I felt my anger melting. It was another verification of the axiom that, in politics, you have no permanent friends or enemies, only permanent interests.

After midnight, the committee called on Minnie Liddell, the African-American leader of a community group in North St. Louis who, along with her son, had been an original plaintiff in the suit in the 1970s. In a voice slightly slurred by the effects of a stroke, but still powerful, Mrs. Liddell said:

"Everybody is asking whether integration works. Well, let me tell you what didn't work. Segregated education didn't work. You owe it to the children of St. Louis to provide them with choices and with a quality education. If you don't each and every one of us is going to pay for it."

The audience gave Minnie, who was to die in 2004 at age fifty-nine, a standing ovation. Now, with a bit of momentum, we worked through the 1998 session of the State legislature to find a solution. What emerged was a change in the funding formula that would provide more funding for districts with highly concentrated poverty. The formula was weighted so that poor children who went to very poor schools would be counted as 1.5 or 1.75 children. The principal beneficiaries of the change were in St. Louis and Kansas City. The formula made sense because all the research showed that concentrated poverty provided a poor environment and that more resources were needed to help children. At the same time, the state budget was in good enough shape that no sacrifices had to be made by other districts to accommodate the needs of the two big urban districts. The job would have been much harder if we had been in a period of budget austerity.

The compromise finally emerged in both houses. With the help of Stoll and House; Senator Lacy Clay, son of Congressman Clay; and in the end Governor Mel Carnahan, the bill secured majority support when African-American legislators in the St. Louis area reluctantly agreed to a provision that required that part of the revenue for school improvement in St. Louis come from a city, wide referendum on a sales tax increase to be held the following February.

With enactment of the legislation, we needed to secure a settlement among the parties. Not surprisingly, that proved to be a very difficult task. At Christmas, I took a brief vacation in London, while my colleagues Dianne Piche and Mike Middleton braved a major snowstorm to get back to St. Louis for negotiations. When I arrived during the first week in January, a few big questions still remained unresolved. The suburban county school districts wanted the right to opt out of a new agreement at almost any time. Jay Nixon said he was ready to enter into a new settlement but it would be a contract that could only be enforced in state court, not in federal court. We went down to the wire on these and other issues. The suburbs made a few concessions regarding the notice they would have to give to opt out and told us that the wealthiest area—Ladue—insisted on leaving almost immediately. We reluctantly agreed on Ladue, which I described as a "little citadel of white privilege" in the *Post-Dispatch*. None of the other districts opted out in 1999 or since. I also got Bill Clay to call Jay Nixon to read him a little lecture on the Constitution, and Jay finally agreed that we could sue for any breach in the federal court. Finally on January 6 we had an agreement, which we announced to the public at the Yeatman School (the school attended in the 1970s by the Liddell children) the next day.

There was one more hurdle to surmount. As stated above, voter approval was needed for a two-thirds of a cent increase in the city sales tax to finance school improvements in St. Louis. Dianne Piche and I had negotiated a substantially revised program in 1998 to replace the unsuccessful one in the original agreement. This one relied on providing more professional development for teachers, using proven learning strategies in the early grades, holding schools accountable for student progress, and reconstituting or closing them when they failed. But these improvements were no guarantee of success on the referendum. In prior efforts to raise taxes, white opposition had often overcome black support, sending the levies down to defeat.

This time, however, Bill Danforth and the business community were taking no chances. They hired a public relations company to mount an ad campaign for the referendum and I worked with them on the messages. The campaign had to be suspended during the last week because a papal visit to St. Louis pushed everything else out of the media. In a delusional state I had thought that perhaps we could get Pope John Paul to pronounce some words that might help our chances—maybe something like "suffer the little children." I called a friend who was in charge of domestic affairs for the U.S. Catholic Conference. Without laughing at me he patiently explained that the pope's speeches had been meticulously scripted for months and that not a word could be added or changed at such a late date.

We won anyway. On February 2, the voters approved the sales tax increase by an almost 2–1 vote, with majorities in both the white and African-American communities. We then had a "fairness" hearing in federal court, a process by which the judge could give the community an opportunity to comment on the settlement and assure himself that the agreement was fair to the class of children we represented. By this time Judge Gunn had died and Judge Limbaugh presided over the hearing. On March 12, Limbaugh approved the agreement and entered it as a court order. "Rarely, if ever, in school desegregation cases . . . have government entities and the public shown such amazing support for a settlement," Limbaugh said.

This was true. In the nineteenth century, Missouri had been the site of the Dred Scott case, in which the Supreme Court decreed that a black man had no rights a white man was obliged to respect, and the state legislature made the teaching of black people a criminal act. In the twentieth century, Missouri embraced racial segregation in the public schools long after the Supreme Court had declared it unconstitutional. In the '80s, our efforts to bring about desegregation evoked ugly expressions of prejudice from public officials and private citizens. But fifteen years later, people had come to terms with a new reality. Some people still feared contact with people of another race, but by now many had experienced it in the schools and workplace and had come to accept, and in some cases even welcome, such interaction. Public officials had come to recognize that the old order had passed. As the Court noted, Attorney General Jay Nixon, who had fought desegregation until the bitter end, "accepted blame on behalf of the state and apologized for this inequity."

In the end, the leadership of a relative handful of people made an important difference. I have never understood why the business leadership of so many cities appears indifferent to the miseducation of so many students. Ill-prepared generations of young people cannot be good for the business climate of a community. Yet in 1991 in St. Louis, the head of a major corporation had written to the judge suggesting he terminate the case because of the embarrassment caused by having city schools regulated by federal courts. The letter did not mention any embarrassment that might be caused by the dreadful condition of the schools or what the court might do to change this. All of this was changed by Bill Danforth's involvement in the case, which persuaded the leaders of Civic Progress—the business establishment's civic association—to take a more positive interest in the case.

It was also very helpful to have a newspaper, the *St. Louis Post-Dispatch*, that was ready to devote ample space on its news and editorial pages to bringing information and thoughtful views about public education to the community. Bill Freivogel, an editorial page editor for most of the period, persevered in the effort to promote public understanding, better education, and racial reconciliation.

(Interestingly, in Fort Wayne, another successful case I had in the 1990s, business and journalistic leadership were key elements. Ian Rolland, head of a very large insurance company with headquarters in Fort Wayne, backed our litigation because of his dedication to education for poor children, though he had to endure nasty attacks from some people in the community. Larry Hayes, editorial page editor of the *Fort Wayne Journal Gazette*, kept the equal opportunity issues before the public. These two, along with Helen Brown, a leader in the African-American community, exercised a steady moral force for change. In the end a narrow-minded school board and superintendent were replaced by more capable and progressive people and the schools were desegregated and significantly improved.)

Most important in St. Louis, leadership was provided by community people—by Minnie Liddell and Dr. James DeClue, a longtime NAACP leader, and by a cadre of organization leaders, civil rights activists, and educators, who took ownership of the agreement and agreed to monitor it and make sure that it was carried out.

St. Louis has not reached nirvana. While the interdistrict program continues to turn out capable students who go on to college and while a few city schools have made notable progress since the new agreement, the city still struggles in its efforts to attract strong educational leadership and qualified teachers. But I have to think that, if one more Supreme Court justice in the Detroit case had exhibited the courage to support a metropolitan school desegregation remedy, more cities would have been able to follow the St. Louis model and the nation would by now be farther along the way toward equal educational opportunity.

School Reform

As I became more deeply involved in the dynamics of public schools through my cases in St. Louis, Cincinnati, and Fort Wayne, I reflected on the question of what makes school desegregation a successful strategy in communities where it has produced positive results. The answers were not very complicated. In most places, the schools that were desegregated were predominantly middle class. Parents and teachers in these schools had generally high expectations of their students. While that might not have been true initially of lower-income students of color who were entering the school pursuant to a desegregation plan, unless there was rigid tracking in the school (in which students were locked in low-ability classes in which little was taught and little expected), soon there would be higher expectations of students of color, too. If the expectations were high, students would be tested on whether their academic performance was at high levels. And, if significant numbers of children were falling short, attention turned to principals and teachers. If the educators were not performing well, parents were prepared to replace them.

These of course were not the conditions that existed in poor, racially isolated schools. There the expectations were often very low. Children were not expected to succeed and were often praised for inadequate work. And while many parents wanted a good education for their children, they lacked the clout to deal with inadequate leadership and bad teaching.

Since desegregation efforts were beginning to wane during the increasingly conservative 1980s, I began thinking about whether these conditions for academic success could be replicated in racially isolated schools. For all kinds of reasons, segregation was not a desirable alternative. But if the best that could be done was to improve the learning environment in poor and racially isolated schools, it was absolutely critical to take the necessary initiatives.

I discovered that this analysis of what was needed paralleled in many ways the thinking of people involved in school reform—a movement that focused on changing the educational environment in inner-city schools. In 1987, I was recruited by David Hornbeck to help the Council of Chief State School Officers draft a model proposal for the education of at-risk children. Hornbeck at the time was the state superintendent of schools for Maryland and the president of the council, which was the national trade association of state commissioners and superintendents. He was, I came to learn, something of a visionary. He had advanced degrees in education, law, and theology. But his strong point was not his academic erudition—it was an ability to see the education problem whole and to put forward a set of principles designed to make public schools work for poor children.

Working with a small advisory committee, we were able to put together the elements of a policy that all states could use to improve opportunity for the many students at risk of educational failure. It included a heavy investment in preschool programs for poor children and in reading strategies in the early grades. The report also outlined the rudimentary elements of an accountability system, giving parents the right to opt out of schools that persistently failed and giving states the authority and responsibility to intervene to restructure such schools.

In November 1987 all the state superintendents convened in Asheville, North Carolina, for their annual meeting. The agenda included approval of the new policy for at-risk students which Education Week termed "a bold proposal." Hornbeck invited me to the meeting but I was asked to stay in the background, lest some of the more conservative state superintendents discover that the chief adviser on the project was a civil rights activist. I did attend a luncheon at which the speaker was Arkansas Governor Bill Clinton, already a leading advocate for education reform. This was only a few months after I had met him for the first time during the battle over the Bork nomination. At the meeting of the chief state school officers, he spoke eloquently and persuasively, and without any visible notes, about the urgent need to make public schools work for poor children. By the time he was finished, I was convinced that Clinton should be our next president. The Hornbeck proposal was adopted and helped influence the course of public school reform in states around the country over the next few years.

In 1990, Hornbeck undertook a much more ambitious venture. He helped put together a commission consisting of twenty-eight educators, child advocates, and researchers to assess how economically disadvantaged children were being served by Title 1 of the Elementary and Secondary Education Act of 1965, the largest program of federal assistance to public schools. The working hypothesis of the commission was that, although Title 1 (then called Chapter 1) had contributed to educational gains for poor children over its twenty-five-year history, it was in need of a major overhaul and wasn't doing enough for children.

I was asked, along with my colleague Dianne Piche, who had become the principal associate in my law firm after serving an internship in my program at Catholic University Law School, to serve as counsel to the new commission to help draft new proposals and to make the case for reform. It was an assignment I undertook with enthusiasm. The Commission on Chapter 1, as it was called, had some extraordinarily thoughtful and creative people. A few of them were women I had known for years—Cindy Brown, who worked for the Chief State School Officers, had been a civil rights official in the Carter administration, and Phyllis McClure, who had worked for me at the Civil Rights Commission in the 1960s and who now was the education expert for the NAACP Legal Defense Fund. But others were new to me—among them, Kati Haycock, who emerged as a leader of the reform movement with an ability to muster research to demonstrate both the need and the possibilities and a passion for fairness to poor children, and Bob Slavin, a Johns Hopkins educator who had put together reading strategies for the early grades that were being adopted all over the country.

A broad consensus that federal policy needed to be fixed, emerged early in our deliberations. When enacted in 1965, Title 1, a part of the Elementary and Secondary Education Act, was an adornment of the Great Society's aim to help the disadvantaged and twenty-five years later it was a hardy survivor of the programs of that time. The legislation had brought needed federal dollars to schools in the poorest areas of the nation, particularly parts of the South. Although federal assistance still was only about 7 percent of overall educational expenditures in some of the poorest districts, it accounted for as much as 25 to 30 percent of the budget. And, once some elemental controls were imposed on the use of the money, children began to make progress.

But over time, large fissures in the federal policy began to appear. The program was run on the same set of notions that had come to dominate urban education—that little could be expected of poor and minority children, and that the task was to give them a "basic" education, while their more affluent peers were learning higher-level skills that would prepare them for work in a post-industrial society. Title 1 had evolved into a new bureaucracy with children being pulled out of regular classrooms for remedial work. In sum, despite the mandate of *Brown v. Board of Education* that dual systems of education were to be eliminated, a new dual system had arisen in almost all states. Like the old systems, the new one consisted of a lower track populated in the main by children of color and poor children. They received a second class education while most others had access to real opportunity.

The defects of these state-run systems of public education were multiple. Wealthy districts wanted to preserve their advantages—low taxes and high revenues based on wealthy property bases—even at the expense of poor education for the most disadvantaged. Teachers' unions wanted to protect the tenure of even those who were not competent, and refused to agree to merit pay for those who took on the greatest challenges. Administrators presided over rigid and unaccountable bureaucracies. Racial bias lurked beneath the surface. And children had few advocates.

While we were largely in agreement on the diagnosis of what was wrong and on the need for a major overhaul of Title 1, coming up with a workable proposal was going to be a major challenge. I don't remember whose idea it was, but we smartly decided to constitute our group as a kind of legislative committee and to subject ourselves to the same discipline that members of Congress would undergo by drafting specific legislative language and seeking a consensus among ourselves. In June 1991, Dianne and I as counsel to the Chapter I Commission began preparing drafts for the commission, which were reviewed in detail and revised.

This process forced us to focus on how specific provisions would work, how the pieces fit together, and whether our proposals were based on the best evidence available. While more difficult than simply seeking agreement on broad principles, when we were done we could have much more confidence that we were not concealing major problems and that our prescriptions might actually do some good.

After almost eighteen months of work, we reached agreement on a proposed new Title 1 with explanatory and supporting text. Given the diversity of our group, in both our backgrounds and the roles we played in education, from classrooms to state boards of education and universities, I found the degree of consensus we reached quite amazing. Only two members of the twenty-eight-member commission were in fundamental disagreement with the final product.

The keystone of the report was a central finding that there is compelling evidence, based on social science research, that all children, regardless of economic circumstances in which they are born and live, can learn and that virtually all have the capacity to acquire high-level knowledge and skills that will enable them to participate fully in the economic and political life of the nation. From that finding flowed the recommendation that high standards should be set by states for all children, with content standards defining what they should know and performance standards defining what constitutes proficiency at particular grade levels. If all children can learn, we concluded, it also follows that school officials should be held accountable for student progress. Accountability should focus not as it had on the expenditure of dollars, a system that had the perverse effect of withdrawing money from schools that were succeeding, but on results, providing rewards and incentives to schools where students were making progress and taking strong steps to deal with schools that persistently failed.

The report also pointed to the importance of good assessments as the means for linking high standards with determinations of student progress for purposes of accountability. Many states and districts still relied on norm-referenced testing, which compared students to each other rather than providing a picture of what they know and can do. Many also relied solely on multiple-choice, fill-in-the-bubble tests that provided no measure of the reasoning abilities of students. The commission called for the adoption of assessments that provided more accurate measures of skills that were emerging around the country, assessments that would gauge not rote learning but a student's ability to think analytically and creatively.

There was much more in the report, including a call to invest more in the recruitment and professional development of teachers, principals, and other adults in the school; and the integration into schools of health and social service support, so that learning is not impaired by nutritional or health deficiencies. Specific problems were addressed, such as the need for much greater effort to help children with limited English proficiency, a problem exacerbated by the notion of some local officials that these children, although mostly poor and Title 1–eligible, should be able to draw only on the much smaller pot of money available for bilingual education. We also sought greater matching of the allocation of funds to the areas of greatest need, a tricky challenge since Title 1 had survived so long in part because every member of Congress had education money flowing to his or her district.

When the commission's report was published in December 1992, we immediately began lobbying for its inclusion in the Clinton administration's proposal for reauthorization of Title 1, which was scheduled for 1994. We were helped in this effort by the fact that one commission member—Mike Smith—had been named deputy secretary of Education and was a strong supporter of the proposed reforms. Amazingly, considering the complexity of the legislation, the administration adopted the great bulk of our work in its own proposal. I then decided that I would work with members of the group to lobby a new Title 1 through Congress.

As had been the case with every important civil rights measure, our leader in the Senate was Ted Kennedy, who chaired the education committee at this time. In the House, George Miller, a longtime congressman from San Francisco who had a deep commitment to educational opportunity for poor children, provided intellectual energy and passion. For the most part, we found that we were able to fly under the radar in moving the bill forward. Most Republicans favored block grants to the states and waivers of requirements, ideas that were antithetical to the principle that school authorities should be held accountable for student progress. But many were also amenable to separate legislation that would make accountability a part of reform. Many also favored federal vouchers for private schools, but garnered little support for them. Most suburban families were satisfied with the education their children were receiving in advantaged public schools and, as evidenced by their negative votes on several state referenda proposing vouchers, saw little need for federal aid to a private school program.

Among the education organizations that lobbied on school legislation —associations of school superintendents and principals, teachers' unions, the national PTA, and others—there was generally little interest either pro or con in reform, I think because most did not take the notion that they might be held accountable for their performance seriously at that time. With some exceptions, the dominant interest of these groups was in increasing federal appropriations, and their motto seemed to be Oliver Twist's "please, sir, I want some more."

In this environment we were able to make progress in moving the bill through Congress. But we encountered one major obstacle—the unwillingness of many legislators to support what were called "opportunity to learn" standards. The problem grew out of extraordinary inequities that existed in many states in the distribution of education resources to school districts. The source of the problem was that, in almost all states, public education was financed through local property taxes. Ordinarily, the areas with the greatest property wealth were suburban districts that served affluent families. Those with the smallest property base were often urban and rural areas with large proportions of poor and minority children. This meant that wealthy suburban areas could often support public schools at a much higher level than their urban and rural counterparts, and with lower property taxes.

While states could redress this situation by changing the basis of funding public education or by ensuring that state education payments compensate for the inequitability of local financing, few have done so. In 1973, the Supreme Court had decided by a 5–4 vote that, even where there were gross disparities in school finances between districts where the wealthy lived and those where poor and minority children lived, there was no denial of the right to equal protection of the laws under the Constitution. In the 1980s, lawyers for children began suits in state courts invoking state constitutional provisions that called for equity or adequacy in public education. A few of these suits were successful, but often judicial victories were followed by lengthy wrangling in state legislatures that delayed any real relief to poor areas. In 1991, Congressman Augustus Hawkins of California, who was then chairman of the House Committee on Education and Labor, asked Dianne Piche and me to conduct a study of state inequities as they related to Title 1.

In our report, *Shortchanging Children*, published by the House Labor and Education Committee, we found that the generally held belief that Title 1 met the special needs of disadvantaged children was not accurate. Title 1 was built on the fiction that Congress was providing federal education dollars on a level playing field provided by state and local funding. In fact, the playing field was anything but level. In a wealthy community like Princeton, New Jersey, we discovered that multiple special needs of poor or disabled students or English language learners could be addressed adequately out of local resources, whereas in depressed urban areas like Camden or Trenton, Title 1 could help meet only one or two of the multiple needs in the student population. The answer, we thought, was not to treat the issue as just one of dollars but to identify the key educational needs and call upon states to meet them in an equitable way.

That was what was meant in proposals for "opportunity to learn" standards. Local school districts were already required by Title 1 to ensure comparability in the offerings of schools within their districts. The comparability requirement could be extended to require states to ensure equity in the provision of services from district to district. Alternatively, we suggested that Congress could establish an "adequacy" requirement calling upon states to ensure that resources would be provided to enable districts to meet their fundamental obligations under the act—including that students are taught by highly qualified teachers, that curriculum and materials are geared to enabling students to meet standards, that class sizes are reasonable, and that counseling is provided.

Neither of these proposals made headway. Jack Jennings, a long-time education committee staffer for the House Labor and Education Committee with a good deal of political savvy, pointed out to me that Congress was now dominated by suburban interests. Obviously, these interests would not be pleased by measures that either would raise their taxes to support the education of children elsewhere in the state or cut services in their districts to ensure that they were provided more equitably. Fearing that an impasse was looming, I turned to the Leadership Conference on Civil Rights. I had not done so earlier for a couple of reasons. Some of the Leadership Conference member groups had strong constituencies in suburban areas and might not support equalization. Other civil rights groups thought that testing was the major problem in education and were attacking tests in the courts. My view was that, while bad testing should be challenged, the major harm being done to children was not by testing which revealed, however imperfectly, the state of their progress, but by educational neglect or miseducation which should be attacked through school reform measures.

Despite the possible opposition I knew I might encounter, I decided to make my case before the Leadership Conference. In fact, the opposition came from an unexpected source. On the day I was scheduled to make my proposal to the Executive Committee, Jane O'Grady, the lobbyist for the AFL-CIO, took me aside and suggested I defer my presentation. The proposal would be opposed, she said, by the American Federation of Teachers (AFT) and, since the Leadership Conference operated by consensus, we would not be able to go forward.

I was surprised for a couple of reasons. The AFT represented teachers in big cities who would clearly benefit from fiscal reforms that would direct more resources their way. In addition, the union was then led by Albert Shanker, who did not ordinarily shrink from controversy. (In Woody Allen's film *Sleepers*, the protagonist who has been preserved cryogenically after his death is brought back to life fifty years into the new millennium. He discovers that the world has been destroyed and is gradually being rebuilt by a handful of survivors. He asks how this happened. "We don't know for sure," is the reply, "but we understand that someone named Albert Shanker got hold of a nuclear device.")

I scheduled a meeting with Shanker to find out what his reasoning was. He told me that he had learned a lesson from the California experience with fiscal reform. In 1971, the California State Supreme Court decided that the state constitution required strong equalization measures in the financing of schools. Legislation was adopted to spur increases in expenditures in property-poor districts while restraining them in property-wealthy districts. High-revenue districts then were hurt by several developments, including declines in enrollment. In 1978, California approved a statewide referendum—Proposition 13—which severely limited the amounts of money that could be collected through property taxes. The result was that, while equity improved, the state's tax collections declined steeply and California became a state that did not appear to care much about the public education of children.

The lesson he drew from this experience, Shanker told me, was that affluent parents demanded a superior education for their children and that this was the price that he and others had to pay to retain adequate support for public education. I never heard Shanker offer this analysis in public and I can understand why. To the extent his analysis is correct, it is a depressing commentary on the commitment of Americans to equality of opportunity for all the nation's children.

In the end, the best we were able to do was to prod the states to provide more resources to disadvantaged students. We secured the insertion of a provision stating that, in the required State Title 1 plan, each state should describe the steps it would take to help local districts and schools develop the capacity to carry out their obligations (such as providing high-quality teachers and up-to-date curriculum material) under the act. It was something less than a firm enforceable requirement for equity but it did at least state a federal policy.

When the bill became a law in October 1994, our Citizens' Commission decided to give priority to monitoring its implementation. The record of the Clinton administration was decidedly a spotty one. For one thing, Dick Riley, the secretary of Education, while a wise and caring person, presided over a department that had become less than vigorous in enforcing laws and policies seeking equality of opportunity. On several occasions when I went to the department to lobby for strong enforcement, I was told by an assistant secretary or other high-ranking official that I did not understand the limitations on the agency.

One tale, recounted several times, was of how the department had sought to enforce desegregation in Chicago in the 1960s and was rebuffed by President Johnson. It was a situation I knew in detail since I had been on the scene. The cabinet Department of Health, Education, and Welfare (which during the Carter administration was split into separate departments for Health and Human Services, and for Education) had responded to a complaint about segregation in Chicago public schools. The complaint came at a time when the Supreme Court had not yet ruled in a Northern school desegregation case and the governing constitutional principles were not yet clear. Moreover, HEW took on the most powerful mayor in the nation, Richard Daley, and a powerful senator, Minority Leader Everett Dirksen, at a time when Lyndon Johnson needed the help of both in order to enact his program. It was, I told the officials at the department, like deciding to fight for the heavyweight championship without having fought any preliminary bouts.

It was also interesting that, while the Chicago debacle had become lore at the Education Department, there was virtually no mention of how school desegregation had come about throughout the South due to the determination and courage of John Gardner, Johnson's secretary of HEW, who threatened to withhold Title 1 money from any district that refused to desegregate its schools. Nevertheless (and although I wrote a detailed memo to Education Department officials trying to set the historical record straight), a kind of culture of nonenforcement malaise had enveloped the agency and people were regularly told that federal officials would provide technical assistance, not carry out its enforcement responsibilities.

The same lack of political will was reflected in the department's giving in to an Iowa governor who urged that each school district be allowed to develop its own standards and that these be used instead of a uniform set of state standards. This was clearly contrary to the language of the statute and it threatened to recreate the very situation we were trying to eliminate—one type of education for the affluent children of suburban Bloomfield Hills or Grosse Pointe, Michigan, and another for the poor and minority children of inner-city Detroit. Fortunately, this precedent was not extended.

In defense of the Clinton administration it may be said that the first years of implementation were largely a gearing up period with states developing and putting in place their performance, assessment, and accountability standards. It is also a fact of life that, one month after passage of Clinton's bill, the Republicans captured the House, and the administration then had to deal with the reality of Newt Gingrich and his cohorts who loathed the very idea of a Department of Education.

But it is also a fact that, after the 1994 Congressional defeat, the administration changed its tactics on many fronts. Now, Clinton rarely spoke in the same moving and eloquent terms about providing opportunities for disadvantaged children that had drawn me to him in the first place. He did some courageous things in civil rights, such as rejecting conservative staff advice in order to save affirmative action after a 1994 Supreme Court defeat, but he seemed no longer to aspire to be the education president; he did not provide inspirational leadership for young people to enter the field of teaching. Instead, Clinton embarked on short-term political hits. One was urging the adoption of school uniforms. Later, he was attracted by Chicago's policy of ending "social promotions," i.e., holding students back if they had not acquired the reading and math skills that were prescribed for their grade level. The fact was that policies of social promotion or leaving students back are both bad medicine. The former leads to students being graduated without having acquired the skills needed for them to become productive citizens. As for the latter, research shows that it leads to students dropping out of school. Instead of this Hobson's choice the better answer is to focus heavy resources on seeing that children are prepared to move forward. It took about four visits to the White House for me and civil rights colleagues to persuade Clinton's aides that pushing a campaign against social promotion would jeopardize the administration's reform efforts.

These were hardly halcyon days for the president. Late in the Clinton administration, two of his senior aides, Chris Edley and Maria Echeveste, became engaged. The Clintons decided to throw them a party at the White House. I was one of about seventy-five people privileged to attend. When it came time for the hosts to say a few words, Hillary Clinton made a gracious speech. She was followed by her husband, who said with a smile, "I can't believe this affair was going on in the White House right under my nose and I knew nothing about it." I looked around the room to find that everyone had a straight face. When the party was over I walked out with my friend Rabbi David Saperstein and asked him what he made of Clinton's statement. "I think it is just an extreme example of his ability to compartmentalize," David said.

Around the nation the picture of progress under school reform was varied. The Citizens' Commission decided to examine the operation of Title 1 in Alabama in both urban and rural areas. I went south to Birmingham, Montgomery, and Selma in 1999, places I had not visited since the 1960s. In a meeting with the state superintendent of schools, Ed Richardson, and his top aides, I was accused of holding an outdated Yankee view of Alabama. The facts were that Alabama, like other Southern states, had changed in its race relations in important ways. African Americans had been elected to public office in Alabama and much overt discrimination had been eliminated. But, as our report documented, Alabama schools were in terrible shape. A handful of schools in the communities we studied (including one in Gadsden named after a civil rights advocate, Oscar Adams, who had become a judge) were making good progress with the aid of Title 1 funds. But they were the exception rather than the rule.

Alabama, a very poor state, did not and does not make even a respectable effort to use the resources it has to support public education. The governor at the time of my visit was Don Siegelman, whom I had known in 1970 when, as a college student at the University of Alabama, he had served as a campaign worker with Allard Lowenstein. It felt strange meeting with him in the state capital in the cradle of the old Confederacy and answering his questions about where certain liberals he had met in those years had ended up. Siegelman wanted to strengthen the public schools, but the only source of increased revenue he thought might be practicable was the state lottery. His proposal had to go before the voters and was defeated by a concerted effort of fundamentalist church leaders who viewed gambling as a sin. (In 2003, a newly elected, very conservative Republican governor took a look at the schools and was appalled. He proposed a major tax increase. This, too, was defeated by the voters, including a substantial number of poor and minority citizens who would have benefited. Although the newspaper editors I met on my trip were strong advocates for reform, there has just not been enough leadership to carry the day.)

In other places during the 1990s, federal and state reform brought real change to the schools. In San Antonio and El Paso, the Texas reform program, bolstered by local education leaders, produced not just a handful of poor schools that made major advances, but actual clusters of them. The program was instituted by Governor Ann Richards and Democrats, but, interestingly, was carried on by then-Governor George W. Bush. In Kentucky, a distinguished citizens' committee, a coalition of local superintendents and a former governor of the state banded together to seek reform in the courts and in the state legislature. Their legal victories called for both fiscal and structural reform and were followed by monitoring and implementation efforts that converted some of the lowest achieving schools into high performers. In New York City, creative educators in an East Harlem community district established schools that became a model for the state and nation, and a school finance suit brought by a skilled lawyer, Michael Rebell, *Campaign for Fiscal Equity v. Pataki,* resulted in a state court order requiring state officers to furnish adequate education for all children and to provide the resources needed to reach the goal.

I see the picture of public school reform in the 1990s as a very mixed one. The most important variable was leadership at every level—from governors to local citizens' committees and school superintendents. Where there was a default in leadership, as in Alabama and California, schools continued to decay. Where communities were galvanized to support their schools, as in St. Louis, Texas, and Kentucky, students were the beneficiaries. In the new century, leadership remains the key to the survival of the public school system as the instrument for opportunity and the balance wheel of our democracy.

Beachheads

Ashcroft and Hatch

G rowing up during the New Deal, I became a believer in a strong presidency and in the affirmative role of the federal government in helping people in need. With the advent of the McCarthy era in the '50s, I came to the sobering understanding that there was an ugly side to government. Some officials, elected and appointed, were not motivated by a desire for public service but by a thirst for power. And, having attained power, they sometimes used it to subjugate and humiliate those who did not have the ability to fight back. Nor did these officials feel constrained to play by the rules. They engaged in unethical behavior and lied when it served their purposes. Certainly McCarthy himself fit that description, but there have been others as well whom I have observed.

Still, I had thought that the McCarthy period was a momentary aberration in the advance of American democracy and that once it ended we would resume progress under principled leaders. Over the past three decades, the evidence supporting that proposition has hardly been overwhelming. Lately I think that the basis for concern has deepened.

It was my misfortune, along with others, to begin the millennium with the battle over the confirmation of John Ashcroft as attorney general in the administration of George W. Bush. The confirmation fight brought to the fore two of the prime practitioners of the current brand of debased politics—Ashcroft himself and Senator Orrin Hatch.

When President Bush nominated Ashcroft, he shocked many people who had been appalled by Ashcroft's right-wing voting record in the Senate and his brief hard-right campaign for the presidency. The nomination seemed at odds with Bush's promise of conciliatory and compassionate approaches to problems and with the apparent political realities surrounding his narrow victory. As the battle-lines formed, I decided that my own contribution would be to document Ashcroft's conduct in and out of court as Missouri attorney general from 1976 to 1985, as candidate for governor in 1984, and later as governor from 1985 to 1993 during the St. Louis school litigation.

Going back into my records I remembered how defiant and recalcitrant John Ashcroft had been. In 1980, the Court of Appeals, recognizing the limitations of a school desegregation plan that applied to the city of St. Louis alone, encouraged the parties to the case to consider a voluntary plan that would include the largely white suburbs of St. Louis County. Ashcroft resisted and forbade the State Education Department to do anything because, he said, "the attorney general was running the show."

Indeed, Attorney General Ashcroft neglected few details in his resistance. When in 1981 the Court appointed Susan Uchitelle, an employee of Missouri's Department of Education, as interim director of the committee devising a voluntary plan, the State objected strenuously. Meanwhile, a state education official phoned Ms. Uchitelle to relay a threat from Mr. Ashcroft that, if she chose to remain in her court-appointed job, she would have to resign from her state job and "would never receive another appointment or job from (the state)." (As noted in the last chapter, Ms. Uchitelle stayed and provided able leadership to the effort.) Even without knowledge of this threat of retaliation, the district judge, a former congressman named William Hungate, concluded at one point that "the State has, as a matter of deliberate policy, decided to defy the authority of [this] Court" and that it had resorted to "extraordinary machinations" to resist dismantling the dual-race school system.

Late in 1982 all the parties came to the bargaining table and, over a period of months, hammered out a settlement that everyone except the State of Missouri supported. Ashcroft rejected the agreement almost in its entirety, including provisions that dealt with improvement of black schools, not desegregation, and unsuccessfully sought to overturn the agreement in the Federal Court of Appeals and the U.S. Supreme Court. Even after all his appeals had failed, Ashcroft continued to obstruct implementation of the settlement. His tactics led Judge Hungate to conclude in 1984 that "if it were not for the State of Missouri and its feckless appeals, perhaps none of us would be here at this time . . . The compromise settlement was made possible through the cooperation of all parties but the State, which, through opposition and repeated appeals, has delayed implementation of a remedial plan designed to remove the last remaining vestiges of school segregation for which the State . . . remains responsible."

In challenging and risking the ire of the court in 1984, Ashcroft had other fish to fry. He was simultaneously running in the Republican primary for governor, where he was pitted against Gene McNary, the county executive of St. Louis County, who also was an adamant opponent of desegregation. Toward the end of a close and nasty campaign in which the candidates sought to outdo themselves in their opposition to desegregation, Ashcroft ran a decisive television commercial, later dubbed the McFlip-Flop ad. The commercial accused McNary of being soft in his opposition to desegregation, by indicating previously that he could live with a voluntary plan if all the suburban districts accepted it. According to the *St. Louis Post-Dispatch*, this ad turned the tide for Ashcroft in a race in which the newspaper previously said the opponents were "exploiting and encouraging the worst racist sentiments that exist in the state."

Once elected governor in 1984, Ashcroft did not cease his efforts to impede school desegregation in St. Louis. As late as 1989 and 1990, the State's actions moved Judge Steven Limbaugh, ordinarily the mildest of judges in his manner and action, to make the following observations in court opinions:

"It appears to this Court that the extremely antagonistic nature of recent filings indicates that the counsel for the State is ignoring the real objectives of this case—a better education for city students. . . ."

He added, the State's litigation tactics were only serving to "waste the Court's time and taxpayer's money."

And, the State had resorted to "factual inaccuracies, statistical distortions and insipid remarks regarding the Court's handling of this case."

Although Ashcroft by this time had moved from the position of attorney general to governor, he was ultimately responsible for the State's conduct in the case.

Judge Limbaugh warned the State to "desist in filing further motions grounded in rumor and unsubstantiated allegations of wrongdoing." He added that the State in recent years had even resorted to "veiled threats" toward the Court in its effort to thwart implementation of the remedy.

Having completed my review, with assistance from researchers at People for the American Way, I prepared a written statement to file with the Senate Judiciary Committee, which was considering the Ashcroft nomination. After I submitted the statement, I learned that Senator Kennedy had reviewed it, concluded that it was highly relevant to the proceedings, and desired that I be asked to testify in person.

It was only later that I learned the full story of what then transpired. Some background is necessary. As I have recounted, in my years working on civil rights legislation I frequently dealt with Senator Orrin Hatch as a principal adversary. Our encounters were marked by strong substantive differences but were largely without personal rancor. In 1993, however, things changed. That was the year that a Hatch staff member, Sharon Prost, who was on the Judiciary Committee, became embroiled in a battle with her ex-husband, Kenneth Greene, over custody of their two children, then seven and three. The Superior Court judge in the case was my wife, Harriett R. Taylor.

In years past, when, as one of the deans of the matrimonial bar in Washington put it, the prevailing wisdom was that a mother belonged in the kitchen, not the workplace, there would have been an automatic presumption in favor of the woman in a custody dispute. It was assumed that young children naturally belonged in the more nurturing arms of their mothers.

But such stereotypes fell by the wayside with the women's rights movement, and the legal presumption was abolished, leaving judges to decide without presuppositions what custody arrangement was in the best interest of the child. After a twelve-day trial in 1994, Harriett decided that it was the father, Greene, who best "prioritized the care and well-being" of the two children and she awarded custody to him, with liberal visiting rights for the mother, Prost. In a lengthy written opinion, Harriett praised both parents but pointed to numerous instances in which Prost had put her work ahead of the other demands of her life. One instance I recall is of Prost attending one of her children's birthday parties but sitting in the corner reading work memos.

Hatch was incensed by the decision. He somehow decided that it was an indictment of the Senate Child Care Center (though of course it was not) and induced some of his colleagues to protest the decision on that basis. He put pressure on women's right groups that had business before his committee to file friend-of-the-court briefs supporting an appeal. Good lawyers for these groups resisted the pressure, understanding that the decision was fully consistent with the movement for equality among women. But one group, headed by an old friend of mine and Harriett's, capitulated and filed a brief without ever seeing the record in the case.

Prost's appeals were all rejected and Harriett's ruling was implemented. But even after her lawyer had left the case, Prost would not let it go, filing her own motions and stalking my wife outside the courtroom seeking to reargue her case in person. I also learned that Hatch had told people that he was sure I had influenced Harriett to decide as she did because of my dislike for him. Anyone who knew Harriett Taylor would appreciate what a ludicrous idea that was. She was a judge who loved her work, whose greatest desire was to apply the law fairly in ways that would be helpful to people. She rejected suggestions that she allow her name to be submitted for membership on more prestigious courts like the federal district court or the District Court of Appeals because she wanted to continue to deal on a daily basis with real people and their real problems in the District of Columbia. She would not have delegated her duty or allowed herself to be influenced by me or anyone else.

Some time later I learned that Hatch had gone far beyond anything I or anyone else imagined in his quest for vengeance on the Prost decision. Judges on the Superior Court are nominated by the president and confirmed by the Senate. After serving a fifteen-year term, they may apply for reappointment. A judicial tenure commission reviews their service, conducting many interviews. If, at the end, the judge is rated as having been highly qualified, he or she is automatically reappointed without the need for a new vote. Harriett had been nominated in 1979 by Jimmy Carter and confirmed by the Senate. In 1994, the judicial tenure commission had reviewed her service and found her highly qualified. Almost everyone familiar with her work gave her rave reviews, and she began a new fifteen-year term.

I found out about a year later that Hatch had sought to nullify her appointment. He drafted a piece of legislation that would change the method of reappointing judges and he made it retroactive to the day before Harriett's reappointment. This would have had the effect of removing her from office pending confirmation through the new process, which he undoubtedly felt he could block. He spoke to a couple of members of the House of Representatives and got them to agree to cosponsor his legislation. While I do not know this for sure, I do not believe he explained to them what he was really trying to accomplish. Ultimately, he was talked out of proceeding with his plan by a Republican colleague who made him understand how ugly and inappropriate his vendetta would appear if it were made public. The then-chief judge of the Superior Court told Harriett and me details about the episode but asked us not to reveal it for fear that Hatch would direct retaliatory action against the court. Harriett died in 1997 without ever speaking publicly about the incident and I have not said anything until now. But it seems to me that there is no longer any reason to remain silent and that, in this memoir about government and public affairs, it is important for people to know not only about the heights that can be attained in this work but also the depths to which people can sink in pursuing base objectives. Since this incident, I have continued to cross paths with Senator Hatch, as in the Ashcroft nomination, but I have never felt tempted to confront him about his efforts to remove Harriett from the bench. It is unlikely he would be repentant.

Returning now to the Ashcroft nomination, when Kennedy requested that I be invited to testify in person on Ashcroft's record in St. Louis, it came during the short period after the November 2000 election when the Democrats retained control of the Senate. Senator Patrick Leahy was chairman of the Judiciary Committee when I learned that Senator Hatch was vehemently objecting to my appearance as a witness. It is my understanding that Senator Leahy, wishing to be conciliatory during his short reign as chairman, initially acceded to Hatch's request to exclude me. Kennedy, I am told, was more than a little upset about this. In a meeting with the other Democrats, he said that if I was not invited, he would hold his own unofficial but very public hearing to allow me to help him make a record.

Leahy changed his stance and advised Hatch that I would testify. When Ashcroft testified on his own behalf on January 16, 2001, he flat-out lied about the St. Louis case and his own role in it. He said that the State had "done nothing wrong" in St. Louis and was "found guilty of no wrong." His statement was astonishing. The courts had found that the state of Missouri had been instrumental in imposing a system of racially segregated schools and then had refused after the *Brown* decision to help dismantle the segregated system. Recognizing perhaps how absurd this claim was, Ashcroft also argued that he was not a party when the court made its findings of state wrongdoing and therefore was justified in trying to relitigate the issues. That, too, was untrue. He had been a party to the case since 1977, and the courts on numerous occasions after that date had recounted the state's constitutional misdeeds. When the court of appeals ruled on several occasions that the constitutional issues were settled, Ashcroft ignored their decisions and filed yet another appeal. Under questioning from Senator Leahy, Ashcroft corrected some but not all of his most flagrant misstatements.

When I testified as part of a panel on Thursday and Friday morning, several senators, including moderate Democrats, seemed intensely interested in what I had to say, indicating that they viewed Ashcroft's defiance of *Brown v. Board of Education* as perhaps the most egregious part of a record that included savaging the reputation of an African-American judge—Ronnie White—whom President Clinton had nominated for a federal judgeship. Interestingly, Orrin Hatch said nothing during my testimony and asked me no questions at the time. Several of my colleagues said they thought he had prudently decided not to take me on. Later, during an interview on C-SPAN, without ever identifying me by name, he told a caller that I had represented a "radical" organization in the St. Louis case. The group I represented was the NAACP.

At the end of January, Ashcroft was confirmed by a vote of 58–42, with all Republicans voting for him and all but eight Democrats voting against. The result was disappointing but not surprising. In deciding whether to confirm judicial nominations, senators have and should exercise a strong independent role. They are, after all, deciding who should hold lifetime appointments in a separate branch of government. But the president ordinarily is given a good deal more deference in determining who should serve in key roles in the executive branch. The Senate has acted only infrequently to deny the president his choice of cabinet or other high officials to work in his administration. In addition, inducing senators to oppose a former senate colleague is often difficult because personal relations have developed even among legislators who have strong substantive differences.

That latter point was hammered home when I spoke to Senator Paul Wellstone about the Ashcroft nomination and I learned he was undecided on how to vote. He cited both the leeway that should be given to the president and his relations with Ashcroft. After he reviewed the record including the testimony I sent him, he decided to vote against the nomination, saying that Ashcroft's actions in the courts on school desegregation were the central reason to oppose him.

When he took the floor of the Senate, Wellstone first acknowledged the presumption in favor of confirming any presidential nominee to the cabinet and his own friendly relations with Ashcroft. But then he said:

"I consider this to be a civil rights vote and a human rights vote. That is why I am voting 'No.'

"I will highlight Bill Taylor's testimony because I consider him to be a giant. I am proud to say he is one of my teachers. He is a real hero. He is one of those who joined Thurgood Marshall's team in the years just after the *Brown* decision to work for full implementation of *Brown versus Board of Education.*"

Then he quoted my testimony and concluded:

"I think the most troubling aspect of the Missouri school desegregation issue, to me, is that John Ashcroft consistently used his fervent opposition to the federal judge's desegregation order as a political issue in the campaign."

In my mind a fundamental qualification to serve as attorney general is to hold a respect for law. Ashcroft was contemptuous of the Constitution and the laws of the nation. As attorney general and then governor, he had taken the oath prescribed by the Constitution to uphold the laws and then dishonored it. No one had reason to suspect in January 2001 that, only a few months later, the nation would face its most severe test of whether it could protect the security of its citizens and protect their liberties at the same time. Attorney General Ashcroft has failed that test. Instead of demonstrating a willingness to discuss excruciatingly difficult issues with legislators and citizens, he has challenged the patriotism and loyalty of all who dare oppose him.

In the end, I do not believe that we need fear an Ashcroft or a Hatch ascending to the presidency with a platform that would transform our government and way of life. After all, both made a run at the presidency and were found by most people to be unappealing candidates. While both can do a lot of damage in their current positions, there is too much prosperity in the country for masses of people to rally to the kind of negative insurgency that has worked in other nations. And the business establishment has too great an interest in the status quo to embrace or tolerate radical change.

But in an age when commercialism seemingly has taken over every aspect of American life including political dialogue, our continuing drift toward the right is certainly troubling. A president may portray himself as affable and compassionate and still embrace policies that constrict opportunity for the poor, while rewarding the wealthy and that penalize people for daring to be different. In every national campaign over the last three decades, the conservative candidate has to some degree exploited racial divisions and played on economic insecurity and fears of crime. By reshaping the South into an anti–civil rights Republican stronghold, Richard Nixon was able to achieve some of these goals before his downfall. The genius of Bill Clinton was that he found politically effective ways to respond without, in most cases, compromising principle. But then he threw it all away by his unwillingness to take tough stands on judges and economic issues and by his personal conduct. All that we can confidently expect is continuing struggle on these issues for decades to come.

You Can Go Home Again

Only a few months after the unsuccessful struggle to deny Senate confirmation to Ashcroft, I received a most pleasant surprise. The president of Brooklyn College, Christoph M. Kimmich, wrote asking me if I would accept an honorary degree and serve as the commencement speaker at the graduation exercises in May. Of course, I readily accepted. In preparing my speech I thought about what a valuable institution the college had been. It had been founded in 1930 in the midst of the great economic depression with the mission of giving immigrants, largely from Eastern and Southern Europe, opportunities for higher education they would not otherwise enjoy. I entered Brooklyn College after my father decided he did not have enough money to send me to Cornell where I had been accepted. Now more than seven decades after its founding, the college is fulfilling the same mission with young people of different backgrounds—African Americans, Latinos, and Asian Americans, among others. I made this the theme of my speech along with the rewards to be found in a diverse environment if one takes advantage of it.

The *New York Times* ran a story under the headline "College Honors Man It Tried to Discredit." A few weeks later the *Times* ran a follow-up story about the rash of apologies that colleges seemed to be making that year to people they had wronged in the past. Dr. Kimmich was quoted as saying, "We're not here to apologize for history. Who are we to do so? We recognized Bill Taylor because he stands for things we value, like independence of thought and fighting for principles you believe in. He represents Brooklyn College as I think of it—and as I would like it to be." I could not have asked for a better tribute.

In the wake of this honor, my former colleagues at *Vanguard* and I have established an annual journalism award to recognize the work of a Brooklyn College student journalist who demonstrates excellence in writing about the first amendment. In a very small personal way, I regard the *Vanguard* saga as an illustration of Martin Luther King Jr.'s maxim that "the arc of history is long, but it bends toward justice."

Durban, South Africa

During my many years of civil rights work, only rarely had I become involved in issues of discrimination abroad. During the '60s, I was consulted by officials of Great Britain who were seeking to craft laws to deal with discrimination against both East and West Indians. In the '70s and '80s I went to international conferences dealing with employment discrimination and the potential use of affirmative action as a civil rights remedy. But these were sporadic involvements.

It was not that I wasn't interested. Rather, I felt that dealing with domestic civil rights issues was daunting enough and that I would not be using my time productively by trying to acquire expertise on issues elsewhere. But my views on this began to change in the '90s. The advent of globalization and the communications revolution made the world a different and smaller place. Key decisions about employment and trade policy were being made less by governments and more by multinational corporations. The economic opportunities of an American worker could be affected as much by decisions made by corporations with operations in Indonesia or Mexico as by decisions in Washington or South Carolina.

So I decided in 2000 to become part of a nongovernmental organization delegation that the Leadership Conference was sending to the World Conference on Racism, Xenophobia, and Related Forms of Intolerance, which the United Nations had scheduled in Durban, South Africa, for August 2001. The history of the UN's work in this area was in itself a cause for frustration. It was almost forty years earlier that, as a young lawyer at the Civil Rights Commission, I had been asked by the State Department to go to New York to advise the United States delegation to the UN about a proposed covenant against all forms of racial discrimination. It was an interesting experience and, surprisingly, a document was produced about a year later. Then, however, it took the United States almost three decades to ratify the covenant as a treaty. The United Nations was only now beginning to talk about the implementation of the treaty, and in practice each nation had an effective veto over any interference with its own racial policies and practices. Nevertheless, the Durban conference provided an opportunity for people in many nations to document and draw world attention to denials of civil rights.

Those of us who attended a regional preconference in Santiago, Chile, in 2000 learned about the mistreatment of the black underclass in Brazil and of indigenous peoples throughout Central and South America. At Durban, representatives from all parts of the globe came to tell stories of unspeakable acts committed against their peoples because of their race or ethnicity or tribe or caste. Dalits from India—untouchables who numbered many millions of people—spoke of the political murder of local leaders who dared to assert their rights. The Romanys (Gypsies who now live in most European countries) are maltreated wherever they go. The scourge of AIDS engulfs South Africa and the African continent and disproportionately affects the most powerless members of their society—women and children.

Unfortunately, many of these voices were drowned out in Durban by the determination of Palestinians and their Muslim supporters to turn the conference into a jihad against Israel and Jews. These protests were vehement and ugly and directed not simply toward the policies of the state of Israel, but to Jews as a people. Placards were replete with caricatures of hook-nosed Jews. Young women I knew, who worked for Jewish organizations, reported to me that they were verbally attacked. And I was somewhat shaken, too. I did not remember feeling the sting of anti-Semitism in this way since my childhood in New York in the '30s and '40s.

The whole affair was badly handled by U.S. officials. Instead of taking on the issue in a substantive way, Colin Powell's State Department withdrew the United States presence; some thought it was a move less dictated by the issue of anti-Semitism than by other concerns, such as demands for reparations. The NGO forum was allowed by the UN to become the vehicle for the anti-Jewish effort. And since the conflict had little to do with the subject of the conference, the anti-Israel advocates tried to give it relevance by reviving the discredited notion that Zionism was racism. It was a mess.

While I was in South Africa, I wanted to visit some of the great advocates for freedom and independence. So I arranged to go to the Legal Resources Centre in Johannesburg, the legal hub of the liberation struggle. There I met with George Bizos, who had served as Nelson Mandela's lawyer and whose office walls were filled with pictures and documents chronicling the effort.

The story, of course, is inspirational. A struggle for freedom that no one thought could be concluded without a bloody revolution was won through the capitulation of the oppressors.

And some of the fruits of the victory were apparent on my trip.

The newspapers and television featured black elected officials and government administrators and corporate executives. In airports, banks, business centers, hotels, I encountered black professionals and white-collar workers, briskly efficient in their jobs. At the Legal Resources Centre, a multiracial staff of lawyers and aides pursued contemporary cases.

But there is a countervailing reality. Bizos spoke to me matter-of-factly about the prevalence of unemployment and crime in Johannesburg and elsewhere. The lowest estimates of joblessness are about 40 percent. As we drove through downtown, his comments were punctuated by the sight of hundreds of men, mostly young, seeking pay for helping to park cars or vending fruit in the middle of traffic. So, where once there was oppression and apartheid, there is now political liberty often accompanied by economic deprivation.

While I was in Johannesburg I contacted Angus Gibson, a creative artist who had been responsible for planning an Apartheid Museum located between Johannesburg and Soweto. Although the museum had not yet opened to the public, he offered to take me on a tour. The museum's origins are emblematic of how things work in our contemporary capitalist world. It came into being because applicants for casino licenses in South Africa must include in their applications a proposal that will benefit the public. The winning applicant for a casino located between Johannesburg and Soweto was persuaded to include a proposal for a museum. So the Apartheid Museum was born and placed incongruously across the road from the casino.

The museum leaves a powerful impression on a visitor. The sandstone buildings have a narrow outside corridor on one side and a wide expanse with olive trees on the other, a contrast that blends with the theme of confinement and hope. The planners had borrowed from the Holocaust Museum in Washington (separate entrances for black and white visitors and the issuance of identity cards) but they also made their own statement. And, of course, the fact of liberation helps to redeem the oppression (the jail cells of political prisoners, some of whom, like Stephen Biko, died in custody, the massacres that came before).

At the end of the exhibit were recorded interviews with ordinary South Africans about how they viewed their lives today. The comments were a great mixture and, while they had not been finally selected, pessimism predominated. When I put that together with the poverty I had witnessed and with the scourge of AIDS that Mandela's successor, Tabo Umbeki, refused to acknowledge, I could not help but be pessimistic myself.

From South Africa I flew to Nairobi, Kenya, and then on to southern Tanzania to join a group of Washingtonians who were beginning the last week of a two-week safari. The air was clear, the landscape was breathtaking, and it was exciting to be able to observe so many species of animals roaming unconfined. But inevitably I saw evidence of stronger animals marking out their territory and preying on the weaker—lions devouring zebra, for example. I am not sufficiently well versed in biological theories of aggression, in psychology, or in research on economic exploitation to reach any conclusions about either animals or people. But there appears to be in almost all people a deep-seated need to feel empowered and to enjoy high status relative to others, a drive many fulfill by exercising dominion over people who are perceived to be different in color or ethnicity or in some other way. As the world grows more crowded and complex, feelings of powerlessness may grow and stimulate even greater feelings of a need to dominate. Whatever the reasons, or combinations of reasons, the need to feel superior and to subjugate seems to be deeply entrenched in cultures and societies around the world.

As I mulled these pessimistic thoughts in a camp called the Selous, in Tanzania, word came to our safari group by shortwave radio of the attacks on the World Trade Center and the Pentagon. Lacking telephones or newspapers or television, I think we were simultaneously buffered and traumatized. We did not see any pictures of the events until five days later as we were returning home through Dakar, Senegal. In the aftermath, the reports that were most shocking to me were of dancing in the streets of Cairo and celebrations in Palestinian refugee camps. One can understand the happiness that meets accounts of military casualties in a war, since enemy soldiers may be viewed as a threat to one's physical security. But how is it possible for anyone to so demonize a whole people as to derive pleasure from the deaths of men, women, and children innocently going about their everyday tasks?

And yet, despite all the evidence of inhumanity, people continue to struggle and make small gains. Two centuries ago, Jefferson advocated a form of public education that would "uncover the mass of talents which lays buried in poverty . . . for want of means of development." Throughout Africa, very large numbers of young children are not in school because they do not have the money to pay the fees. On a trip to the province of Kwazul-Natal, I encountered children begging not for money but for pens and pencils, since their families must pay for school supplies. And in conversations with Africans wherever I traveled, I found a thirst for knowledge and sensed that there were many talents buried beneath the poverty. Gradually, in some places enrollment is increasing, especially among girls who had been excluded almost entirely.

A year after my South African trip, I was invited to Budapest to consult with a group of young lawyers working for the rights of Romany people to education. With the help of a grant from the Open Society Institute, research had been commissioned showing that isolating Romany children in classes for the mentally retarded is a terrible educational practice and that, given a chance to perform at higher levels, many will do so. Now, the lawyers are advocating for changes that will break down educational isolation.

Soon after, I went to a seminar in the United Kingdom that was devoted in large part to the work of the European Court of Human Rights. That international tribunal has in recent years been issuing increasingly progressive rulings on matters such as capital punishment and its rulings are often accepted by member nations. Increasingly, too, members of our own Supreme Court, notably Justice Ruth Bader Ginsburg, have cited the work of the European Court and other international bodies in their own opinions. Interestingly, too, the moderates on our Court have begun to take account of the evolving opinion of states and communities of our nation on some aspects of human rights. For instance, the Court's recent decision against capital punishment for mentally retarded prisoners reversed a Supreme Court decision issued thirteen years earlier and was predicated in part on the increasing numbers of states that had ruled out such executions.

My recent experience has persuaded me more strongly that there is value in establishing norms of conduct governing equality and due process, even when those norms go unenforced. There is value, too, in documenting violations of these norms and in collecting racial and other data revealing the gaps between the haves and the have-nots. All of this may come under the heading of having a "decent respect for the opinions of mankind." The effort is to establish beachheads where values of equality and fairness prevail. And the work of preserving and expanding these beachheads in a sea of inhumanity is an honorable calling.

I should underline the task of preservation. More than two years after the Durban conference, the Organization for Security and Cooperation in Europe (OSCE) sponsored a conference on anti-Semitism and I attended again as a member of an American delegation of civil rights advocates. The conference was spurred by the anti-Semitic acts that occurred at Durban as well as growing evidence of a resurgence of such bias in several European countries.

For me and other Jews of my vintage, attending such a meeting in Berlin stirred mixed emotions. Speeches by the president of the German Republic and its foreign minister demonstrated a powerful commitment to warding off a revival of religious hatred. A visit to the new Jewish Museum, where groups of young German students moved solemnly through the exhibits, was encouraging to me.

The most stunning moment came in a post-meeting press conference with Solomon Passy, the Bulgarian chair of the OSCE, and German foreign minister Joschka Fischer. Passy, a Jew, said that his father, who had been imprisoned by the Nazis, had told him that "one day we will give our yellow stars [the badge of identification and indignity] back to the Germans." With that, Passy produced an ornate silver box, opened it, revealing a yellow badge, and presented it to Fischer. Fischer was clearly shocked, but recovered and made a graceful acceptance speech.

But here we were, more than sixty years after the events, discussing the recurrence of anti-Semitism. Elie Wiesel, the American conscience of the Holocaust, said that as a young man he thought naively that the revelation of Auschwitz would put an end to anti-Semitism, but that he was wrong. At the conference it was clear that it was not just the growing immigration of Muslim workers to Europe, but a recurrence of the old virus of hatred that afflicted the ruling class, that required attention.

So I came again to believe in the aphorisms that eternal vigilance is the price of liberty and that struggle is the only constant.

Brave New World

As to the future, I do have concerns. One is that, while the capitalist system generates general prosperity in the United States and a few other developed countries, it is also producing ever growing inequities. A great satisfaction for me in 2002 was the work I did in conceiving and writing, with Rob Weiner, a former counsel to President Clinton, a friend-of-the-court brief for the Leadership Conference that we filed in the Supreme Court in the Michigan University affirmative action cases. We, along with many others, supported the university in its contention that racial diversity serves government interests of the highest order.

Part of our argument was that, for two centuries, the central goal of our government has been a strong unified country forged from a population more diverse than any other—building a great nation of immigrants. We contended that the United States had coped with the problems of diversity and even turned into a source of strength, while societies around the world have broken apart under the pressures of ethnic turmoil. The University of Michigan argued that, as an elite institution of higher education, it had an important role in developing the next generation of leadership and that, in doing so, racial and ethnic diversity would be critical in producing a harmonious governing structure. Prominent military officials and business leaders offered similar contentions about the importance of diversity in their own institutions.

By a narrow 5–4 vote, the Court sustained carefully drawn policies designed to promote diversity, with Justice Sandra Day O'Connor articulating the views I have described. It seems to me that we may well be on the way to introducing diversity in our leadership class—in government, business, the military, the arts, and other areas. But it is perfectly conceivable that we will do this while maintaining a deeply submerged underclass that consists disproportionately of people of color. For a number of people, particularly members of some immigrant groups, there may be opportunities for mobility, but for others, most likely black people, their tenure at the bottom of society may be long-term and persistent.

Whether government will do anything significant to ease the plight of those who are worst off is also subject to question. There was a time when two fundamental roles of government were to regulate businesses to guard against corporate avarice and exploitation of consumers and workers, and to provide a safety net for those who were most vulnerable. But, as a people, we appear to have lost a good deal of the confidence we once had in government as an instrument for positive protections and change. Our experience with national leaders since the years of the New Deal and the Great Society has been so negative for so long that people under the age of fifty can hardly be blamed for mistrusting government. Thus, deregulation and the atrophying of policies to ensure competition have opened the way for Enron-style abuses of corporate power. As to the safety net government is expected to provide, the increasing privatization of public functions and the outsourcing of jobs to independent contractors have diminished benefits for many workers. In the last century, economists talked about the need for countervailing government power to restrain the excesses of corporations. These days, the words are rarely heard or heeded.

Moreover, the corrupting influence of money in the political process has clouded the prospects for reform. While legislative fixes have been tried and most recently sustained by the Supreme Court, evasion remains the name of the game. We do not lack for idealistic and talented people who seek elected office to advance a progressive agenda. But the hurdles they face are very high.

The last item on my list of concerns is the unintended consequences of technological advance. It is true that the new information technology can provide opportunities for disadvantaged people, provided we find ways to overcome the digital divide. But we need to consider whether overreliance on computers may become an isolating factor. It is now possible to meet almost every tangible need without ever leaving home. So what is to become of our town halls, voting sites, schoolrooms, and other public places where human contact is possible and which somehow give us a larger sense of public and community purpose?

On a positive note, we have a history of being resourceful enough to ward off dehumanizing forces and to promote freedom and opportunity. Over the past fifty years, many of the chains of discrimination have been broken and many more people have gained the chance to fulfill their dreams and potential. One result is more contact among young people across the racial and ethnic divide, contact that is generally freer and more natural than it was among their elders. I suspect that progress will come by different means in the future. We may rely less on the courts and more on community organization and action. Movements for national change may arise more from grassroots action (including use of the Internet) than before.

In my general optimism, I find myself going counter to the gloomy views of many of my friends who see nothing but trouble ahead in the current conservative resurgence. I find myself growing impatient with the pessimism of people whose intellect and values I have admired for years. It seems to me that many people underestimate their own capacity to effect change. If the communities we live in are overprivileged and exclude those who seek opportunity, we have the ability to launch local efforts to change the rules to become more inclusive. When I am invited to speak to law students these days, I often tell them that, since they are a generally assertive breed, I find it odd that so many of them feel constrained to fit into corporate structures or to take other conventional paths rather than to strike out on their own. For older adults, burdened by family responsibilities and other cares, it may be more difficult to sustain a first or second career as a change agent. I do not exempt myself from this criticism. But, as Eleanor Roosevelt said, "It is better to light a candle than to curse the darkness."

In any case, I wake up these days feeling unaccountably cheerful. I know that there's a good fight to go to—to help restore civil rights remedies, to give people ideas about how to revitalize their school systems, to keep people who oppose constitutional values off the federal bench. Lacking any talent for retirement, I hope to stay in the fray as long as I can.

Notes

Resisting the habits of a professional lifetime, I decided not to employ footnotes in this memoir, because I believe they would distract from the flow. I am prepared, however, to document factual assertions I make in these pages. For chapter 2, "Working for Thurgood and Bob," I have the legal memoranda I wrote to Thurgood Marshall and Bob Carter during the period of my employment from 1954 to 1958. I also have most of the legal briefs which I had a hand in preparing.

For chapter 3, "A Little Democracy," I have the memos I wrote to Harris Wofford and Lee White of the White House Staff and the reports I wrote during the period from 1961 through 1964 when I served as the Secretariat for the Subcabinet Committee on Civil Rights. For chapters 3, 4, and 5, I have detailed minutes of meetings of the U.S. Commission on Civil Rights, usually held on a monthly basis during the period when I was general counsel and later staff director. For chapter 6, "New Beginnings," I have the annual reports and papers of the Center for National Policy Review.

All of these sources and others are available in the collection of my papers at the Library of Congress. In addition, I relied on the sources listed below both for general background and specific information contained in the memoir.

Bibliography

General

Branch, Taylor, *Parting the Waters: America in the King Years 1954–63.* New York: Simon and Schuster, 1988.

Branch, Taylor, *Pillar of Fire: America in the King Years 1963–65.* New York: Simon and Schuster, 1998.

Clark, Kenneth B., *Dark Ghetto.* New York: Harper & Row, 1965.

Ellison, Ralph, *Invisible Man.* New York: Random House, 1947.

Kluger, Richard, *Simple Justice.* New York: Vintage Books, 1977.

Myrdal, Gunnar, *An American Dilemma. (2 Vols.)* New York: McGraw-Hill, 1964.

Wofford, Harris, *Of Kennedys and Kings: Making Sense of the Sixties.* New York: Farrar Strauss, 1980.

Chapter 3: A Little Democracy

Fleming, Harold C., *The Potomac Chronicle.* Athens, Ga.: University of Georgia Press, 1996.

Chapter 4: The Road to Mississippi

Hendrickson, Paul, *Sons of Mississippi: A Story of Race and its Legacy.* New York: Random House, 2003.

Taylor, William L., Civil Rights and Federal Responsibility in *37 Representative American Speeches* 1964-1965 (Thompson ed.). New York: H.W. Wilson, 1965.

United States Commission on Civil Rights, Hearings on Voting. Jackson, Mississippi, February 16–20, 1965.

United States Commission on Civil Rights, Hearings on Administration of Justice. Jackson, Mississippi, February 16–20, 1965.

United States Commission on Civil Rights, Voting in Mississippi. Washington, D.C.: 1965.

United States Commission on Civil Rights, The Voting Rights Act . . . the first three months. Washington, D.C.: 1965.

Chapter 5: Triumph and Despair

Anderson, Elijah, *A Place on the Corner.* Chicago: University of Chicago Press, 1976.

Brown, Claude, *Manchild in the Promised Land.* New York: Macmillan, 1965.

U.S. Department of Health, Education, and Welfare, *Equality of Educational Opportunity.* Washington, D.C.: Government Printing Office, 1996.

The National Advisory Commission on Civil Disorders, *The Kerner Report.* Washington, D.C.: Government Printing Office, 1968.

United States Commission on Civil Rights, *Racial Isolation in the Public Schools.* Washington, D.C.: Government Printing Office, 1967.

United States Commission on Civil Rights, *A Time to Listen A Time to Act, Voices from the Ghetto of the Nation's Cities.* Washington, D.C., 1967.

Chapter 6: New Beginnings

Dimond, Paul R., *Beyond Busing: Inside the Challenge to Urban Segregation.* Ann Arbor: University of Michigan Press, 1985.

Ford Foundation, *Competence and Impact—And Now for a Strategy: Grants to the Center for National Policy Review.* New York: 1973.

National Revenue Sharing Monitoring Project, *Equal Opportunity Under General Revenue Sharing.* Washington, D.C.: National Clearinghouse on Revenue Sharing, August 1975.

National Revenue Sharing Monitoring Project, *General Revenue Sharing: The Case for Reform.* Washington, D.C.: Center for National Policy Review, February 1976.

Chapter 7: Fighting Back in the '80s

Arrington, Karen McGill and Taylor, William L. (eds.), *Voting Rights in America.* Washington, D.C.: Leadership Conference Education Fund and Joint Center for Political Studies, 1992.

Pertschuk, Michael, *Giant Killers.* New York: W.W. Norton, 1986.

Chapter 8: Fighting Back in the '80s: Part II

Bronner, Ethan, *Battle for Justice: How the Bork Nomination Shook America.* New York: W.W. Norton, 1989.

Citizens' Commission on Civil Rights, *"There is No Liberty . . ."* A Report on Congressional Efforts to Curb the Federal Courts and to Undermine the Brown Decision. Washington, D.C.: October 1982.

Leadership Conference on Civil Rights, *Without Justice—A Report on the Conduct of the Justice Department in Civil Rights in 1981–1982.* Washington, D.C.: February 15, 1982.

Pertschuk, Michael and Schaetzel, Wendy, *The People Rising: The Campaign Against the Bork Nomination.* New York: Thunder's Mouth Press, 1989.

U.S. Senate, Committee on the Judiciary Hearings on the Nomination of Robert H. Bork to be Associate Justice of the Supreme Court of the United States, September 1987.

Chapter 9: The Thomas Nomination

Mayers, Jane and Abramson, Jill, *Strange Justice: The Selling of Clarence Thomas.* New York: Houghton Mifflin, 1994.

Chapter 10: Back to Schools

Citizens' Commission on Civil Rights, *"Choosing Better Schools,"* A Report on Student Transfers Under the No Child Left Behind Act. Washington, D.C.: May 2004.

Commission on Chapter 1, *Making Schools Work for Children in Poverty.* Washington, D.C.: December 1992.

Freivogel, William H., "St. Louis: Desegregation and School Choice in the Land of Dred Scott." *in Divided We Fail: Coming Together Through Public School Choice.* Washington, D.C.: Century Foundation, 2002.

Taylor, William L., "Standards, Tests and Civil Rights" in *Education Week*, Nov. 15, 2000, p. 56.

Wells, Amy Stuart and Crain, Robert L., *Stepping Over the Color Line: African-American Students in White Suburban Schools.* New Haven: Yale University Press, 1997.

Chapter 11: Beachheads

Taylor, William L., Racial equality: "The World According to Rehnquist" in *The Rehnquist Court: Judicial Activism on the Right* (Herman Schwartz, ed.) New York: Farrar, Strauss & Giroux, 2002.

U.S. Senate, Committee on the Judiciary Hearings on the Nomination of John Ashcroft to be Attorney General of the United States, January 2001.

Acknowledgments

T hree people, Taylor Branch, David Wigdor and my daughter Lauren R. Taylor, were good enough to review the entire manuscript and to offer helpful suggestions.

Toinnette Marshall, my assistant, patiently got me through the numerous drafts. Robin Reed provided research assistance.

Milly Marmur, my agent, did far more than was contemplated by her job description. She believed in the book, spurred me to greater effort, made good suggestions before we got in the formal editing process. I owe her a special debt of gratitude.

Philip Turner, my editor at Carroll and Graf, has offered recommendations that have made this a better book than it originally was.

All three of my children, Lauren, Deborah and David, have been supportive in a variety of ways.

I have many other debts to people who have served as mentors, colleagues and coconspirators during my fifty-year journey in civil rights work. The reader will meet many of them in the pages of this book, but my appreciation for their generosity of spirit goes far beyond words.

Index

About the Author

M r. Taylor is a graduate of Brooklyn College and the Yale Law School. He began his legal career in 1954 as an attorney on the staff of the NAACP Legal Defense and Education Fund. In the 1960s he served as General Counsel and later as staff director of the United States Commission on Civil Rights where he directed major investigations and research studies that contributed to the civil rights laws enacted in the 60s. Among the studies was *Racial Isolation in the Public Schools*, the first major interdisciplinary study of northern public schools.

In 1970, Mr. Taylor founded the Center for National Policy Review, a civil rights research and advocacy organization funded by private foundations that he directed for 16 years. At the Center, as counsel for black school children and other plaintiffs, Mr. Taylor helped secure major desegregation victories in Wilmington, Delaware; Indianapolis; St. Louis; and Cincinnati.

On the legislative front, Mr. Taylor has long been a leader of the Leadership Conference on Civil Rights and currently serves as Vice Chairman. Working with the Leadership Conference in 1982 he played a major role as a legislative strategist bringing about the extension and strengthening of the Voting Rights Act of 1965. He was a leader in the coalition of civil rights organizations that successfully blocked the confirmation of Robert Bork to the Supreme Court in 1987. More recently, he helped lead successful efforts to enact the Civil Rights Restoration Act of 1988, the Civil Rights Act of 1991, and the 1993 National Voter Registration Act. Mr. Taylor was a founder and now serves as the Chair of the Citizens' Commission on Civil Rights, a bipartisan group of former federal officials which has monitored federal civil rights policies and enforcement efforts since the early 1980s. For the Citizens' Commission, he has served as co-editor for a series of reports since 1986 that have documented failures of civil rights enforcement and made recommendations for change.

In his private practice, established in 1986, Mr. Taylor continues to represent minority and low-income children in litigation seeking equal educational opportunity. In 1987, he was retained by the Council of Chief State Schools Officers to draft a model state statute providing educational entitlements for at-risk students. The model statute was adopted in principle by the Council and is being widely promoted by state education departments. In 1987, he also was retained as a legal consultant to Senator Kennedy's Committee on Labor and Human Resources to provide assistance on the Civil Rights Restoration Act which was enacted into law in 1988.

In 1989, as counsel for black school children, he negotiated a plan for desegregation and educational improvements in the Fort Wayne, Indiana, school system and, in 1984, a settlement with the State of Indiana, which significantly increased the resources for educational improvement. As a consultant to the New York City Board of Education, he drafted an affirmative action plan covering employment throughout the system which the Board adopted.

In 1990, he and a colleague, Dianne Piché, completed a study of school finance for the House Education and Labor Committee, published by the Committee under the title *Shortcoming Children: The Impact of Fiscal Inequity on the Education of Students At-Risk*. For several years, he has served as counsel to a group of leading educators and advocates in the drafting of comprehensive reforms to Title I (formerly Chapter 1) of the Elementary and Secondary Education Act. Many of the reforms proposed were adopted by Congress in the Improving America's Schools Act of 1994.

For fifteen years, Mr. Taylor taught civil rights law at Catholic University Law School and operated a clinical program for law students. In 1996-97, Mr. Taylor served as Phleger Visiting Professor of Law at Stanford Law School.

He now teaches education law as an adjunct professor at Georgetown University Law School. He has written widely about public law and policy issues for legal and education journals, magazines, and newspapers, and is the author of the book *Hanging Together:*

Equality in an Urban Nation, published in 1971. He is a member of the Bars of the District of Columbia and New York and various federal courts, and serves on the boards of several civil rights and public interest organizations. Among the honors he has received is the first Thurgood Marshall Award conferred by the District of Columbia Bar in 1993.

He lives in Washington, D.C. His late wife, Harriett R. Taylor, was a judge of the Superior Court of the District of Columbia. Their children are Lauren, Deborah, and David.